*I Never Knew That*
*About*
THE SCOTTISH

Christopher Winn has been a freelance writer and trivia collector for over twenty years. He has worked with Terry Wogan and Jonathan Ross, and sets quiz questions for television as well as for the *Daily Mail* and *Daily Telegraph*. He is the author of the bestselling *I Never Knew That About England*. Books in the same series cover Ireland, Scotland, Wales, London, Yorkshire, the Lake District and New York, and he has written further books on the River Thames and Royal Britain. He is also the Associate Producer for a TV series by ITV about Great Britain. He is married to artist Mai Osawa, who illustrates all the books in the series.

# CHRISTOPHER WINN

## *I Never Knew That About*
## THE SCOTTISH

ILLUSTRATIONS BY
Mai Osawa

EBURY
PRESS

5 7 9 10 8 6

Ebury Press, an imprint of Ebury Publishing,
20 Vauxhall Bridge Road,
London SW1V 2SA

Ebury Press is part of the Penguin Random House group of companies whose
addresses can be found at global.penguinrandomhouse.com

 Penguin
Random House
UK

Text © Christopher Winn 2009
Illustrations © Mai Osawa 2009

Christopher Winn has asserted his right to be identified as the author of this Work
in accordance with the Copyright, Designs and Patents Act 1988

First published by Ebury Press in 2009
This edition published by Ebury Press in 2015

www.eburypublishing.co.uk

A CIP catalogue record for this book is available from the British Library

ISBN 9780091960247

Typeset by Palimpsest Book Production Limited,
Falkirk, Stirlingshire
Printed and bound by Clays Ltd, Elcograf S.p.A.

Penguin Random House is committed to a sustainable future
for our business, our readers and our planet. This book is made from
Forest Stewardship Council® certified paper.

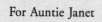

For Auntie Janet

# CONTENTS

————◆◆◆◆●————

[vii]

# PREFACE

————◆•◆•◆————

I N ORDER TO be able to fully appreciate the stories in this book
it is helpful to know a little of their history and where they come
from.

The Scotland of today is primarily a fusion of four races.

1) The Irish Gaelic Scotii from Dal Riata (see below).
2) The Picts, or 'painted people' from the north.
3) The Norse from Norway who occupied Orkney and Shetland, the Western
   Isles and parts of Caithness and Sutherland.
4) The Normans who came north from the court of Henry I of England with
   the Scottish King David I in 1124, and settled mainly in the Borders and the
   south. The Normans and the Norse were, of course, from the same origins
   – the Norman family of Robert the Bruce, for instance, was descended from
   the Earls of Orkney.

## Monarchs of Scotland

The monarchs of Scotland traditionally trace their descent from Fergus Mor,
King of the ancient Irish Gaelic kingdom of Dal Riata, which covered an area
more or less equivalent to the modern County Antrim. He led a group of
'Scotii' from Ireland to settle in Kintyre in the late 5th century.

Dal Riata, or Dalraida in Scotland, grew to occupy much of the western
seaboard of present-day Scotland (Argyll, Bute and some of Wester Ross) as
well as the original territory in the north of Ireland.

The inhabitants of Dalraida were referred to as Scotii, from the Latin name
for the people of Ireland.

In the 9th century Dalraida, under Kenneth MacAlpin of the Scotii, united
with the kingdom of the Picts in the north to form the land of the Scotii or
Scotland.

## House of Alpin (848–1034)

| | |
|---|---|
| Kenneth MacAlpin | 843–58 |
| Donald I | 858–62 |
| Constantine I | 862–77 |
| Aed | 877–78 |
| Giric and Eochald | 878–89 |
| Donald II | 889–900 |
| Constantine II | 900–43 |
| Malcolm I | 943–54 |
| Indulf | 954–62 |
| Dubh | 962–66 |
| Culen | 966–71 |
| Kenneth II | 971–95 |
| Constantine III | 995–97 |
| Kenneth III | 997–1005 |
| Malcolm II | 1005–34 |

## House of Dunkeld   (1034–1286)

### Duncan I (1034–40)

Maternal grandson of Malcolm II and son of Crinan, hereditary lay abbot of Dunkeld – hence House of Dunkeld.

### Macbeth (1040–57)

Also a maternal grandson of Malcolm II and therefore cousin of Duncan. Son of the Mormaer of Moray.

### Lulach (1057–58)

Stepson of Macbeth.

## Malcolm III (1058–93)

Known as Malcolm Canmore (Big Head). Son of Duncan, he slew Macbeth at Lumphanan.

| | |
|---|---|
| Donald III | 1093–94 |
| Duncan II | 1094 |
| Donald III (restored) | 1094–97 |
| Edgar | 1097–1107 |
| Alexander I | 1107–24 |

## David I (1124–53)

Youngest son of Malcolm III, David spent much of his youth at the court of his brother-in-law Henry I of England, who was married to David's sister Matilda. When he came north to rule Scotland David brought with him many Norman knights to whom he gave land and titles. In what is termed the 'Davidian Revolution' he introduced Norman feudalism, consolidated the system of primogeniture and founded a number of monasteries.

| | |
|---|---|
| Malcolm IV | 1153–65 |

## William I (1165–1214)

Known as William the Lion from his standard, a red lion rampant on a yellow background, which is still the Royal Standard of Scotland.

| | |
|---|---|
| Alexander II | 1214–49 |

## Alexander III (1249–86)

He succeeded in wresting the Western Isles from Norway and bringing them under Scottish rule. When he died without a male heir Scotland's monarchy was plunged into chaos.

## House of Fairhair (1286–1290)

### Margaret (1286–90)

Known as the 'Maid of Norway' she was the grand-daughter of Alexander III and daughter of King Eric Fairhair of Norway. She never set foot in Scotland but was drowned off Orkney at the age of 7 while on her way to her new kingdom. Her death left the throne of Scotland without an obvious heir by primogeniture, and a number of candidates came forward to claim the throne, including Robert de Brus, grandfather of the future Robert I (Robert the Bruce). Edward I of England was asked to choose between them and he decided upon John de Balliol, a great grandson of David of Huntingdon, brother of William the Lion.

**Interregnum**                                              1290–92

## House of Balliol  (1292–1296)

### John de Balliol (1292–96)

John was eventually deposed by Edward I who then annexed Scotland to the English crown. This move resulted in the Scottish Wars of Independence which started with William Wallace in 1297, saw the crowning of Robert the Bruce as Robert I of Scotland in 1306 and ended with Scottish independence after the Battle of Bannockburn in 1314.

**Interregnum**                                              1296–1306

### The Ragman Rolls

In 1296 Edward I of England persuaded many of the Scottish nobels to sign a document swearing their allegiance to him. The document became known as the Ragman Rolls after a previous record compiled by a papal tax collector called Ragimunde.

## House of Bruce  (1306–1371)

Robert I (the Bruce)                                        1306–29
David II                                                    1329–71

## House of Stewart/Stuart (1371–1567)

### Robert II (1371–90)

Grandson of Robert I and High Steward of Scotland – hence the name Stewart.

| | |
|---|---|
| Robert III | 1390–1406 |
| James I | 1406–37 |
| James II | 1437–60 |

### James III (1460–88)

He married the daughter of King Christian of Denmark and received sovereignty of Orkney and Shetland as an unredeemed dowry.

| | |
|---|---|
| James IV | 1488–1513 |
| James V | 1513–42 |
| Mary I | 1542–67 |

### James VI (I of England) (1567–1625)

On the death of Elizabeth I of England in 1603 the crowns of England and Scotland were united and James VI of Scotland became also James I of England.

| | |
|---|---|
| Charles I (I of England) | 1625–49 |
| Charles II (II of England) | 1649–85 |
| James VII (II of England) | 1685–89 |
| Mary II (II of England) | 1689–94 |
| William II (III of England) | 1694–1702 |

### Anne (1702–7)

After the death of Anne, the last Stuart monarch, the term King or Queen of Scots was no longer used. The Hanoverians and all subsequent monarchs have been British monarchs.

In 1707 the Parliaments of Scotland and England were united into the Parliament of Great Britain and the separate Kingdoms of Scotland and England became a single United Kingdom.

N
W E
S

Shetland

Orkney

Caithness

Outer Hebrides

Sutherland

A : Nairn
B : Kincardine
C : Kinross
D : Clackmannan
E : West Lothian

Ross and
Cromarty

Moray

A

Inverness

Banff

Aberdeen

Aberdeen

Inner Hebrides

Inverness

B

Angus

Perth

Dundee

Argyll

Perth

Fife

C

D

Edinburgh

Stirling

Dunbarton

E

East
Lothian

Renfrew

Glasgow

Midlothian

Berwick

Bute

Lanark

Peebles

Selkirk

Roxburgh

Ayr

Dumfries

Kircudbright

Wigtown

ENGLAND

IRELAND

# THE CLANS AND COUNTIES
# OF SCOTLAND

◆◆◆◆

T HE WORD CLAN comes from the Gaelic 'clann', meaning children, descendants or tribe – members of a clan share a common descent and most usually share a surname taken from the founder of that Clan. If Gaelic, this surname was often derived from a physical characteristic (eg Campbell – gaelic for 'crooked mouth'), or from 'mac', or 'son of' as in MacDonald, son of Donald. If Norman, the surname was usually based on territory, as in Robert de Brus, or Robert of Brix in Normandy, and Adam de Gordon, Adam of Gourdon in France. I have used the European dynastic term 'House' rather than 'Clan' for some of the families of Norman descent, eg House of Gordon.

Because these surnames refer back to a single ancestor it follows that most people bearing that surname, wherever in the world they now live, share the same family roots and are hence of Scottish descent. It is on this basis that in each chapter I feature some notable people who share the same surname.

After the Battle of Culloden in 1746 the Clans and their old loyalties were suppressed by the Act of Proscription, and many Clan members became scattered around the world as a result of the emigrations caused by such repression and also the Clearances of the 18th and 19th centuries. Consequently many Clan Chiefs and their relatives reside outside Scotland.

In the late 19th century, however, there was a movement, led by Sir Walter Scott, to revive the customs, loyalties, dress and traditions of the Clans, and today many Clan societies flourish. Clans now hold annual gatherings at their ancestral castles which are attended by Clan members from all over the world.

Most Clans and families were associated with, or settled in, a particular part of Scotland at a time when the country was divided into kingdoms, mormaerdoms and provinces, rather than counties. Because these older divisions were somewhat vague and constantly changing, I have divided the chapters of this book into more recognisable counties, and each chapter features the Clans and families who hail from the territory now known by those county names, as well as other figures who were born there or are associated with the county in some other way.

# Aberdeenshire

HOUSE OF GORDON ✦ THE HUNTLYS
✦ DUKES OF GORDON ✦ GORDONS OF HADDO
✦ THE ABERDEENS ✦ THE WICKED EARL ✦ LORD ABERDEEN
✦ GEORGE OSBORNE ✦ MARQUESS OF ABERDEEN
✦ SOME NOTABLE GORDONS ✦ THE SPANISH GORDONS
✦ CLAN FORBES ✦ SOME NOTABLE FORBES

*Castle Fraser — one of the grandest of Aberdeenshire's great tower houses, built in the late 16th century by the Aberdeenshire branch of the Fraser family, who also founded the town of Fraserburgh.*

◀ ABERDEENSHIRE FOLK ▶

Bertie Charles Forbes ✦ John Barbour ✦ James Gregory ✦ William Forsyth
✦ Revd Alexander John Forsyth ✦ Alexander Milne Calder ✦ Mary Slessor
✦ Sir Patrick Geddes ✦ Andy Beattie

[1]

## The House of Gordon

————◆◆◆◆————

The Gordons came, it is thought, from Gourdon, near Quercy in France, in the 11th century, and gave their name to the border lands where they settled. They later fought for Robert the Bruce, and in 1320 SIR ADAM DE GORDON, from the village of HUNTLY in Berwickshire, accompanied the Declaration of Arbroath to the Papal court in Avignon to plead with the Pope to recognise Scottish independence and lift Bruce's excommunication for killing John Comyn at Dumfries in 1306. Gordon's reward for his efforts was to be granted the lands of Strathbogie in Aberdeenshire, once belonging to the Earl of Fife.

In 1445 Sir Adam's descendant through marriage, Sir Alexander Seton, became the 1st Earl of Huntly, and his son married a daughter of James I.

## The Huntlys

————◆◆◆◆————

HUNTLY CASTLE, in the heart of Aberdeenshire, was the seat of the Chiefs of the House of Gordon for nearly 400 years from the 14th to the 17th century. Originally known as the Peel of Strath-bogie, the first castle to be built on the site was a motte

and bailey, put up in 1190 by the Earl of Fife to guard the crossing where the rivers Bogie and Deveron meet.

Around 1400 the Gordons replaced the wooden castle with a stone tower house, and then in 1450 the 1ST EARL OF HUNTLY built a grand new structure more in keeping with his status as one of the pre-eminent men of his time. In 1496 James IV, always keen to ruffle the feathers of the English, came to Strathbogie to celebrate the marriage of his beautiful young cousin Lady Catherine Gordon to Perkin Warbeck, pretender to the throne of Henry VII.

The 3RD EARL OF HUNTLY, one of the few survivors of the Battle of Flodden in 1513, changed the name of Strathbogie Castle, and the nearby town, to Huntly.

The 4TH EARL OF HUNTLY, GEORGE GORDON, Lord Chancellor of Scotland, converted the castle into a noble house just in time for a visit in 1556 by Mary of Guise, widow of his childhood friend

James V. The Earl later fell out with Mary of Guise's daughter Mary Queen of Scots and was defeated by Mary's forces at the Battle of Corrichie in 1562, dying of apoplexy not long after. The Huntly title was temporarily forfeited, but was restored two years later to his son, another George Gordon, who became the 5TH EARL OF HUNTLY.

In 1599 the 6th Earl was created the 1ST MARQUESS OF HUNTLY by James VI. This title is THE OLDEST EXISTING MARQUESSATE IN SCOTLAND, and the second oldest in Britain, after that of Winchester. The 1st Marquess began to transform Huntly into a lavish palace, the impressive remains of which we see today. Just in case the casual passer-by might have been unaware who was the proud owner, his name and that of his wife are splashed in huge stone letters across the oriel windows of the upper floor. 'George Gordon First Marquis of HU' and, below, 'Henriette Stewart Marquesse of HU'. The French spellings (Marquis instead of the English Marquess) provide a clue as to why Huntly Castle was more like a sumptuous French château than a northern Scottish castle – Gordon grew up in France and clearly picked up some tips on comfort from the French aristocracy. Even in its ruinous state, Huntly still exudes luxury and extravagance, with its huge rooms and elaborately carved windows and fireplaces. The castle's greatest treasure,

famous far and wide, is the extraordinary carved heraldic frontispiece above the main courtyard entrance, which is UNIQUE IN BRITAIN.

The Gordons eventually lost Huntly Castle after the 2nd Marquess, who was the first to sport the Gordon nickname 'COCK O' THE NORTH', backed King Charles in the English Civil War, and Huntly began a slow decline until, in the 18th century, much of the building was ransacked for stone to make houses in the town.

Accessed from the town via a stone archway and a broad avenue of trees, Huntly Castle is now in the care of Historic Scotland.

## Dukes of Gordon

The 4th Marquess of Huntly was created 1ST DUKE OF GORDON in 1684, and from this time on Gordon Castle in Morayshire, built in the 1470s by the 2nd Earl of Huntly, became the main seat of the House of Gordon (*see* Morayshire). The dukedom died out in 1836 with the death of the 5th Duke, but the marquessate of Huntly survived, passing to the Duke's cousin the Earl of Aboyne, who became 9th Marquess of Huntly. GRANVILLE GORDON, 13TH MARQUESS OF HUNTLY, born in 1944, is the present CHIEF OF THE HOUSE OF GORDON, and resides at ABOYNE CASTLE.

The 5th Duke of Gordon's nephew, Charles Gordon-Lennox, 5th Duke of Richmond, inherited most of the Gordon estates, and in 1876 his son was created Duke of Gordon of the second creation, becoming Duke of Richmond and Gordon. The holder of this title thus holds four dukedoms (Richmond, Lennox, Gordon and Aubigny), more than any other duke.

## Gordons of Haddo

In 1469 JAMES GORDON, a cousin of the Gordons of Huntly, acquired the lands of HADDO, near Tarves, and settled there. His descendant SIR JOHN GORDON OF HADDO, was an ardent Royalist and was created a Baronet of Nova Scotia by Charles I in 1642 (*see* Clackmannanshire). He was later locked up in Edinburgh's St Giles Cathedral by the King's enemies for kidnapping the Provost of Aberdeen, who was a staunch believer in the National Covenant renouncing the religious innovations of Charles I. Gordon, whose cell in St Giles, known as Haddo's Hole is still there, was then beheaded, earning the distinction of becoming THE FIRST ROYALIST TO BE OFFICIALLY EXECUTED IN SCOTLAND.

Sir John's eldest son was restored to the title and estates at the Restoration of Charles II, and *his* son, George, was created 1ST EARL OF ABERDEEN.

## The Aberdeens

In 1732 WILLIAM, 2ND EARL OF ABERDEEN, set about building a sumptuous mansion at Haddo to replace the run-down old 'Place of Kellie' tower house that had served as the family home up until then. William was later described by the family historian Archie Gordon, 5th Marquess of Aberdeen, as 'ambitious, financially accumulative and a thumping snob' – qualities he exhibited splendidly by marrying first the daughter of the Earl of Leven and Melville, then the daughter of the Duke of Atholl and thirdly the daughter of the Duke of Gordon, each of whom brought with them a considerable dowry of land and money.

HADDO HOUSE was designed in Palladian style by William Adam, the leading Scottish architect of the day. As one of the first stately houses in the north of Scotland it must have amazed the people of Aberdeenshire, who were more used to stern castles and rugged tower houses.

## The Wicked Earl

In 1745 the 2nd Earl of Aberdeen went to join Bonnie Prince Charlie's rebel forces at Edinburgh, but died of natural causes before he could be implicated in the rebellion, a stroke of luck for his heir, the 3rd Earl, who thus inherited his father's estates intact, and became the largest landowner in Aberdeenshire. Known as 'THE WICKED EARL', he was something of a rake, and was harried into marrying the cook of a Yorkshire hostelry after he paid his compliments to the chef rather too personally – when he went back for seconds the good lady held him at gun-point until he agreed to make an honest woman of her.

In 1787 the Wicked Earl took the opportunity to increase his landholdings even further by buying the Castle of Gight, adjoining the Haddo estate, off his cousin Catherine Gordon for a knock-down price. Catherine's father, George Gordon of Gight, a descendant of James I, had committed suicide and Catherine, his heiress, had married a fortune-hunter called Captain John Byron who dissipated her wealth and then fled to France. Catherine was forced to sell her ancestral home, which should have been passed on to her son, George Gordon, the poet Lord Byron.

The Wicked Earl, whose lifestyle eventually drained the estate, was predeceased by his son and there was little left for his grandson, who became the 4th Earl of Aberdeen, to inherit.

# Lord Aberdeen
## 1784–1860

*'First in the cat-fed phalanx shall be seen
The travell'd thane, Athenian Aberdeen'*

George Gordon, orphaned as a boy, and ignored by his grandfather the Wicked Earl, was brought up in London by Henry Dundas, later Viscount Melville. With Dundas and the Prime Minister, William Pitt, as his guardians, his early days were much influenced by politics. He was educated at Harrow, after which he travelled widely throughout Europe, spending much of his time in Greece. On his return to London he founded the Athenian Society, whose membership was confined to those who had visited Greece – hence the name 'Athenian Aberdeen' given to him by his cousin Lord Byron (*see* above). Gordon later purchased the foot of Hercules, which had been a part of the Parthenon in Athens for thousands of years, and had it transported to Haddo, from where it has since disappeared.

In 1813 Aberdeen was sent to Vienna by the new Prime Minister, Lord Liverpool, to negotiate an alliance between Britain, Russia and Austria against Napoleon, which was formalised as the Treaty of Toplitz. While in Europe he was witness to the Battle of Leipzig, the bloodiest battle ever seen in Europe until the First World War, an experience which turned him against war for ever.

He was Foreign Secretary under the Duke of Wellington, until they both resigned over the Great Reform Bill of 1832, and then again under Sir Robert Peel, during which time he was responsible for drawing up the boundaries between the USA and what would become Canada. A believer in free trade, he was forced to resign a second time, along with Peel, over the Repeal of the Corn Laws in 1846.

In 1852, after the resignation of the Earl of Derby, Aberdeen became the prime minister of a coalition government which, against his better judgement, led Britain into the Crimean War. Lord Aberdeen was personally – and somewhat unfairly – blamed for the mismanagement of the conflict and resigned in 1855.

Lord Aberdeen was remembered as honest, generous and cultured, worthy rather than charismatic, a man whose 'strength did not equal his goodness'. Although he remarried, he never really recovered from the death of his beloved first wife, a noted beauty, at the age of 28, and the subsequent loss of all three of his daughters before they were 20.

Memorable Quote:
*'I do not know how I shall bear being out of office. I have many resources and many objects of interest; but after being occupied with great affairs, it is not easy to subside to the level of common occupations.'*

## George Osborne

The Prime Minister's grandson, the 6th Earl of Aberdeen, overwhelmed by his inheritance, ran away to sea and joined the United States merchant marine under the name of GEORGE OSBORNE. He never saw his family again, but turned out to be a fine sailor and was much mourned when he was swept overboard during a violent storm while on passage to Australia.

## Marquess of Aberdeen

'George Osborne's brother became the 7TH EARL OF ABERDEEN

1916 the Earl was created 1ST MARQUESS OF ABERDEEN AND TEMAIR.

The present holder of the title is ALEXANDER GEORGE GORDON, 7TH MARQUESS OF ABERDEEN AND TEMAIR.

## Some Notable Gordons

ROBERT GORDON OF STRALOCH (1580–1661), THE FIRST GRADUATE OF THE UNIVERSITY OF ABERDEEN'S MARISCHAL COLLEGE and SURVEYOR OF THE FIRST ACCURATE ATLAS OF SCOTLAND. His grandson Robert Gordon founded the Robert Gordon University.

in 1870. He twice served as Lord Lieutenant of Ireland and was Governor-General of Canada from 1893 until 1898. His wife, Ishbel Marjoribanks, became a promoter of women's rights and founded the Onward and Upward Association for the education and betterment of women in service. She was the daughter of Sir Dudley Coutts Marjoribanks, 1st Baron Tweedmouth, the originator of the Golden Retriever dog, and was responsible for introducing the breed to Canada. In

*Marischal College*

GORDON'S GIN, established in London in 1769 by Alexander Gordon. The recipe is known to only 12 people in the world at any one time and has been kept a secret for over 200 years.

BAZIL GORDON (1768–1847) emigrated to America from Scotland and settled in Falmouth, Virginia, in 1786. He started a small shop handling imported goods, and then made a fortune exporting tobacco from the plantations along the Rappahannock River to England. The enterprise made him one of America's first millionaires.

ADMIRAL SIR JAMES ALEXANDER GORDON (1782–1869), born in Kildrummy, served in the Royal Navy for over 70 years. He fought at the Battle of Cape St Vincent in 1979, and at the Battle of the Nile in 1798, and was present when the British fleet bombarded Fort McHenry outside Baltimore during the War of 1812, the action that inspired Francis Scott Key to write 'The Star Spangled Banner'. He became Governor of Greenwich Royal Hospital and was made Admiral of the Fleet in 1868, the last survivor of the group of young captains, known as the Band of Brothers, who had served with Nelson 70 years earlier at the Nile. Gordon is thought to have been one of those on whom C.S. Forester based his naval hero Horatio Hornblower.

GENERAL CHARLES GORDON (1833–85), known as 'Chinese' Gordon for his exploits during the second Opium War, when he successfully defended Shanghai against the Taiping rebels, leading his troops into battle armed only with a walking stick. He gained a reputation for being incorruptible when he put down a mutiny sparked by his refusal to allow looting, and turned down a bribe from the Chinese emperor. He was later made Governor of Sudan, and in 1884 was ordered to conduct the evacuation of Europeans from Khartoum, which was under threat of attack from rebels led by the al-Mahdi. Having managed to get over 2,000 women, children and wounded out of the city, Gordon then held Khartoum against huge odds until 26 January 1885, when he and his troops were overwhelmed and massacred. A British relief force, which had been delayed by political wrangling in London, arrived three days later. 'Chinese' Gordon was hailed as a hero and became even better known as Gordon of Khartoum.

JULIETTE GORDON LOW (1860–1927), known affectionately as 'Daisy Gordon'. She founded the Girl Scouts of America in Savannah, Georgia, in 1912. The first registered member was her niece Margaret 'Daisy Doots' Gordon.

## The Spanish Gordons

❧❧❧

Some time in the 18th century, ARTHUR GORDON, of the Gordons of Wardhouse in Aberdeenshire, who was a Catholic, left Protestant Scotland and emigrated to Spain where he set up a wine business in Cadiz. He was followed by his nephew, John David Gordon, and other Catholic members of the Gordon family, who all married into Spanish families, settled in the Jerez region and began making sherry. The first major shipment of sherry, or Jerez wine, sent to England was shipped by J. Gordon and Co. in 1798.

Their sherry also proved popular with the Spanish royal family and inspired a friendship that has lasted until the present day. In 1906 the grandparents of King Juan Carlos of Spain, King Alfonso XIII and Queen Victoria Eugenia, spent their honeymoon at Wardhouse as guests of Rafael Gordon, Count de Mirasol, the last Laird of Wardhouse.

In Scotland, Wardhouse is now a ruin, but Beldorney Castle, the original home of the Wardhouse Gordons, is still in use as a private house. In Spain, the sherry business, Gonzalez Byass, is still run by the family, headed by Gabriel Gonzalez-Gordon Gilbey.

## Clan Forbes

❧❧❧

Forbes is a grand old Aberdeenshire name. The Forbes, Premier Barons of Scotland, have been one of Aberdeenshire's leading families since the 13th century, when they were awarded a tranche of land known as the Braes of Fourbois. There is a colourful story of how they came by their land and their name, which tells of a brave warrior from Ireland named Ochonchar, who came to Aberdeen in pursuit of his sweetheart, a local heiress named Bess. In order to impress her, he slew a rampaging bear that was menacing the neighbourhood – an act of heroism which, as he put it, was 'For Bess'. It worked – he won Bess and her estates, as well as a name for his family.

For 600 years the seat of the Forbes family has been Castle Forbes, which sits above the River Don on the land won by Ochonchar. The present castle was built in 1815 for the 17th Lord Forbes. The present Master of Forbes is Malcolm, son of the 22nd Lord Forbes. His wife, Jinny, runs what could be the world's smallest private perfumery out of a former dairy shed in the grounds.

## Some Notable Forbes

GENERAL JOHN FORBES (1707–59) led the 1758 Forbes Expedition that captured the French outpost at Fort Duquesne. He renamed it Fort Pitt, after his Prime Minister, William Pitt the Elder, and the settlement eventually grew into the modern city of Pittsburgh, Pennsylvania.

JOHN FORBES (1740–83) travelled to America to serve as the only British clergyman in America's oldest settlement, St Augustine in Florida. He had three sons who went on to establish the Forbes family in America. One of his descendants is JOHN FORBES KERRY, presidential nominee for the Democratic Party in the 2004 presidential election won by George W. Bush. As a young man Kerry spent many summer holidays at Les Essarts in Brittany, France, the estate of his grandfather James Grant Forbes. Another of Forbes's grandsons, Kerry's cousin BRICE

LALONDE, served as mayor of the local village St-Briac-sur-Mer and ran for election as President of France in 1981.

JAMES DAVID FORBES (1809–68) designed an early seismometer to measure earthquakes at Scotland's earthquake centre, Comrie in Perthshire. He WAS THE FIRST PERSON KNOWN TO HAVE CLIMBED THE CUILLINS ON

SKYE, and became THE FIRST HONORARY PRESIDENT OF THE ALPINE CLUB, which was founded in 1857 as THE WORLD'S FIRST MOUNTAINEERING CLUB.

His son, PROFESSOR GEORGE FORBES (1849–1936), reported for *The Times* as THE ONLY BRITISH WAR CORRESPONDENT WITH THE RUSSIAN ARMY DURING THE RUSSO-TURKISH WAR OF 1877. A prolific inventor, he also pioneered the use of electricity for the world's first electric railway, the City and South

London Railway, forerunner of the world's first underground network, and invented the CARBON BRUSH still universally used in electric motors today.

*Well, I never knew this*
*about*
ABERDEENSHIRE FOLK

BERTIE CHARLES FORBES (1880–1954), financial journalist and publisher who founded *Forbes Magazine* in 1917. Born in New Deer, he emigrated to New York in 1904.

JOHN BARBOUR (1320–95), the poet described as 'the Father of Scots Literature', was born in Aberdeen. Best known for his epic narrative poem, *The Brus*, an account of the struggles and triumphs of Robert the Bruce, he was THE FIRST MAJOR ARTIST TO WRITE IN THE SCOTS VERNACULAR.

'Fredome is a noble thing'
John Barbour: *The Brus*

## James Gregory
◄ 1638–75 ►

Born in Drumoak, James Gregory became a very young professor at the University of St Andrews. At the age of 25, in a document called *Optica*

*Promota*, he put forward a design for a reflecting telescope, which was eventually built ten years later by Robert Hooke. Although Isaac Newton built the world's first reflecting telescope in 1670, it was not as efficient as Hooke's Gregorian telescope, which is regarded as THE WORLD'S FIRST PRACTICAL REFLECTING TELESCOPE. Gregorian optics are used today in many of the world's modern radio telescopes and observatories such as the world's largest fully steerable radio telescope at Greenbank in West Virginia, the Las Campanas Observatory in Chile and the Arecibo Observatory in Puerto Rico, which featured in the dénouement of the 1995 James Bond film *Goldeneye*.

WILLIAM FORSYTH (1737–1804), the botanist after whom Forsythia is named, was born in Old Meldrum. As curator of the Physic Garden in Chelsea, he is credited with creating BRITAIN'S FIRST ROCK GARDEN, and he was one of the founders of the Royal Horticultural Society in 1804.

THE REVD ALEXANDER JOHN FORSYTH (1769–1843), inventor of the PERCUSSION CAP, was born in Belhevie. A keen shot, particularly of game birds, he was greatly vexed by the unreliability of the flint-lock in the damp conditions prevalent in his Aberdeenshire parish. He designed a new priming system, which he patented in 1807, whereby a percussion cap ignited an enclosed (and dry) charge when struck with a hammer. The invention was the forerunner of the modern bullet and proved so effective that the Emperor Napoleon offered a considerable amount of money for the design – his offer was rejected.

# Alexander Milne Calder
## ◄ 1846–1923 ►

Alexander Milne Calder was born in Aberdeen, the son of a stonemason who made his living carving tombstones. Alexander picked up some useful techniques from his father, which he was able to put to good use when he moved to London to work on the Albert Memorial. In 1868 he emigrated to Philadelphia in the United States and a few years later received a commission that would occupy him for the next 20 years, to make sculptures for America's largest municipal building, PHILADELPHIA CITY HALL.

Out of the 250 pieces he created, Calder's masterpiece was undoubtedly

*Philadelphia City Hall*

the bronze statue of Philadelphia's founder, William Penn, which still crowns the tower of City Hall and helped, for a few years at the start of the 20th century, to make it the tallest building in the world. At 548 ft (167 m) high, it is still the tallest *masonry* building in the world. The statue is 37 ft (11.3 m) high and is THE TALLEST STATUE TO BE FOUND ON TOP OF A BUILDING ANYWHERE IN THE WORLD.

Alexander Milne Calder's grandson, SANDY CALDER, invented the 'MOBILE', a type of kinetic sculpture, smaller examples of which can often be seen hanging above a baby's cot to entertain the occupant.

MARY SLESSOR (1848–1915), missionary and THE FIRST WOMAN TO PRESIDE OVER A COURT UNDER BRITISH JURISDICTION, was born in Gilcomston, Aberdeen, the daughter of an alcoholic shoe-maker. She became a missionary in Nigeria when she was 28 and was appointed to sit in judgement at the native courts in 1891. Though petite, she was fearless and unconventional, socialising with the natives, stopping ritualistic killings, and setting up schools, churches and hospitals all over West Africa. She was greatly loved by the local tribespeople, who called her 'Ma'. Her image appears on the £10 note issued in Scotland by the Clydesdale Bank.

# Sir Patrick Geddes
◄ 1864–1932 ►

*'This is a green world, with animals comparatively few and small, and all dependent on the leaves . . . Some people have strange ideas that they live by money . . . we live not by the jingling of our coins, but by the fullness of our harvests'*

Pioneer ecologist, one of the founders of modern town planning, and THE FIRST BRITISH CITIZEN TO USE 'LANDSCAPE ARCHITECT' AS A PROFESSIONAL TITLE, Patrick Geddes was born in Ballater. Using observations he made from his camera obscura in Edinburgh's Outlook Tower, he was responsible for the renovation of much of the Royal Mile, replacing cramped and squalid tenements with spacious new buildings such as Ramsay Garden. He also pioneered the use of moats to separate animals in Edinburgh Zoo from the public, in place of the old Victorian cages. In 1915, in his book *Cities in Evolution*, he coined the word 'CONURBATION', and in 1925 he designed the centre of TEL AVIV in Israel as a garden city.

ANDY BEATTIE (1913–83), appointed in 1954 as THE FIRST MANAGER OF THE SCOTLAND FOOTBALL TEAM, was born in Kintore.

# Angus

EARLS OF ANGUS ✦ MONTROSE ✦ GRAHAM
✦ THE GREAT MONTROSE ✦ DUKES OF MONTROSE
✦ SOME NOTABLE GRAHAMS ✦ BONNIE DUNDEE
✦ THANE OF GLAMIS ✦ GREY LADY
✦ EARL OF STRATHMORE AND KINGHORNE

*Dudhope Castle on Dundee Law in Dundee. Built*
*by the Scrymageous family in the late 13th century,*
*the present castle dates from 1580. Home in the*
*17th century to Viscount, 'Bonnie' Dundee*

◄ ANGUS FOLK ►

Hector Boece ✦ William Small ✦ James Tytler ✦ Neil Arnott
✦ Revd Patrick Bell ✦ James Bowman Lindsay ✦ Sir Robert Watson-Watt
✦ Iain Macmillan ✦ Ian McDiarmid

[15]

# Earls of Angus

A NGUS, the county, is named after Oengus, the oldest of seven sons of Fergus, a king of the Pictish kingdom of Alba in the 8th century. Each son occupied his own province, and when the Picts combined with the Scots to form the kingdom of Scotland these provinces became known as mormaerdoms, a Gaelic term, and their rulers were called mormaers. The first of these to be recorded was Dubacan of Angus, who was Mormaer of Angus in the 10th century.

Matilda, daughter of the last Gaelic Mormaer of Angus, Maol Choluim, married the Norman Gilbert de Umfraville, who used the Anglo-French title Earl of Angus. The title was eventually forfeited on the death of his grandson in 1325 and went to the Stewart family.

# Montrose

T he title DUKE OF MONTROSE was created in 1488 by James III for David Lindsay, the Earl of Crawford, who became THE FIRST SCOTSMAN NOT OF ROYAL BLOOD TO BE MADE A DUKE. The title then died out until WILLIAM GRAHAM was created Earl of Montrose in 1505,

since when it has stayed in the Graham family. The present Duke of Montrose is the Chief of Clan Graham and is THE ONLY ELECTED DUKE IN THE HOUSE OF LORDS. He resides at Drymen, near Loch Lomond.

# Graham

T he name GRAHAM could come from the Celtic 'greamach', meaning grim, or the Saxon 'grem', meaning stern or fierce, but is most likely of Norman origins. The first recorded Graham is the Norman knight SIR WILLIAM DE GRAHAM, who rode north from England with David I in 1128 and possibly got his name from Greag Ham, now Grantham in Lincolnshire. Sir William witnessed the charter to found the abbey of Holyrood and was granted lands in West Lothian, at Abercorn and Dalkeith, and as his descendants were building their reputation as the 'Gallant Grahams', so they gained more lands and honours, a process helped on occasion by marrying into the royal family.

SIR PATRICK GRAHAM died at the Battle of Dunbar in 1296, the only Scottish noble not to retreat, and his son SIR JOHN DE GRAHAM was William Wallace's stalwart friend, by his side throughout Wallace's campaign for independence. In early 1297, near

Queensberry in Dumfriesshire, the Scots were surprised by a body of English cavalry led by Sir John Graystock, whereupon Graham, aided by a few chosen men, led a hopeless charge, killing Graystock and giving his companions time to escape unscathed into the forest. Graham was wounded at Stirling Bridge and finally slain at the Battle of Falkirk.

Sir John's son DAVID GRAHAM was a faithful supporter of Robert the Bruce and received the lands of Montrose in return. In 1451 Patrick Graham was made THE 1ST LORD GRAHAM, and in 1488 William, the 3rd Lord Graham, who sat in the first

parliament of James IV, was created EARL OF MONTROSE. Along with his king, he died at the Battle of Flodden in 1513.

## The Great Montrose

JAMES GRAHAM, 5TH EARL AND 1ST MARQUESS OF MONTROSE (1612–50) was most likely born at Mugdock Castle in Stirlingshire. He became Earl of Montrose on his father's death in 1626, was educated at St Andrews University and learned the art of war in France. He was one of the four Scottish nobles who drew up the National Covenant in Greyfriar's Kirkyard in 1638, declaring the right of Scots to worship God without papist bishops. He went on to fight for the Covenanters in the 1640 Bishops' War against Charles I, but became disillusioned when he realised that many of the Scottish nobles were using the conflict for their own ends. As a result he refused to support the Scottish Parliament when it advocated union with Cromwell's English Parliamentarians, for which he was briefly imprisoned in Edinburgh Castle.

In gratitude, Charles I made Montrose his Lieutenant in Scotland, and created him 1st Marquess of Montrose. The new Marquess raised the King's standard at Blair Atholl to rally the Clans to the King's cause. To get the feuding clans to agree to anything was no easy task, and the fact that Montrose was able to lead them to a succession of stunning victories, culminating at the Battle of Kilsyth in August 1645, is testament to his skill as a leader, as well as his tactical genius.

His forces eventually became too dispersed, and he was finally defeated at Philphaugh, near Selkirk, in September 1645 and fled to Norway.

Shocked by Charles I's execution, in 1649 Montrose returned to Scotland determined to avenge the King. His forces were depleted in a shipwreck off Orkney, however, and his remaining men were easily overcome at the Battle of Carbisdale in 1650. Montrose escaped but was betrayed and held at Ardvreck Castle by MacLeod of Ardvreck until he could be handed over and taken to Edinburgh, where he was hanged without trial and disembowelled.

At the Restoration, Charles II ensured that Montrose was given a hero's funeral, and he was laid to rest beneath a grand monument in St Giles Cathedral.

# Dukes of Montrose

James Graham, 4th Marquess of Montrose (1682–1742), was elevated to 1ST DUKE OF MONTROSE by Queen Anne in 1707 in recognition of his support for the Act of Union.

JAMES GRAHAM, 6TH DUKE OF MONTROSE (1878–1954), was a naval engineer and President of the British Institution of Marine Engineers, who conceived and designed THE FIRST PRACTICAL AIRCRAFT-CARRIER and also took THE FIRST-EVER FILM OF A TOTAL ECLIPSE OF THE SUN.

JAMES GRAHAM, 7TH DUKE OF MONTROSE (1907-92), lived most of his life in Southern Africa and in 1965, in Salisbury, Rhodesia (now Harare, Zimbabwe), signed the Rhodesian Declaration of Independence along with Ian Smith.

## Some Notable Grahams

PATRICK GRAHAM (d.1478), grandson of Robert III, was THE FIRST ARCHBISHOP OF ST ANDREWS, from 1465 until his death.

# Bonnie Dundee

JAMES GRAHAM OF CLAVER-
HOUSE (1648–89) was the 1st and
only VISCOUNT DUNDEE. In 1672,
as a young lieutenant fighting for a
Scots regiment on the Continent, he
saved the life of the young Prince
William of Orange, whose horse had
become trapped on muddy ground.
The Prince later recommended
Graham as a soldier to the Duke of
York (later James VII of Scotland and
II of England), whose brother Charles
II sent Graham to suppress the
Covenanters in southern Scotland –
a task he pursued so vigorously that
he earned himself the nickname
'Bluidy Clavers'.

After the Glorious Revolution of
1688, in which James was removed
from the English throne by William
of Orange, Graham remained loyal to
James, who was his uncle, and was
created Viscount Dundee. He led
James's troops to a famous, but ultimately fruitless victory at the Battle
of Killiecrankie in 1689 (aided by Rob
Roy McGregor), but died leading the
final charge and was later immortalised in poem and song by Sir Walter
Scott as 'Bonnie Dundee'. The title
Viscount Dundee was forfeited in
1690.

*Come fill up my cup, come fill up my
    can,
Saddle my horses and call out my men,
And it's Ho! for the west port and let
    us gae free,
And we'll follow the bonnets o' bonnie
    Dundee!*
        Chorus from 'Bonnie Dundee'
                    by Sir Walter Scott

GEORGE GRAHAM (1674–1751), early
clockmaker who invented the
MERCURY PENDULUM and the DEAD
BEAT 'GRAHAM' ESCAPEMENT. He
also invented and built, in 1704, the
first modern ORRERY, or clockwork
model of the solar system, for Charles
Boyle, 4th Earl of Orrery, who gave
the device its name.

THOMAS GRAHAM (1805–69),
chemist who discovered DIALYSIS
(used in today's kidney dialysis
machines) and Graham's Law on the
diffusion of gases.

CHARLES K. GRAHAM (1824–89), civil engineer who laid out Central Park in New York City.

KENNETH GRAHAME (1859–1932), author of *The Wind in the Willows.*

WINSTON GRAHAM (1908–2003), author of the *Poldark* series of historical novels.

BILLY GRAHAM, born 1918, American evangelist.

BRUCE GRAHAM, born 1925, architect of the USA's tallest building, the 1,730 ft (527 m) high Sears Tower in Chicago.

DANIEL O'GRAHAM (1926–95), prime originator of the USA's controversial Strategic Defense Initiative concept, the defensive missile shield more popularly known as 'Star Wars'.

DAVID GRAHAM, actor and voice-over artist who was the original voice of the Daleks (with Peter Hawkins) in Dr Who, and also Parker and Brains in the original *Thunderbirds* television series.

# *Thane of Glamis*

Although Macbeth was accorded the title THANE OF GLAMIS by William Shakespeare, the first recorded Thane of Glamis was SIR JOHN LYON (c.1340–82), who was granted the lands and title by Robert II in 1372. In 1376 Lyon married Robert's daughter Princess Joanna and then became Chamberlain of Scotland.

The name LYON is derived from a French family called de Leon who came to Scotland at the end of the 11th century and settled in Perthshire, on land that became known as Glen Lyon. Sir John Lyon is recognised as the first of Clan Lyon.

His son John is thought to have built the original tower house at Glamis to replace the hunting lodge that was already there. The younger John's son Patrick was made LORD GLAMIS in 1445.

## Grey Lady

The 6TH LORD GLAMIS married JANE DOUGLAS, who in 1537 was burned as a witch on the orders of James V, during his feud with the Douglas family. In the chapel at Glamis Castle there is a seat at the back in which no one sits, for it is reserved for the Grey Lady, said to be the ghost of Jane – just one of the many hauntings that occur at Scotland's most haunted castle.

## Earl of Strathmore and Kinghorne

The 9th Lord Glamis was made Earl of Kinghorne in 1606, to which title the 3rd Earl of Kinghorne added the name Strathmore.

THE 9TH EARL OF STRATHMORE AND KINGHORNE assumed his wife's name of Bowes, as stipulated in the will of her father, a wealthy Durham coal mine owner, and the family name thereafter was BOWES-LYON.

The 10th Earl and his common-law wife Mary Milner had a son who was known as JOHN BOWES. Unable to claim his father's title, which went to the Earl's younger brother, John Bowes instead claimed his grandmother's coal-rich estate in Durham and eventually married a French actress, Joséphine Benoîte Coffin-Chevalier. They were both passionate collectors of art and antiques and endowed the BOWES MUSEUM in Barnard Castle to house their collection.

*Princess Margaret,*
*born in Glamis Castle in 1930*

The 13th Earl married FRANCES DORA SMITH, grandmother to Queen Elizabeth the Queen Mother and great-grandmother to Queen

Elizabeth II. Through her mother, Frances was a kinswoman of George Washington, thus making our Queen one of the closest living relatives of the first President of the United States.

*Well, I never knew this about*
## ANGUS FOLK

HECTOR BOECE (1465–1536), philosopher and FIRST PRINCIPAL OF THE UNIVERSITY OF ST ANDREWS, born in Dundee. In 1527 he published his *History of the Scottish People*. Written in Latin, it was only the second Scottish history to be published, and when it was translated into English for Holinshed's *Chronicle* it provided the basis for Shakespeare's *Macbeth*.

WILLIAM SMALL (1734–75), mathematician and philosopher, born in Carmyllie. As Professor of Natural Philosophy at the College of William and Mary in Virginia, he had a profound influence on his student Thomas Jefferson, principal author of the Declaration of Independence, who described him as 'a man profound in most of the useful branches of science, with a happy talent of communication, correct and gentlemanly manners, and a large and liberal mind'. When he returned to Britain in 1764, Small was elected on the recommendation of Benjamin Franklin to the Lunar Society, a prestigious club of scientists, industrialists and philosophers, which included James Watt, Erasmus Darwin, William Murdock and Josiah Wedgwood. They were all aware that they were changing the world and eagerly sought Small's philosophical and moral advice. He was much missed when he died tragically young at 41.

## James Tytler
◄ 1747–1804 ►

Styled by the *Edinburgh Advertiser* as the 'FIRST PERSON IN GREAT BRITAIN TO HAVE NAVIGATED THE AIR', Tytler was born in Fern. A successful imbiber but an unsuccessful medical student and inventor, Tytler fed his family by editing the second and third editions of the *Encyclopaedia Britannica* between 1776 and 1784.

Tytler then became swept up in the enthusiasm for ballooning provoked by the Montgolfier Brothers' successful flight at Versailles in September 1783, and in August 1784 he rose into the air from Abbeyfield in his own hot-air balloon and sailed for half a mile (0.8 km) across Edinburgh at a height of 350 ft (107 m), before landing at Restalrig. Unfortunately, no one was looking and when he tried to repeat the feat in front of massed press and public he couldn't get off the ground. He did manage flight once more, in October that year, but crashed into the crowd causing much pandemonium.

Tytler's achievement was rather overshadowed by the flamboyant Vincenzo Lunardi, who flew over Hertfordshire in September that year with much fanfare, but there were enough people to witness that James Tytler, if nothing else, was THE FIRST SCOTSMAN TO FLY.

In 1793 Tytler was forced to flee after publishing some seditious material and he ended up in Salem, Massachusetts, where he drowned in 1804.

NEIL ARNOTT (1788–1874), inventor and physician, born in Arbroath. Travels to discover the ancient wonders of China as surgeon for the East India Company inspired an inventive streak in Arnott, which bore fruit in the mid 1820s when he came up with a highly efficient smokeless stove called an ARNOTT STOVE, along with a chimney ventilation valve. In 1832 he invented the WATERBED, to provide comfort to his bedridden patients and to prevent bedsores. His de luxe version, a water chair intended to prevent seasickness, was less successful, merely exacerbating the problem.

THE REVD PATRICK BELL (1799–1869) was born at Auchterhouse, near Dundee. In 1827 he invented an ingenious REAPING MACHINE, which he then spent 15 years perfecting. When it was unveiled in 1843, the same year he was ordained as minister at Carmyllie, it was an immediate success and the design led directly to the modern combine harvester.

JAMES BOWMAN LINDSAY (1799–1862), inventor and author, born in Carmyllie. Educated at St Andrews University, he settled in Dundee as science and mathematics lecturer at the Watt Institution. Motivated by the need to find a safe method of lighting for the city's jute factories, after a number of fires caused by naked flame, Lindsay came up with an ELECTRIC LIGHT whereby he could 'read a book at a distance of one and a half foot'. He demonstrated this at a public meeting in Dundee's Thistle Hall in 1835, some 40 years before Joseph Swan unveiled his light bulb in Gateshead. Lindsay was not business-minded enough to establish or develop his invention, as with the system of submarine telegraphy he put forward in 1854, but his vision of the 'information society' and 'cities lit by electricity' inspired scientific advance for the next two centuries.

*James Bowman Lindsay*

SIR ROBERT WATSON-WATT (1892–1973), inventor of the first practical RADAR, born in Brechin. He was a descendant of the inventor of the steam engine, James Watt.

IAIN MACMILLAN (1938–2006), the photographer who took the iconic cover photograph for the Beatles' *Abbey Road* album, born in Dundee.

IAN McDIARMID, the actor who plays the Emperor in the *Star Wars* film series, was born in Carnoustie in 1944.

# Argyll

DUKE OF ARGYLL ✦ CAMPBELL ✦ LORD CAMPBELL
✦ EARLS OF ARGYLL ✦ DUKES OF ARGYLL
✦ SOME NOTABLE CAMPBELLS ✦ LORD CLYDE
✦ SIR HENRY CAMPBELL-BANNERMAN

*Inverary Castle, seat of the Chief of Clan Campbell, the Duke of Argyll. The Armoury Hall has the highest ceiling in Scotland, at 70ft (21m).*

◄ ARGYLL FOLK ►

David Colville ✦ Archibald Mitchell ✦ Neil Munro
✦ John Smith ✦ Sylvester McCoy

# Duke of Argyll

The title DUKE OF ARGYLL has been held by the Campbell family since 1701. The Duke is also Chief of Clan Campbell, known as MACCAILEAN MÒR – Gaelic for 'Son of Great Colin', which refers to the Great Sir Colin Campbell, who was killed fighting the MacDougall Lord of Lorne in 1294.

The Campbell rise to power is based on the impregnable nature of their Highland strongholds, and on their acting as agents of the Scottish crown in subduing the rebellious and semi-independent Lords of the Isles. The latter also partly explains the stories of a legendary feud between the Campbells and the MacDonalds.

# Campbell

The first officially recorded member of the Campbell family is Gillespie, or Archibald, who was granted lands in Menstrie in Clackmannanshire in 1263. Gillespie was the father of Cailean Mór, the GREAT SIR COLIN CAMPBELL, ancestor of all the MacCailean Mòrs up to the present Duke of Argyll.

The Campbells had held lands around Loch Awe for several generations before then, and the Great Sir

Colin's grandfather, Dugald of Loch Awe, was given the name 'Cam Beul', meaning 'crooked mouth', since he had a habit of talking out of the side of his mouth. One of their strongholds was the hopelessly romantic KILCHURN CASTLE, which stands in Loch Awe on what was once an island.

# Lord Campbell

The Campbells acquired their ever-increasing land and power by supporting Robert the Bruce and by marrying well. They fought for Bruce at Bannockburn, and the Great Sir Colin's son Neil married Bruce's sister Mary. In the early 15th century, Duncan Campbell married Marjorie, daughter of Robert Stewart, Duke of Albany and brother of Robert III, thus cementing their relationships to both the royal houses of Scotland. Duncan was made 1st Lord Campbell in 1445 by James II. Around this time the Campbells moved their seat from Loch Awe to Inverary on Loch Fyne.

## Earls of Argyll

D uncan's grandson Colin, 2nd Lord Campbell (1433–93), was made IST EARL OF ARGYLL by James III in 1457 as a reward for supporting James II against the Black Douglases. He was Lord Chancellor for both James III and James IV.

ARCHIBALD, 2ND EARL OF ARGYLL, was killed alongside James IV at Flodden in 1513. His younger son married the kidnapped daughter of the Thane of Cawdor and became the first Campbell of Cawdor (*see* Nairnshire).

ARCHIBALD, 5TH EARL OF ARGYLL (1537–73), was at first opposed to Mary Queen of Scots, and was implicit in the murders of both Rizzio and Lord Darnley, but he baulked at deposing Mary and came round to her side, leading her army at the Battle of Langside in 1568. Well, not quite leading, because he fainted as battle was joined, but certainly supporting. Once recovered, he was made Lord High Chancellor of Scotland in 1572.

ARCHIBALD, 7TH EARL OF ARGYLL, earned himself the nickname, reminiscent of his 14th-century ancestor the Earl of Douglas, of 'Archie the Grim', for his ruthless pursuit of the clans Donald and Gregor – he is suspected of having had a hand in the massacre of the Colquhouns at Glenfruin in 1603, which resulted in the proscribing of the MacGregors (*see* Dunbartonshire). He also gained the lands of Kintyre from the MacDonalds of Islay and in 1618, in an effort to civilise the natives, he began the transformation of the little burgh of Lochhead into CAMP-BELTOWN, which became a royal burgh in 1700. At the end of his life he converted to Rome and surrendered his lands to his son.

ARCHIBALD CAMPBELL, 8th EARL OF ARGYLL (1607–61), was created the one and only MARQUESS OF ARGYLL in 1641 by Charles I, who expected him to look after his royal interests in Scotland, but Argyll was a Covenanter and ended up fighting against Charles' man Montrose, who gathered together an army of disaffected MacDonalds to inflict a heavy defeat on Argyll at Inverlochy in 1645. Campbell was quite happy to see Montrose eventually hang at Edinburgh, but his own turn came at the Restoration, when he was executed at Edinburgh Cross by the gruesome Scottish guillotine, the Maiden, and his head displayed on top of the Tolbooth, where Montrose's head had previously been the attraction. The Marquessate of Argyll died with him.

ARCHIBALD CAMPBELL, 9TH EARL OF ARGYLL (1629–85), was a Royalist who fought for Prince Charles at the Battle of Worcester in 1651. He was also a Protestant, however, and James VII's overt Catholicism provoked Campbell into leading an invasion of Scotland in 1685 as the Scottish wing of the Monmouth Rebellion. He was defeated by the Marquess of Atholl, captured and, like his father, executed. The 9th Earl was responsible for the building of the exquisite Argyll's Lodging in Stirling, the most complete example of a 17th-century town house in Scotland.

## Dukes of Argyll

ARCHIBALD CAMPBELL, 9TH EARL OF ARGYLL (1658–1703),

did not support his father's rebellion in 1685 but was rebuffed when he tried to approach James VII and so transferred his loyalty to William of Orange, being one of the two commissioners who offered William the Scottish crown. In 1689 he raised and was the nominal colonel-in-chief of the Earl of Argyll's Regiment of Foot, which was involved in the Glencoe Massacre in 1692. The Earl himself played no part in the outrage, the regiment being commanded by his distant kinsman Captain Robert Campbell (1630–96). In 1701 William made the Earl the 1ST DUKE OF ARGYLL. A hearty swordsman, he is credited with inventing the CONDOM.

The 1st Duke clearly passed the notion of the condom on to his son, JOHN CAMPBELL, 2ND DUKE OF ARGYLL (1680–1743), who is referred to, in a letter that provides the first known use of the word, as travelling from London to Edinburgh in possession of a 'certaine instrument called a Quondam, which occasioned ye debauching of a great number of Ladies of qualitie, and other young gentlewomen'. The 2nd Duke took command of government forces to defeat the Jacobite Earl of Mar at the Battle of Sheriffmuir in 1715, and in 1736 he became ONE OF THE FIRST TWO FIELD MARSHALS appointed in the British army.

ARCHIBALD CAMPBELL, 3RD

DUKE OF ARGYLL (1682–1761), helped his brother, the 2nd Duke, at Sherrifmuir, and in 1727 was co-founder and FIRST GOVERNOR OF THE ROYAL BANK OF SCOTLAND. Since 1987 his portrait, based on a painting by Allan Ramsay, has appeared on the front of all Royal Bank of Scotland banknotes. He began the building of Inverary Castle, which was completed by his cousin the 4th Duke.

JOHN CAMPBELL, 5TH DUKE OF ARGYLL (1723–1806), married, in 1759, ELIZABETH GUNNING, widow of the Duke of Hamilton and one of the 'beautiful Miss Gunnings'.

JOHN CAMPBELL, 9TH DUKE OF ARGYLL (1845–1914), married, in 1871, PRINCESS LOUISE CAROLINE ALBERTA, fourth daughter of Queen Victoria. In 1878, Campbell was appointed as THE YOUNGEST EVER GOVERNOR-GENERAL OF CANADA, where they took up residence. Lake Louise and the province of Alberta were named for the Princess.

The 11th Duke's third wife, MARGARET WHIGHAM, found fame in the gossip columns for having an affair with a number of high-profile men including the actor Douglas Fairbanks Jnr and Minister of Defence Duncan Sandys. During divorce proceedings in 1963 the Duke produced a picture of the 'dirty duchess', wearing her full set of pearls, having her way with a man whose face was not shown. The identity of this 'headless man' has remained an intriguing mystery ever since.

The present incumbent and MacCailean Mòr, Chief of Clan Campbell, is TORQUHIL CAMPBELL, 13TH DUKE OF ARGYLL. His seat is INVERARY CASTLE.

## Some Notable Campbells

JOHN CAMPBELL OF LUNDIE (d. 1712), banker. In 1692 Campbell set up as a goldsmith banker at the sign of the Three Crowns in the Strand in London, one of the first people to offer a comprehensive banking service, discounting bills, taking deposits and making loans. His kinsman, the rich and powerful Duke of Argyll, was one of Campbell's first clients, and introduced him to Queen Anne, who commissioned Campbell to create the regalia for the Order of the Thistle. Some 60 years later the bank that John Campbell founded became Coutts Bank.

## Field Marshall Sir Colin Campbell, Lord Clyde
### 1792–1863

Born in Glasgow, the son of a carpenter, Campbell adopted his mother's name to gain a commission in the army in 1807. He served with distinction in the Peninsula War (including Corunna), then the Opium Wars in China, where he was promoted to brigadier-general. Next

came the Second Sikh War (1848–9) in India and command of the outpost at Peshawar on the North-West Frontier. In 1854, at the age of almost 60, he led the Highland Brigade to victory at Alma, the first battle of the Crimean war. At Balaclava his courageous leadership inspired the Brigade's 'thin red line' to hold fast against the Russian cavalry. His heroism was not yet done with, and he was sent to take command in India during the Mutiny of 1857, where he relieved Lucknow for the second time. Popular with his men and admired by his fellow officers, Sir Colin Campbell is remembered as one of the British army's greatest commanders.

CAMPBELL'S CONDENSED SOUP, the world's best-selling soup, was first sold in 1897 by John Campbell of New Jersey, born 1817. The red and white labelling was introduced in 1898 and immortalised in a 1961 painting by Andy Warhol.

## Sir Henry Campbell-Bannerman
### 1836–1908

SIR HENRY CAMPBELL-BANNERMAN, Liberal MP for Stirling and FIRST PRIME MINISTER. 'CB', as he was

known, was the first person to be called Prime Minister. Before then the leader was referred to as First Lord of the Treasury, and that is the title still written on the brass plate on the door of No. 10, Downing Street. CB was obliged to add Bannerman to his surname in 1871 as a condition for inheriting a fortune from his uncle. While in office from 1905 to 1908, he oversaw the introduction of sick pay and the old age pension, and negotiated entente with Russia.

In 1907 he became THE ONLY SERVING PRIME MINISTER TO ALSO BE FATHER OF THE HOUSE.

In April 1908 he resigned because of ill health, brought on, some say, by a broken heart after the death of his beloved wife Charlotte in 1906. He was too ill to be moved out of Downing Street and died there three weeks after resigning – THE ONLY PRIME MINISTER TO DIE IN No.

10. His last words were 'This is not the end of me.'

CB and his wife, who had poor health, went every year to take the cure at Marienbad in Bohemia. He would consult his wife on everything and called her 'my final Court of Appeal'.

He did not like exercise. 'Personally I am an immense believer in bed, in constantly keeping horizontal: the heart and everything else goes slower, and the whole system is refreshed.'

He loved trees. As one of his guests at Belmont Castle, his home in Perthshire, remarked, 'When he passed those [trees] of which he was particularly fond he would bow to them and wish them good morning.' When selecting a walking stick, he would apologise to the ones left behind.

He loved bulldogs, at one time owning 30 of them. They were known to bite, and CB's private secretary would sometimes have to defend himself, and other guests, with a fire poker, during tea.

CB was something of a bon viveur and enjoyed French cuisine. He took long lunches and would always finish with gingerbread and butter – a Scottish custom.

He was one of the few Prime Ministers everyone seemed to like. In the words of Lloyd George: 'I have never met a great public figure who so completely won the attachment and affection of the men who came into contact with him. He was not merely admired and respected; he was absolutely loved by us all', and '. . . he has the one great and essential qualification in a Liberal [leader] of being a liberal himself.'

Memorable Quotes:

*'Good government can never be a substitute for government by the people themselves.'*

*'The people of this country are a straightforward people. They like honesty and straightforwardness of purpose . . . but they do not like cleverness.'*

SIR MALCOLM CAMPBELL (1885–1948), world speed record holder AND THE FIRST PERSON TO DRIVE AT OVER 300 MPH. Between 1924 and 1935 he broke NINE LAND SPEED RECORDS, three on Pendine Sands in Wales and five at Daytona Beach in Florida. His final record was set on the Bonneville Salt Flats in 1935 with a speed of 301.3 mph (484.8 kph). He also held four water speed records, his highest speed being 141.7 mph (228 kph) in *Bluebird K4* on Coniston Water in 1939. One day before racing at Brooklands, Campbell went to see a play, *The Blue Bird*, by Maeterlinck, about the bluebird of happiness, always tantalisingly out of reach. Next day he painted his

Darracq car blue and christened it 'BLUEBIRD', the name he, and his son Donald, would from then on give to all their cars and boats. The Napier-Campbell *Bluebird* which he drove at a record 174.9 mph (281.4 kph) on Pendine Sands in Wales in February 1927 was THE FIRST CAR EVER BUILT SIMPLY FOR BREAKING THE LAND SPEED RECORD.

Memorable Quote:

*'Life is an eternal challenge, a variant on Maeterlinck's theme that the Bluebird of happiness is by the side of each and every one of us, always within reach, yet, if pursued to catch and possess, is beyond our grasp.'*

DONALD CAMPBELL (1921–67), world speed record holder, son of Sir Malcolm Campbell, and THE ONLY PERSON EVER TO HOLD LAND AND WATER SPEED RECORDS IN THE SAME YEAR, 1964. Between 1955 and 1964 he set seven water speed records, reaching 276 mph (444 kph) on Lake Dumbleyung in Perth, Australia, in 1964, the same year that he set the land speed record of 403 mph (648 kph) at Lake Eyre in Australia. In 1967 he was killed on Coniston Water, where his father had set so many records, while attempting to become the first person to go over 300 mph on water – he succeeded just before he died.

GEORGE LAW CAMPBELL (1912–2004), linguist who served in the BBC European Service during the Second World War. Campbell appeared in the *Guinness Book of Records* for his ability to write and speak fluently in 44 languages.

PATRICK CAMPBELL, 3RD BARON GLENAVY (1913–80), journalist and television personality remembered for his appearances on the TV panel game *Call My Bluff* opposite Frank Muir.

GLEN CAMPBELL, country singer, born 1936. Amongst his greatest hits are 'By the Time I Get to Phoenix' (1967), 'Wichita Lineman' (1968), 'Galveston' (1969) and 'Rhinestone Cowboy' (1975).

SIR MENZIES CAMPBELL, highly regarded Liberal politician, born 1941.

KIM CAMPBELL, the FIRST FEMALE PRIME MINISTER OF CANADA, born 1947.

NEVE CAMPBELL, actress known for her roles in the *Scream* film series and *Wild Things* (1998), born 1973.

*Well, I never knew this about*
ARGYLLSHIRE FOLK

DAVID COLVILLE (1813–97), founder of Colville Steel, born in Campbeltown. After some time spent helping his father with his coastal shipping business David Colville went into partnership to set up an iron-making company, the Clifton Iron Works, at Coatbridge. Ten years later he moved to Motherwell and established the Dalzell Works, producing malleable iron bars. In 1879 he won the contract to supply the iron bars for the new Tay Bridge. The next step was to build the necessary infrastructure to manufacture the new mild steel for the Forth Railway Bridge. The Dalzell Works also supplied the slabs from which the very first steel plates were rolled in America. By 1912 David Colville's sons had made the Dalzell Steel and Iron Works in Motherwell the LARGEST STEEL WORKS IN BRITAIN, with Harland and Wolff among its customers. In 1954 the Colvilles expanded and built a huge new works at Ravenscraig which in its heyday was THE LARGEST HOT STRIP STEEL MILL IN EUROPE.

SPRINGBANK DISTILLERY, Campbeltown, THE OLDEST INDEPENDENT FAMILY-OWNED DISTILLERY IN SCOTLAND, was founded in 1828 on the site of an illicit still owned by ARCHIBALD MITCHELL (1734–1818). In October 1888, 112 gallons of Springbank's finest whisky was bought at 8s. 8d. per gallon by one Mr John Walker. Today the distillery is still in the hands of the Mitchell family and is THE ONLY DISTILLERY IN SCOTLAND TO CARRY OUT THE FULL PRODUCTION PROCESS, FLOOR MALTING, MATURATION AND BOTTLING ON ONE SITE. It is also

THE ONLY DISTILLERY IN SCOTLAND TO PRODUCE THREE DIFFERENT SINGLE MALTS, Springbank, Longrow and Hazelburn, using three different production methods. J&A Mitchell additionally owns THE FIRST NEW DISTILLERY BUILT IN SCOTLAND in the new millennium, MITCHELL'S GLENGYLE DISTILLERY, also in Campeltown.

NEIL MUNRO (1863–1930), writer, born in Inverary. Munro was a journalist and author (under the name Hugh Foulis) of the Para Handy stories about a Clyde puffer called the *Vital Spark*, which were turned into three BBC television series between 1959 and 1995.

JOHN SMITH (1938–94), Labour Party leader, born in Dalmally. He modernised Labour, bringing the party into the centre left and paving the way for New Labour to win power

with a landslide victory in 1997. He died suddenly of a heart attack and is buried on Iona.

SYLVESTER McCOY, actor, best known for playing the seventh Doctor Who from 1987 to 1989, born in Dunoon in 1943.

# Ayrshire

KENNEDY ✦ DUNURE ✦ EARLS OF CASSILLIS
✦ CULZEAN CASTLE ✦ MARQUESS OF AILSA
✦ SOME NOTABLE KENNEDYS ✦ EARLDOM OF EGLINTON
✦ EGLINTON CASTLE ✦ EGLINTON TOURNAMENT

*Culzean Castle, Robert Adam's finest creation in Scotland, former seat of the Kennedys and Scottish home of President Eisenhower.*

◀ AYRSHIRE FOLK ▶

Robert Hunter ✦ Charles Tennant ✦ Abram Lyle ✦ Andrew Fisher
✦ John Boyd Orr ✦ Sam Torrance ✦ Sir Thomas Hunter

# Kennedy

S outh Ayrshire and Carrick has been Kennedy territory since the 11th century, when it was part of Galloway. The clan was a branch of the Lords of Galloway, descended from Duncan, 1st Earl of Carrick, and Kennedy is thought to come from Kenneth, meaning 'chief', or 'head of the tribe'.

## Dunure

J OHN KENNEDY OF DUNURE received the barony of Casellis in 1350 and, as Sir John Kennedy, married the heiress Marjory Montgomerie, bringing the enormous tower house of CASSILLIS into the family. Nonetheless, they continued to live in mighty DUNURE CASTLE, perched on its rocky outcrop overlooking the Firth of Clyde.

Sir John's descendant, Sir James Kennedy of Dunure, married Mary, daughter of Robert III, and their son Gilbert Kennedy (1406–79) was created LORD KENNEDY in 1458.

# Earl of Cassillis

D avid, 3rd Lord Kennedy, was created EARL OF CASSILLIS in 1509 and died at Flodden Field four years later.

## 3rd Earl of Cassillis

A t the age of 12, GILBERT KENNEDY, 3RD EARL OF CASSILLIS (1515–58), was pressured into signing the death warrant of Patrick Hamilton, Scotland's first Protestant martyr. Many years later he was one of the eight Commissioners appointed to attend the marriage of Mary Queen of Scots to the Dauphin of France in 1558. The French Court were most upset when the Scottish refused to allow the Dauphin to become King of Scotland, and Kennedy was one of the four Commissioners who died in mysterious circumstances in Dieppe on their way home, poisoned, it is supposed, by the French.

## 4th Earl of Cassillis

G ILBERT KENNEDY, 4TH EARL OF CASSILLIS (1541–76), was resolute in his efforts to increase the family holdings when everything was

*Dunure Castle*

up for grabs after the Scottish Reformation. He acquired some of the lands of Glenluce Abbey in Wigtownshire by paying a monk to forge the necessary signatures on the charter, then retrieved the fee by having the monk disposed of, and finally wrapped it all up neatly by hanging the monk's killer on a charge of theft.

This was only a rehearsal. Gilbert had his eye on the juicy estate of Crossraguel Abbey, and since the Abbot there was his uncle, Gilbert fully expected to get everything when his uncle died. Uncle duly obliged in 1564, but the new administrator, sent in to sort out the finances, was a Stewart, and he was not disposed to let Kennedy have anything at all. The disgruntled Gilbert had Stewart kidnapped, brought to Dunure, tied to a spit and roasted over the open fire in the castle kitchens until he agreed to sign over the abbey estates, which Stewart did after two slow rotations.

The lightly browned Stewart was eventually rescued by a Kennedy relative who wanted the lands for himself, but Gilbert had his signed agreement and kept his prize.

Not long afterwards the Kennedys abandoned Dunure and made CASSILLIS HOUSE their main home.

## Culzean Castle

B y 1777 DAVID, 10TH EARL OF CASSILLIS, was awash with cash thanks to a highly efficient and innovative farm manager called John Bulley, who somehow managed to increase the yield of the Kennedy estates tenfold. The Earl therefore commissioned Robert Adam to transform the simple fortified house at CULZEAN, a few miles to the south of the old castle at Dunure, into a prestigious stately home befitting a family of means and ancient lineage. Standing right on the edge of the cliff,

150 ft (46 m) above the Firth of Clyde, with sweeping views across to the Mull of Kintyre, the Isle of Arran and the majestic Ailsa Craig, Culzean is Robert Adam's crowning glory. The jewel in that crown is the ingenious OVAL STAIRCASE at the centre of the house, squeezed in as an afterthought but unsurpassed in beauty.

Since 1987 Culzean Castle has featured on the back of the Royal Bank of Scotland's five-pound note.

## Marquess of Ailsa

❧❧❧❧

ARCHIBALD KENNEDY, 12TH EARL OF CASSILLIS (1770–1846), became a great friend of William IV of England, the 'Sailor King', who created him MARQUESS OF AILSA at the coronation in 1831.

CHARLES KENNEDY, 5TH MARQUESS OF AILSA (1875–1956), handed Culzean

over to the National Trust for Scotland in 1945 in lieu of death duties, with the stipulation that they present the apartment on the top floor of the castle to General Eisenhower for his lifetime, in recognition of Eisenhower's role as Supreme Commander of the Allied Forces in Europe during the Second World War. Eisenhower first visited Culzean Castle in 1946 and stayed there four times, on one occasion while President of the United States, no doubt with an eye to the proximity of Troon and Turnberry golf courses.

Memorable Quote:
*'. . . nothing else that Scotland could have done could so emphatically symbolise for me the feeling of British-American partnership which was such a vital force in bringing the war to a successful conclusion.'*
President Dwight D. Eisenhower

*Eisenhower and the 5th Marquess of Ailsa*

In 1973 the castle starred as the home of Lord Summerisle (played by Christopher Lee) in the cult film THE WICKER MAN, starring Edward Woodward.

ARCHIBALD KENNEDY, 8TH MARQUESS OF AILSA, is the present hereditary Chief of Clan Kennedy and lives at Cassillis House.

## Some Notable Kennedys

SUSANNAH KENNEDY (c.1690–1780), daughter of Sir Archibald Kennedy of Culzean, and third wife of Alexander Montgomerie, 9th Earl of Eglinton, was one of the most beautiful women of her time and produced seven equally beautiful daughters as well as three handsome sons. After her elderly husband died in 1729, when she was not yet 40, she became renowned for giving magnificent dinner parties at Auchans, her house in Ayrshire, and impressed even Dr Johnson with her grace and wit. As she grew older she became a trifle eccentric and began to give dinner parties for the Auchans' rat population, summoning them to the table by tapping on one of the wall panels. Once they had feasted she would give a quiet word of command and the rats would disperse in an orderly fashion back into the wainscotting. Lady Eglinton found them to be much more satisfactory guests than her human friends. 'Rats,' she would say, 'know when to go home.'

SIR LUDOVIC KENNEDY, journalist, broadcaster and author, born 1919. Often addressed as 'Ludo' by politicians who mistakenly tried to ingratiate themselves with him during interviews. He was married to the dancer and actress Moira Shearer, who died in 2006, for 56 years.

CHARLES KENNEDY, popular leader of the Liberal Democrats from 1999 until 2006, born 1959.

## *Earldom of Eglinton*

The Eglinton estate came into the Montgomerie family in the late 14th century when SIR JOHN

MONTGOMERY OF EAGLESHAM married ELIZABETH, heiress to SIR HUGH DE EGLINTON, brother-in-law of Robert II.

The Earldom of Eglinton was created for Lord Hugh Montgomerie in 1508 by James IV, for whom the Montgomeries had fought at the Battle of Sauchiebrun in 1488.

## Eglinton Castle

T he Montgomeries built themselves a small 'fare castell' at Eglinton when they acquired the estate, but they continued to live mainly at Poltoon Castle, their family seat at Eaglesham in Renfrewshire, until Hugh Montgomerie (1739–1819) returned from military action in America and succeeded as the 12th Earl in 1769.

He had a distinguished record as a soldier, serving with the 77th Regiment, which was raised by his kinsman the 11th Earl and was known as Montgomerie's Highlanders. He fought alongside George Washington during the Forbes expedition to recapture Fort Duquesne (now Pittsburgh) from the French in 1758.

Once home, and established as Earl, Hugh Montgomerie decided to indulge in some serious construction, and his first project was the building of a huge castellated Gothic fantasy at Eglinton. When it was finished the new EGLINTON CASTLE was rivalled in Ayrshire only by Culzean for grandeur. At the same time, the Earl began to construct a deep-water dock at Ardrossan along with a canal linking the dock with the coalfields on his estate and the booming industrial towns of Glasgow and Paisley.

*Eglinton Castle*

# Eglinton Tournament

Archibald Montgomerie, 13th Earl of Eglinton (1812–61), grandson of the 12th Earl and a keen *aficionado* of the turf, completed his grandfather's great building works (although the canal never made it to Ardrossan) and still had enough money left over to fund and organise one of the most lavish and talked-about extravagances ever witnessed in Scotland, the Eglinton Tournament of 1839.

The tournament was to consist of four days of carnival, pageantry and feasting, and was designed to compensate those who had been disappointed by the muted celebrations for Queen Victoria's coronation the previous year. As the main attraction the Earl had arranged a jousting tournament, a brave choice bearing in mind that in 1559 his kinsman Gabriel, Comte de Montgomery, had killed Henry II of France by piercing the King's eye with his lance during a joust.

The Eglinton Tournament drew a crowd of over 50,000 people, and amongst those attending were the 'Mad' Marquess of Waterford, the Earl of Craven in a magnificent suit of Milanese armour, inlaid with gold, that his ancestor had worn at the Battle of Crecy, the Duke of Atholl with a retinue of his new Atholl Highlanders, Lady Seymour, granddaughter of the playwright Richard Brindsley Sheridan, as Queen of Beauly, the Hungarian Baron Esterhazy and the exiled Prince Louis Napoleon of France, later Napoleon III, who kept falling off his horse and rolling around on the ground in his armour, unable to get up. It poured with rain every day.

Eventually the Eglinton fortunes sank in the Ardrossan docks, and in the early 20th century Eglinton Castle was abandoned. Much of it was demolished when the army used it for target training in the Second World War, and now just a few bare walls are left standing, although the ornamental bridge built across the River Lugton for the tournament, survives at the heart of what is now a country park.

In 1859 the 13th Earl of Eglinton was created Earl of Winton and the two earldoms were united. The present incumbent is ARCHIBALD MONTGOMERIE, THE 18TH EARL OF EGLINTON AND WINTON, who is Chief of the Name and Arms of Montgomerie. The present seat of Clan Montgomery is SKELMORLIE CASTLE near Largs.

*Well, I never knew this*
*about*
## AYRSHIRE FOLK

ROBERT HUNTER (1664–1734), grandson of the Laird of Hunterston, family seat of the Clan Hunter. He joined the British army, and saw service in Flanders and at the Battle of Blenheim in 1704. In 1707 he was appointed Lieutenant Governor of Virginia and later, in 1710, became the Governor of New York and New Jersey, where he was described as 'one of the few popular Royal Governors in American history'. A poet and play-wright, he was friends with Joseph Addison and Jonathan Swift, and in 1714 he co-authored, with Lewis Morris, a satirical comedy called *Androborus*, THE FIRST PLAY TO BE WRITTEN AND PRINTED IN AMERICA. He went on to be Governor of Jamaica from 1727 until his death in 1734.

CHARLES TENNANT (1768–1838), industrial chemist, was born in Ochiltree, one of 16 children of a farmer. As an apprentice weaver he soon discovered that methods for bleaching cloth were not keeping up with the development of weaving in other areas, and after some research in partnership with Charles Macintosh he invented BLEACHING POWDER, using a combination of chlorine and lime. In 1800 he set up a factory at St Rollox in Glasgow to produce this bleaching powder, and by 1830 it had become the LARGEST CHEMICAL WORKS IN THE WORLD. Tennant's wealth spawned a colourful dynasty that included Lord Glen-conner, the supermodel Stella Tennant and Stephen Tennant, the 'bright young thing' who partly inspired Evelyn Waugh's Lord Sebastian Flyte in *Brideshead Revisited*, and spent the last 20 years of his life in bed.

ANDREW FISHER (1862–1928) born in Crosshouse, the son of a miner. At 17 he was elected as secretary of the local branch of the National Union of Miners, but after leading a number of strikes he was blacklisted and in 1885 he decided to emigrate to Australia. After some time working in the mines there he once more joined the union and was then elected to the Queensland Assembly. Rising to leader of the Labour Party in the new Federal government he became Prime Minister three times between 1908 and 1915, and ranks second to Bob Hawke as Australia's longest-

*Andrew Fisher*

serving Labour Prime Minister. Fisher's second administration in 1910 was AUSTRALIA'S FIRST FEDERAL MAJORITY GOVERNMENT and THE FIRST LABOUR MAJORITY GOVERN-MENT IN THE WORLD.

JOHN BOYD ORR (1880–1971), doctor and biologist, was born in Kilmaurs. He served as a medical officer in the trenches at the Battle of the Somme, for which he won a Mili-tary Cross, and at Passchendaele, for which he received the DSO. Part of his success was the result of research Boyd Orr had done before the war into nutrition and health, and he carried on this work afterwards at the Rowlett Research Institute, which he set up in Aberdeen. One of the recommendations of the Institute was for FREE MILK IN SCHOOLS. He was appointed FIRST DIRECTOR GENERAL OF THE UNITED NATIONS FOOD AND AGRICULTURE ORGAN-ISATION, and in 1949 he was awarded the NOBEL PEACE PRIZE for his contribution to helping the starving nations of the world.

SAM TORRANCE, professional golfer, born in Largs in 1953. He played for the European team in eight Ryder Cup competitions and is remembered for sinking the winning putt in 1985 that wrested the trophy away from the Americans for the first time in 28 years. He also won the Ryder Cup as non-playing captain of the European team in 2002.

SIR THOMAS HUNTER, born in New Cumnock in 1961, a grocer's son, was recorded in 2007 as the FIRST SCOTS-BORN BILLIONAIRE. He began his career selling trainers out of the back of a van, a business that grew into Sports Division, which he sold to JJB Sports in 1998 for £292 million. After this he set up the Hunter Foundation for donating to educational and business projects in Scotland.

# Banffshire

MACDUFF ✦ WILLIAM DUFF ✦ DUFFTOWN
✦ WILLIAM GRANT ✦ GLENFIDDICH
✦ THE BALVENIE ✦ GRANT'S WHISKY

*Duff House, regarded as one of the finest Georgian houses
in Britain, was built by William Adam in 1740 for Earl
Fife and modelled on the Villa Borghese in Rome.*

### BANFFSHIRE FOLK

St John Ogilvie ✦ James Blair ✦ Captain George Duff
✦ Admiral Archibald Duff ✦ George Stephen

# *Macduff*

❖◄●●●►❖

The Macduffs were descended from Dub, King of Alba 962–6. Dub, or Duff, comes from the Celtic word for dark and refers to the King's black hair and swarthy looks. Dub's heir, Kenneth III (grandfather of Lady Macbeth), was killed in battle by Malcolm II, but the sons of Dub, the Macduffs, held on as Mormaers of Fife, the highest ranking nobles in the Kingdom.

It was MACDUFF who, according to Shakespeare, actually killed Macbeth, but even if in reality he didn't strike the fatal blow, Macduff was certainly the architect behind Macbeth's downfall.

The story goes that Macduff was reluctant to answer Macbeth's call for help in building his castle at Dunsinane, and this angered the King. Macduff fled, crossing the Firth of Forth at the spot today named Earlsferry while his wife delayed the pursuing Macbeth until she saw her husband was safely in the middle of the river. (This occurrence gave rise to the tradition, still adhered to, that any fugitive taking a boat from Earlsferry should be free from pursuit until he has got half-way across the river.)

Macduff then went to England to meet Malcolm, the son of King Duncan who had been murdered by Macbeth. With Macduff's help, Malcolm returned to Scotland and avenged his father by slaying Macbeth at Lumphanan in 1057 and eventually ascending the Scottish throne.

In gratitude, Malcolm granted Macduff and his heirs the BOON OF MACDUFF, the privilege of leading the king to his throne at a coronation. The most famous occasion when the Boon of Macduff was exercised was at Scone in 1306 when Isabella, Countess of Buchan and sister of Duncan, Earl of Fife, led Robert the Bruce to his coronation seat.

*Robert the Bruce*

Earl Duncan had been a supporter of John Balliol, and in order to ingratiate himself with the new King Robert he relinquished to him the position of hereditary Mormaer of Earl of Fife. After being handed around various Bruces and Stewarts the title eventually went dormant in 1425.

It was this noble heritage that William Duff of Braco and the House of Macduff laid claim to in 1759.

# William Duff of Braco
## 1696–1763

William Duff's inheritance (apart from Braco farm) was the largest rent revenue in the north of Scotland. Largely through marriage, allied to good husbandry, the Duffs, an ancient Banffshire family of farmers and merchants, owned the estates of Aberlour, Monymusk, Keith, Mortlach and many more throughout the north-east.

William carried on the Duff tradition of marrying well, first to Janet Ogilvie, the daughter of the Earl of Findlater, and then to Jean Grant, daughter of Sir James Grant. From 1727 to 1734 he served as Member of Parliament for Banffshire, and in 1735 he decided to build himself a home worthy of his exalted position. For this purpose he hired the foremost Scottish architect of the day William Adam, and the result was DUFF HOUSE, in Banff, said to be modelled on the Villa Borghese in Rome, and regarded as one of the finest Georgian houses in Britain.

Duff gave Adam a free hand but then complained about the cost, forcing Adam to abandon the intended wings and colonnades. He then refused to live in the house, which now forms part of the National Galleries of Scotland.

In 1759, after managing to prove his descent from the Macduffs, Mormaers of Fife, Duff was created 1st Earl Fife.

His son, JAMES DUFF, 2ND EARL FIFE (1729–1809), completed Duff House and developed the little village of Doune, across the River Deveron from Banff, into the finest harbour on the Moray Firth – renaming it, with due modesty, MACDUFF.

His nephew, THE 4TH EARL FIFE (1776–1857), went off after the death of his young wife, to fight against Napolean in Spain, and served bravely at Talavera and Cadiz. When he came home, as a means of giving employment to soldiers returning from the Napoleonic Wars, he founded DUFFTOWN, alongside an ancient settlement called Mortlach in Glenfiddich.

ALEXANDER DUFF, 6TH EARL FIFE, married Princess Louise, eldest daughter of the future Edward VII, and was elevated to Duke of Fife. Since then the title has been passed around various members of the royal family, resting today with the 1st Duke's grandson, James Carnegie, born in 1929, who lives at Elsick House in Kincardineshire.

## Dufftown

Dufftown, home at one time to 10 different distilleries, proudly claims to be The Whisky Capital of the World.

Standing high on a knoll above the confluence of the Fiddich and the Dullan Water, about one mile (1.6 km) to the north of the town, is the original Mortlach, Balvenie Castle, one of Scotland's earliest stone castles and home in turn to the Black Comyns, the Douglases and the Dukes of Atholl. Now ruined and in the hands of Historic Scotland, Balvenie Castle looks down upon the Balvenie and Glenfiddich distilleries, founded in the fields below by William Grant.

## William Grant
### 1839–1923

WILLIAM GRANT was born in Dufftown in 1839, into a distinguished family who had settled on Speyside in the 14th century. At the age of seven he was sent out into the fields to herd cattle, and was then apprenticed to a shoemaker. Eventually, in 1866, he joined the Mortlach distillery as a clerk.

Grant quickly rose to become the manager and for 20 years patiently learned the art of distilling, while always dreaming of starting his own distillery and creating the 'best dram in the valley'.

# Glenfiddich

In 1886, after saving up enough money, Grant bought a field beneath the walls of BALVENIE CASTLE and with the assistance of his nine children, laid the foundation stones for his very own plant. Glenfiddich malt whisky first flowed from the new GLENFIDDICH distillery of William Grant & Sons on Christmas Day, 1887.

# The Balvenie

In 1892 Grant purchased an 18th-century manor house next door to the Glenfiddich distillery and converted it into another distillery, THE BALVENIE, and on 1 May 1893, The Balvenie malt whisky made its debut.

# Grant's Blended Scotch Whisky

In 1898 Pattison's, the largest whisky blender in Scotland at the time, went out of business. William Grant saw his chance, expanded into blending and Grant's Blended Scotch Whisky was born.

William Grant remained active in the company he had built until he died in 1923, aged 84. Four generations later, Grant's is the largest of the few whisky companies still in the hands of the families who founded them.

In 1957 Grant's unveiled their iconic TRIANGULAR BOTTLE. In 1963 Glenfiddich became THE FIRST SINGLE MALT TO BE EXPORTED OUTSIDE SCOTLAND and remains THE ONLY HIGHLAND MALT THAT IS DISTILLED, MATURED AND BOTTLED AT ITS OWN DISTILLERY.

*Well, I never knew this*
*about*
**BANFFSHIRE FOLK**

## St John Ogilvie
◄ 1579–1615 ►

JOHN OGILVIE was born near Keith. Educated on the Continent, he became a Catholic and determined to return to Scotland to minister to the Catholics who were being persecuted there as a consequence of the Scottish Reformation. He slipped back into the country in 1613, disguised as a soldier, and started to preach and celebrate mass at secret locations and in private homes. He was soon found out, arrested and thrown into gaol in Paisley, where he was ferociously tortured for information, but refused to betray his fellow Catholics or their identities. He was convicted of high treason, paraded through the streets of Glasgow and hanged at Glasgow Cross, on 10 March 1615, aged just 36.

As he was dying he threw his rosary beads into the crowd, where one of his tormentors caught them and subsequently became a devout Catholic.

AS THE FIRST MARTYR OF THE COUNTER-REFORMATION IN SCOTLAND, John Ogilvie was beatified in 1929 and canonised in 1976 – THE ONLY PERSON TO BE MADE A SAINT IN SCOTLAND SINCE THE REFORMATION.

JAMES BLAIR (1656–1743), clergyman, was born in Banff. An Episcopalian, Blair was ordained into the Church of England and sent by the Bishop of London to revive the church in the Virginia Colony. In 1693 he was granted a charter to found The College of William and Mary in Virginia, the second-oldest institution of higher education in America. US Presidents Thomas Jefferson, James Monroe and John Tyler were all educated there.

CAPTAIN GEORGE DUFF (1764–1805), Royal Navy officer, born in Banff. Great-nephew of Admiral Robert Duff, victor at the Battle of Quiberon Bay (1759) and colonial governor of Newfoundland, he served with the admiral in the Mediterranean and saw action in a number of conflicts. He was killed at the Battle of Trafalgar in 1805 while in command of HMS *Mars*.

ADMIRAL ARCHIBALD DUFF (1792–1862), Royal Navy officer who saw action at the Battle of Trafalgar, where his father was killed. He fought in Chesapeake Bay during the war of 1812 and eventually rose to the rank of vice-admiral. In 1847 he commissioned Thomas Mackenzie to build him a Victorian baronial house in a wooded glen between Dufftown and Keith, which he called Drummuir Castle. It is now Diageo's Home of Scotch Whisky.

# George Stephen, 1st Baron Mount Stephen
## ◄ 1829–1921 ►

George Stephen, banker and railway baron, was born in Dufftown, the son of a carpenter. Having gained experience as a draper with apprenticeships in Aberdeen and Glasgow, he emigrated to Canada in 1850 and took control of a relative's drapery business. This provided the funds to go into banking, at which he proved to be a master, and he ended up as the

*Drummuir Castle*

PRESIDENT OF THE BANK OF MONTREAL in 1876.

In partnership with other Scots Canadians, Stephen purchased the bankrupt St Paul and Pacific Railway in Minnesota, restored it and sold it on for a tremendous profit, which he

then ploughed into a company, set up in partnership with the Canadian government, to build a railway across Canada. As FIRST PRESIDENT OF THE CANADIAN PACIFIC RAILWAY, Stephen personally oversaw the massive project, which was finished on time and under budget, making him an even greater second fortune. When the last spike on the railway was driven, Stephen christened the spot CRAIGELLACHIE, in honour of his birthplace.

Stephen retired to Britain in 1891 and was created Baron Mount Stephen, taking the title from a mountain named after him in the Canadian Rockies. He was THE FIRST CANADIAN TO BE MADE A PEER.

# Berwickshire

HOME ✦ HUME CASTLE ✦ EARL OF HOME
✦ SIR ALEC DOUGLAS-HOME
✦ SOME NOTABLE HOMES AND HUMES
✦ HAIGS OF BEMERSYDE ✦ SOME NOTABLE HAIGS
✦ BEMERSYDE HOUSE

*Thirlestone Castle, seat of the Maitland family, Earls of Lauderdale. The present building dates from the late 17th century and is largely the work of William Bruce.*

◄ BERWICKSHIRE FOLK ►

Thomas Learmouth ✦ Thomas Boston ✦ James Small ✦ Robert Fortune

## Home

The name HOME, pronounced Hume, originates from the lands of Home, which in turn take their name from the old English word 'hom', meaning 'hill' or 'height' – which perfectly describes the site of the magnificent HUME CASTLE, 13th-century 'Sentinel of the Merse' and earliest stronghold of the ancient Home, or Hume, family.

The Homes are descended from Malcolm II of Scotland by his great-grandson the 1st Earl of Dunbar, whose own grandson Cospatrick married Ada, the natural daughter of King William the Lion, thus bringing the lands of Home to the Dunbars.

In 1214, these lands were granted to Ada, daughter of the 6th Earl of Dunbar, and when she married her cousin William of Greenlaw, he became known as WILLIAM OF HOME, the first to take the name.

## Hume Castle

William set about building a mighty fortress, to act as a power base from which to subdue and control his territory, and as a lookout and beacon to warn of any invasion forces approaching across the border from England.

The result, Hume Castle, was one of the earliest castles in Scotland to have a rectangular courtyard plan, and it dominates the Merse, an area of Berwickshire between the Tweed and the Lammermuirs, commanding fine views as far south as Carter Bar.

In 1460, during the time of ALEXANDER, 1ST LORD HOME, James II stayed at Hume Castle while directing the siege of Roxburgh Castle, one of the last castles to be held by the English after the Wars of Independence. James was a great believer in the newfangled cannons, and he had brought along some of his finest for the siege. On the morning of 3 August one of them exploded, blowing his leg off, and James bled to death.

In 1651, after Hume Castle was captured and dismantled by Oliver Cromwell's forces, the Homes abandoned their ancestral home and established THE HIRSEL, outside Coldstream, which remains the family seat to this day.

## Earl of Home

Alexander, 6th Lord Home, was created 1ST EARL OF HOME in 1605, and the Earls of Home are CHIEFS OF CLAN HOME.

In 1832 COSPATRICK ALEXANDER HOME, 11TH EARL, married LUCY

*The Hirsel*

MONTAGUE. When she inherited the estates of her cousin, the 4th Lord Douglas, her husband Earl Home was made Baron Douglas of Douglas and added Douglas to his surname, which from then on was DOUGLAS-HOME.

## *Sir Alec Douglas-Home*
### *1903–95*

Alexander, or Alec, Douglas-Home was the 14th Earl of Home from 1951 until 1963, when he was chosen by the Queen to lead the ruling Conservative party after the unexpected resignation of Prime Minister Harold Macmillan. Douglas-Home thought it would be wrong to serve as Prime Minister from the House of Lords and he disclaimed the earldom so that he could contest a by-election for the safe seat of Kinross and West Perthshire.

He was duly elected as THE LAST PEER TO BE PRIME MINISTER and THE ONLY PRIME MINISTER TO RESIGN FROM THE HOUSE OF LORDS TO ENTER THE HOUSE OF COMMONS. He was also THE LAST PRIME MINISTER TO BE CHOSEN PERSONALLY BY THE MONARCH, THE FIRST TO HAVE BEEN BORN IN THE 20TH CENTURY and THE ONLY PRIME MINISTER TO HAVE PLAYED FIRST-CLASS CRICKET. When the Conservatives under Edward Heath won power in 1970, Douglas-Home took up the post of Foreign Secretary, making him THE LAST FORMER PRIME MINISTER TO SERVE IN A SUBSEQUENT PRIME MINISTER'S CABINET.

Memorable Quotes:
*'There are two problems in my life. The political ones are insoluble and the economic ones are incomprehensible.'*

*'It isn't really necessary for a Prime Minister to be popular.'*

*'Oh God, if there be cricket in heaven, let there also be rain.'*

On the death of Lord Home of the Hirsel in 1995, the earldom was revived for his son David Douglas-Home, who thus became the 15th Earl of Home. He is chairman of Coutts Bank and also serves as chairman of the Duke of Westminster's Grosvenor Group.

# Some Notable Homes and Humes

## *David Hume*
## *1711–76*

D AVID HUME, philosopher and one of the leading figures of the Scottish Enlightenment, was one of the first advocates of the philosophy of empiricism, the belief that knowledge arises from experience rather than reasoning. His first work, *A Treatise on Human Nature*, was written over four years while he was staying in France. Not well received when it was published in 1739, the *Treatise* is somewhat heavy but repays study and has gained a better press over time.

Back in Edinburgh, Hume next produced *Political Discourses*, which had a great influence on the econo-

mist Adam Smith. As the philosopher Robert Adamson later wrote, 'the main errors of the *Wealth of Nations* are to be found in the deviations from the principles of the *Political Discourses.*' Between 1753 and 1761 Hume worked on his monumental and hugely successful *History of England*, which was regarded as the definitive work on the subject until Macaulay's *History of England* came out almost 100 years later.

Memorable Quotes:
*'Beauty in things exists in the mind which contemplates them.'*

*'Avarice, the spur of industry.'*

HAMILTON HUME (1797–1873), the first Australian-born explorer. He was the author of the Hume and Hovell expedition, which discovered the overland route from Sydney to Port Philip Bay, where the city of Melbourne now stands. Between 1953 and 1966 Hume's portrait appeared on the Australian one-pound note.

WILLIAM DOUGLAS-HOME (1912–92), playwright and younger brother of Prime Minister Sir Alec Douglas-Home. After serving as a tank officer in the Second World War he wrote over 40 plays, many of which are still being performed. He is best known for *The Chiltern Hundreds* (1947), *The Reluctant Debutante*

(1955), twice adapted into a film in 1958 and 2003, *The Secretary Bird* (1967), and *Lloyd George Knew My Father* (1972).

CARDINAL BASIL HUME (1923–99), Archbishop of Westminster from 1976 until his death. He was THE FIRST ROMAN CATHOLIC PRELATE TO ATTEND THE INSTALLATION OF AN ANGLICAN ARCHBISHOP OF CANTERBURY (Archbishop Runcie in 1980) and organised THE FIRST-EVER VISIT TO BRITAIN BY A REIGNING POPE (John Paul II), in 1982. He was also the first head of the Roman Catholic Church for over 400 years officially to play host to the British monarch, head of the Church of England, when he invited Queen Elizabeth II to visit Westminster Cathedral in 1995.

# Haigs of Bemersyde

*Tyde what may, what'er betyde,*
*Haig shall be Haig of Bemersyde*
Thomas the Rhymer

The first HAIG OF BEMERSYDE was PETRUS DE HAGA, who settled in Berwickshire in 1162.

His origins are uncertain. The name would suggest that de Haga was from a Norman family, although the fact that 'haga' is an Old English word, meaning 'enclosure', points towards the more romantic story that he was descended from Druskine, King of the Picts, who was killed by Kenneth, King of the Scots, at the Battle of Camelon in 839. Druskine's son, Haga, escaped to Norway and Petrus de Haga, his descendant, fought with Harald IV of Norway. Petrus was shipwrecked off Eyemouth and befriended by the Earl of March, later marrying the Earl's daughter and receiving the lands and barony of Bemersyde as a dowry. The Haigs have been there ever since, as prophesied by Thomas the Rhymer in the 13th century.

JOHN, 3RD BARON HAIG OF BEMERSYDE, signed the Ragman Roll of obedience to Edward I in 1296, but then marched against Edward alongside William Wallace at Stirling Bridge in 1297. His son Petrus, 4th Baron, fought at Bannockburn at the age of 17 and survived, but died 19 years later defending Berwick from Edward III at the Battle of Halidon Hill in 1333. John, the 5th Baron, died at Otterburn in 1388.

WILLIAM, 10TH BARON HAIG OF BEMERSYDE, died at Flodden in 1513. His great-great grandson, James, the 14th Baron, had eight sons, of whom the four eldest were killed in the service of the King of Bohemia. The line was carried on by his fifth son, but in 1854 the Rhymer's prediction looked shaky when the succession fell to three daughters. However, the daughters signed over the succession to their cousin ARTHUR BALFOUR HAIG, who was descended from the 17th Baron, and he became the 28TH BARON HAIG OF BEMERSYDE.

In 1921, after Balfour Haig put the Bemersyde estate up for sale, a public subscription from the people of the British Commonwealth raised enough funds to purchase it. Bemersyde was then presented to FIELD-MARSHAL EARL HAIG, Commander of the British Expeditionary Force in France and Belgium from 1915 to 1918, in recognition of his service during the First World War. Thus the estate was kept in the Haig family, in line with Thomas the Rhymer's prediction.

EARL HAIG was the son of John Haig, chairman of the family whisky distillers HAIG & HAIG, which was founded with an illicit distillery on Robert Haig's farm in Stirlingshire in 1627. The dimpled Haig whisky bottle is unique.

When Earl Haig died in 1928 the title passed to his son George Haig, who became the 2ND EARL HAIG. He was a page of honour to George VI at the Coronation in 1937 and served in the Royal Scots Greys during the Second World War, ending the conflict as a prisoner of war at Colditz. During his incarceration he learned to draw, and after the war he studied to become a professional artist, becoming an associate member of the Royal Scottish Academy. He lives with his family at Bemersyde, and has an heir, Alexander Haig, Viscount Dawick.

## Some Notable Haigs

JACK HAIG (1913–89), actor, fondly remembered from the BBC TV situation comedy *'Allo 'Allo*, in which he played Monsieur LeClerc, the incompetent counterfeiter and pianist known for his bad disguises.

Memorable Quote:
*'It is I, LeClerc!'*

ALEXANDER HAIG, born 1924, US Army general, Supreme Allied Commander Europe, White House chief of staff for Richard Nixon and Gerald Ford. He took over after Bob Haldeman had resigned during the Watergate affair and is credited with persuading Nixon to resign. He was then US Secretary of State under President Ronald Reagan. Haig won two Silver Stars in the Korean War and a Distinguished Service Cross, Distinguished Flying Cross and Purple Heart in the Vietnam War. In 1979, as commander of NATO forces in Europe, he survived an assassination attempt by Baader Meinhof terrorists.

Memorable Quotes:

*'That's not a lie, it's a terminological inexactitude.'*

*'I am in control here!'* (After the assassination attempt on President Reagan in 1981)

DAVID HAIG, born 1955, actor. Fondly remembered for his appearance as Bernard the Bridegroom in the 1994 film *Four Weddings and a Funeral*, and as Detective Inspector Grim in the BBC TV situation comedy *The Thin Blue Line*. He won an Olivier Award for 'Actor of the Year in a New Play' for his performance in *Our Country's Good* at the Royal Court Theatre in 1988 and is the only male actor to have performed an Alan Bennett *Talking Heads* monologue on television, other than Bennett himself.

Memorable Quote:
*'. . . your cock-up, my arse!'* (As Detective Inspector Grim)

### Bemersyde House

BEMERSYDE HOUSE, which lies close to the River Tweed about 3 miles (5 km) east of Melrose, began as a huge peel tower erected in 1535 and rebuilt ten years later after being damaged by the marauding English. It was enlarged in 1690 and had wings added in the 18th century to make it into a more comfortable dwelling. In the writing room in the old part of the house, Field Marshal Earl Haig's huge map of the Western Front can be seen.

The elaborate gardens, which are open to the public in summer, were laid out by Arthur Balfour Haig and include a huge chestnut tree believed to be at least 500 years old.

Sir Walter Scott, a frequent visitor to Bemersyde, thought that 'almost a wizard spell' hung over the place. His last visit in 1831 was with the artist Turner, who made a sketch of the occasion to illustrate an edition of Scott's poems, showing Scott, his biographer Lockhart and Miss Haig standing in the sunken garden.

The view from BEMERSYDE HILL above the house, looking across the Tweed towards the Eildon Hills, was described by Walter Scott as 'the grandest and most extensive panorama in the Borderland', and has become known as SCOTT'S VIEW. On the day of Scott's funeral his own horse, which was drawing the hearse from Abbotsford to Dryburgh Abbey, stopped at the view of its own accord, no doubt to give its master a final look.

Earl Haig is buried at Dryburgh Abbey, as are Sir Walter Scott and his wife.

*Well, I never knew this*
*about*
BERWICKSHIRE FOLK

## Thomas Learmouth

◄ 1220–98 ►

Seer and poet, better known as THOMAS THE RHYMER, Learmouth was born in Earlston, on the Roxburghshire border, where his family were landowners. A writer of ballads and a collector of Scottish folk tales, the Rhymer is credited with authorship of *THE ROMANCE OF SIR TRISTREM*, THE OLDEST KNOWN PIECE OF SCOTS POETRY, but is best remembered for his prophesies, which foretold many of the great events in Scottish history, including the death of Alexander III: 'On the morrow, afore noon, shall blow the greatest wind that ever was heard before in Scotland' – on 19 March 1286 Alexander was thrown from his horse and killed while riding along the Fife cliff tops in a storm, and his death without an heir brought about years of war and strife as the Scots squabbled over the throne and fought to keep their independence.

Thomas also predicted the Battle of Bannockburn, Flodden, the Jacobite uprisings of 1715 and 1745, and the accession of James VI to the English throne.

His story is told in the ballad 'Thomas the Rhymer', which Sir Walter Scott included in his collection *Minstrelsy of the Scottish Border*.

No one knows how the Rhymer died. He simply walked out of his tower house and was never seen again, although legend has it that he will return to Scotland's aid in her hour of greatest need.

THOMAS BOSTON (1676–1732), theologian, born in Duns, the son of Covenanters. Educated at Edinburgh and licensed by the presbytery of Chirnside, he took on the ministry of the tiny parish of Simprin in 1699. His name became known when he published, with notes, a religious compendium called MARROW OF MODERN DIVINITY, which sparked the Marrow Controversy, a dispute over the nature of atonement. In 1707 he was moved to Ettrick, where his kindliness and reputation for brilliant preaching brought the congregations flocking. He wrote his sermons out in full and so they were able to be collected together and published in book form, but the book for which he is best remembered is his HUMAN

NATURE IN ITS FOURFOLD STATE, which ranked second only to the Bible in many Scottish homes of the 17th and 18th centuries.

JAMES SMALL (1740–93), inventor of the IRON PLOUGH, was born in Ladykirk. He later bought a small farm at Blackadder Mount where he experimented with various kinds of plough and his greatest innovation was the use of cast iron, which made his SWING PLOUGH much lighter and less cumbersome than the wooden Scotch ploughs in use before. In 1784 he published a book called *A Treatise on Ploughs and Wheel-Carriages*, setting out the scientific principles of plough design, which remained the standard text on the subject for many years. Small did not patent his design, not wanting to profit from an invention intended to make life easier for the farmer, and although his plough was widely copied he died in poverty.

# Robert Fortune
◄ 1813–80 ►

ROBERT FORTUNE was a botanist who was responsible for founding India's tea industry. Born in Blackadder, he began his career in the Edinburgh Botanical Gardens and later moved to the Royal Horticultural Society gardens at Chiswick in London. In 1843, following the Treaty of Nanking, which ended the First Opium War, he went out to China on behalf of the Society and sent many new and exotic plants back to Britain.

In 1848 he entered the employ of the East India Company, and disguised as a Chinese courtier 'from a distant province', he began to smuggle out tea from China to Darjeeling in India, on a specially adapted Chinese junk, a crime that was punishable with death by decapitation. He shipped out some 20,000 seedlings and in this way established the Indian tea industry, breaking China's monopoly.

He was also responsible for introducing many plants to Britain, such as camellia, jasmine and japonica, and has a camellia, a hosta and a rhododendron named after him, as well as two roses, Fortune's Double Yellow and Rosa Fortuneana.

# Buteshire

SHERIFF OF BUTE ✦ EARLS OF BUTE
✦ MARQUESS OF BUTE ✦ JOHNNY DUMFRIES
✦ EARL OF ARRAN ✦ BRODICK CASTLE

*Mount Stuart House, Scotland's finest Victorian Gothic
House, home to the Stuarts of Bute.*

◄ BUTESHIRE FOLK ►

William Bannatyne ✦ William MacEwen
✦ (George) Leslie Hunter ✦ Adam Crozier

## Sheriff of Bute

The office of SHERIFF OF BUTE was granted to ALAN FITZWALTER, 2ND HIGH STEWARD OF SCOTLAND (c.1140–1204), by King William I of Scotland (William the Lion) in about 1200. Bute had not long ago been part of the Norse empire of the Western Isles, and FitzWalter was charged with keeping the newly won territory in Scottish hands, a task at which he and his heirs were largely successful, and the Stewarts have held the position ever since.

FitzWalter's first move was to build a wooden castle to protect Rothesay Bay, Bute's best natural harbour, and in 1230 his son Walter replaced the wooden fortifications with a powerful circular stone castle, which was added to at the end of the 13th century. It became a favourite retreat of the Stewart kings.

In 1385 John Stewart (1360–1449), known as the 'Black Stewart', to distinguish him from his brother John Stewart of Dundonald, the 'Red Stewart', was granted the lands of Bute, Arran and Cumbrae and the hereditary office of Sheriff of Bute by his natural father Robert II. Black Stewart's older brother Robert III died at Rothesay Castle on 1406.

Robert III's son David was made Duke of Rothesay, Scotland's second oldest dukedom, and a title that has remained in royal hands to this day, the present Duke of Rothesay being Charles, Prince of Wales.

## Earl of Bute

James Stuart, seventh in descent from Black Stewart (Mary Queen of Scots changed the spelling of the name after living in France), was created Baronet of Bute in 1627, and his grandson, the 3rd Baronet, was one of those who negotiated the Union with England in 1703, for which he was made EARL OF BUTE.

## John Stuart, 3rd Earl of Bute 1713–92

JOHN STUART, 3RD EARL OF BUTE (1713–92), was a favourite of George III, and in 1762 he became

the FIRST SCOTSMAN TO SERVE AS PRIME MINISTER – and the FIRST TORY PRIME MINISTER.

Being the first Scottish Prime Minister was no easy ride. The English were still uneasy about the Scots after the Jacobite Rebellions, the last of which had happened less than 20 years before, and furthermore, Bute's fellow politicians didn't like the fact that he owed his position to King George's good offices. As some wag remarked, 'Why, there is a Scotchman got into the Treasury and they can't get him out!'

When Bute was made Prime Minister, the Bishop of Gloucester William Warburton wrote, 'Lord Bute is a very unfit man to be a Prime Minister of England. First, he is a Scotchman; secondly he is the King's friend; and thirdly, he is an honest man.'

As his way of relaxing, Bute would put on amateur dramatic productions at his family home, often dressing up as Lothario, which is perhaps why he was unfairly suspected of having an affair with King George's mother, the Dowager Princess Augusta, widow of Frederick, Prince of Wales, the first man to die after being hit by a cricket ball. It was most unlikely, because Bute was happily married and had been a close friend of Frederick's, whom he had met at Egham races in 1747, when invited to play whist in the royal tent.

Nonetheless, the mob burned effigies of Bute in the street and he was portrayed in cartoons as a 'Jack Boot', an unkind play on his name John Bute.

In the end he only lasted as Prime Minister for 317 days, the sixth shortest term of office. Yet in that time he broke the predominance of the Whigs and brought peace by ending the Seven Years War.

Bute devoted the rest of his life to his estates and to his beloved botany, helping to establish Kew Gardens and having the flowering plant genus 'Stuartia' named after him. Independently wealthy through his wife, the heiress Mary Wortley Montagu, he became a great patron of the arts, helping, amongst others, Dr Johnson, Tobias Smollett and Robert Adam, whom he commissioned to build Luton Hoo, his mansion in Bedfordshire.

In November 1792, while foraging for plants at his home in Highcliffe, Hampshire, Bute fell over a cliff and died not long afterwards. He is buried on the Isle of Bute.

Memorable Quote:
*'Oh my God! It's all over!'* (Upon hearing the news of Lord Cornwallis's surrender at Yorktown in 1781, the moment when Britain lost her American colonies)

# Marquess of Bute

The Prime Minister's son, JOHN STUART, 4TH EARL OF BUTE (1744–1814), married Charlotte Windsor, daughter of Viscount Windsor, and through her acquired vast estates in South Wales. In 1796 he was made 1ST MARQUESS OF BUTE, and after his first wife died in 1800 he married Frances Coutts, the daughter of banker Thomas Coutts.

The Marquess's heir married Lady Elizabeth McDouall-Crichton, the daughter of the Earl of Dumfries, but predeceased his father in 1794. Thus John Stuart's grandson became 2ND MARQUESS OF BUTE in 1814, and he added his mother's name of Crichton to the family name which thus became CRICHTON-STUART.

The 2nd Marquess (1793–1848) risked his entire inheritance on developing the Bute docks at Cardiff, then a small town serving his Welsh estates, and was handsomely rewarded when Cardiff became the biggest coal port in the world.

JOHN CRICHTON-STUART, THE 3RD MARQUESS, built the fantastical Gothic masterpiece that is Mount Stuart out of the ashes of a previous Queen Anne house that had gone up in flames in 1877. It was such a massive project that Mount Stuart was only completed in the 1980s. The house is now open to the public.

## Johnny Dumfries

B efore he inherited the title, the
present (7th) Marquess of Bute
had a successful career as a racing
driver. His courtesy title as the oldest
son of the Marquess was Earl of
Dumfries, and competing under the
name JOHNNY DUMFRIES, he won
the British Formula Three Championship in 1984, drove in 16 Grand
Prix for the Lotus Formula One team,
where his team-mate was Ayrton
Senna, and in 1988 won the Le Mans
24-hour race in a Jaguar.

## Earl of Arran

T he title Earl of Arran was created
in 1503 for James, 2nd Lord
Hamilton, as a reward for negotiating
the marriage of his cousin James IV
to Margaret Tudor, sister of Henry
VIII of England.

## Brodick Castle

I n 1510 the Earl rebuilt Brodick
Castle on Arran, replacing the 13th-
century castle of the Stewarts of
Menteith with a powerful tower
house. For the next 150 years it was
fought over by Henry VIII, Oliver
Cromwell and the Campbells, but the
Hamiltons did finally get to keep it
as a summer retreat.

In the middle of the 19th century
the 10th Duke of Hamilton,
enriched by his marriage to the
daughter of England's richest man,
William Beckford, transformed the
modest Brodick into a grand stately
home as a wedding present for his
eldest son, who was married to
PRINCESS MARIE OF BADEN (1817–
88), granddaughter of the Emperor
Napoleon.

In 1957 Brodick was handed
over to the National Trust for Scotland.

*Well, I never knew this*
*about*
## BUTESHIRE FOLK

WILLIAM BANNATYNE, LORD BANNATYNE (1743–1833), a distinguished lawyer who inherited Kames Castle, ancestral home of the Bannatynes, through his mother. As well as being a lawyer and judge he contributed to the *Mirror* and the *Lounger* magazines, and was one of the great literary masters of the late 18th century who could write with wit and flair on wide-ranging subjects such as philosophy, politics and science. After adding a fine mansion to the 14th-century tower house at Kames he went broke and had to sell up.

ANDREW BANNATYNE (1798–1871), lawyer and businessman, born on the island of Bute, the son of a Glasgow

postmaster. He founded one of the world's first intercity railways, the Edinburgh and Glasgow railway, which opened in 1842.

## Sir William MacEwen
#### ◄── 1848–1924 ──►

A pioneering surgeon, born in Rothesay, WILLIAM MACEWEN studied surgery at the University of Glasgow under Sir Joseph Lister, and further developed Lister's techniques of antiseptics and sterilisation while working at the Glasgow Royal Infirmary.

Once able to work in a perfectly sterile surgical environment, MacEwen was free to attempt more difficult surgery, in particular on the brain and spine. In 1876 he became THE FIRST SURGEON TO OPERATE ON A BRAIN ABSCESS and followed this by removing a brain tumour in 1878. His other interest was in bone growth and in 1879 he performed the FIRST-EVER BONE GRAFT.

In 1892 he was appointed to the position held by Joseph Lister when MacEwen was a student, the Regius Chair of Surgery at the University of

Glasgow. In 1895 he was elected as a Fellow of the Royal Society and in 1902 he was knighted.

He spent as much of his free time as he could on the Isle of Bute, at Garrochty, and is buried in St Blane's Chapel churchyard.

# (George) Leslie Hunter
## ——◄ 1879–1931 ►——

Born in Rothesay, LESLIE HUNTER emigrated to California with his family at the age of 13 and developed a burgeoning career as an illustrator and painter. When he was 29, and on the verge of considerable success, the San Francisco earthquake of 1906 destroyed all his early work and, disheartened, he returned to Scotland to settle in Glasgow. He slowly began

to work up a strong portfolio again and in 1916 held his first one-man exhibition at Glasgow's Reid Gallery.

During the 1920s he became one of a group of artists known as the Scottish Colourists, taking forward the ideas and influences of the Glasgow Boys. Along with Francis Cadell, Samuel Peploe and John Duncan Fergusson, Hunter reworked the purity, vibrant colours and deft brushwork of the French Impressionists and Post-Impressionists and endowed it with a recognisably Scottish character.

ADAM CROZIER, chief executive of the Royal Mail, was born in 1964 on the Island of Bute, where his father was estate manager for Lord Bute. From 2000 to 2002 he was chief executive of the Football Association.

> The Glasgow Boys were a group of late 19th-century painters who rebelled against Victorian sentimentality and painted fresh, vibrant portraits of everyday subjects. Amongst their numbers were John Laurey, George Henry and E. A. Hornel.

# Caithness

EARL OF CAITHNESS ✦ STEWART EARLS
✦ SINCLAIR EARLS ✦ NOTABLE ST CLAIRS OR SINCLAIRS

*The castle of Mey was built by the Earl of Caithness
in 1572 and later became the late Queen Mother's
favourite home. It is the most northerly castle
on the British mainland*

◄ CAITHNESS FOLK ►

Richard Oswald ✦ Alexander Keith ✦ Alexander 'Sandy' Keith
✦ Alexander Bain ✦ Donald Swanson ✦ Sir William Alexander Smith
✦ John Barneson

# Earl of Caithness

The first EARL OF CAITHNESS in the modern sense is held to be Maol Íosa V, Earl of Strathearn, who owned the earldom of Caithness in his position as Earl of Orkney. When Maol was accused of treason and forced to forfeit his titles in 1344, Orkney went to Norway, while Caithness came to the Scottish king.

## Stewart Earls

In 1375 Robert II gave the Castle of Braal in Caithness to his son David Stewart (1357–86), and in 1377 made him Earl of Caithness.

David's brother Walter Stewart then got hold of the title, but rashly forfeited it by killing James I, for which he was also disembowelled and beheaded.

## Sinclair Earls

After a slight blip, when Sir George de Crichton, the Lord High Admiral, was awarded the title and then wasted it by dying soon afterwards, the earldom of Caithness eventually came to rest at its rightful home, with the 'lordly line of high St Clair'.

In 1455 James II conferred the earldom of Caithness on WILLIAM SINCLAIR, builder of Roslin chapel, who already held the Norse earldom of Orkney by virtue of being the grandson of Henry Sinclair the explorer, who was made Earl of Orkney by the Norwegian King Haakon in 1379.

In 1468 James III took possession of Orkney and Shetland as part of his dowry from the King of Norway (*see* Orkney and Shetland), and in 1470 he persuaded Sinclair to give up the earldom of Orkney to the Crown in return for lands in Fife, leaving Sinclair as just Earl of Caithness.

The title Earl of Caithness has remained with the Sinclair family to this day, and the present incumbent is MALCOLM SINCLAIR, 20TH EARL OF CAITHNESS, who was born in 1948.

# 2nd Earl of Caithness

WILLIAM SINCLAIR, 2ND EARL OF CAITHNESS, built the impregnable family seat of GIRNIGOE CASTLE on a rocky promontory just north of Wick around 1470, and was later killed along with James IV at the Battle of Flodden in 1513.

furious that his son had not been ruthless enough in the task, leaving witnesses alive to reveal the Sinclairs' involvement in the outrage.

The Earl imprisoned his son in the dungeon at Girnigoe and left him there to die. John hung on inconsiderately and was still there seven years later, so the Earl fed him nothing but salted beef – 'and then, with holding all drink from him, left him to die of a raging thirst'.

## 4th Earl of Caithness

GEORGE SINCLAIR, 4TH EARL OF CAITHNESS, was chairman of the jury who acquitted the Earl of Bothwell, third husband of Mary Queen of Scots, of the murder of her second husband, Lord Darnley.

He also built the CASTLE OF MEY, overlooking the Pentland Firth, in 1572, which nearly 400 years later became the Queen Mother's favourite home.

The 4th Earl is better remembered, perhaps unfairly, for a slightly more sinister reason. In 1571, ostensibly in his capacity as Chief Justice of Caithness, he arrested his own son and heir John for sacking Dornoch and burning down the Cathedral. In fact, John had been acting under his father's orders, and the Earl was

## 5th Earl of Caithness

It has been suggested that the story above was put about by the Earl's enemies, and that in fact John died peacefully in Knockinnon Castle. However, to add spice, John's son GEORGE, 5TH EARL OF CAITHNESS, became known as 'Wicked Earl George' for allegedly killing his father's keepers at Girnigoe, David and Ingram Sinclair.

The 5th Earl also locked his own daughter up in the attic of the Castle of Mey when she fell in love with a local ploughman. Driven mad by her confinement she flung herself out of the window and is reputed to haunt the castle today, in the guise of the 'Green Lady'.

# 14th Earl of Caithness

JAMES SINCLAIR, 14TH EARL OF CAITHNESS, gained a reputation as an imaginative inventor. His achievements included a steam carriage, a tape loom arranged so that the weaver could stop any one of the shuttles without halting the whole loom, and his favourite, the CAITHNESS GRAVITATING COMPASS, which is very steady and still used by modern shipping companies today.

## Notable St Clairs or Sinclairs

## *Arthur St Clair*
## *1737–1818*

Born in Thurso, ARTHUR ST CLAIR served in the British army in North America during the Seven Years War, helping General Wolfe take Quebec in 1759. He then settled in Pennsylvania, becoming one of the state's largest landowners, and to defend his holdings fought with the Continental Army in the American War of Independence. He was aide-de-camp to General Washington at Yorktown, when the British under Cornwallis surrendered. Later he served a term as President of the Confederation Congress, during which the Congress enacted the United States Constitution, and was then appointed Governor of the vast Northwest Territory, which covered the area now occupied by the states of Ohio, Indiana, Illinois, Michigan, Wisconsin, and the north-eastern part of Minnesota.

In 1791 St Clair led a punitive expedition against native Indian settlements on the Wabash River, a tributary of the Ohio River, which resulted in the worst defeat the American army ever suffered at the hands of native American Indians, with more than 600 soldiers, women and children killed in what became known as the Columbia Massacre.

Although St Clair was exonerated, he resigned from the army, but continued as Governor of the Northwest Territory at Washington's request.

He died in Pennsylvania, somewhat impoverished after business losses. There are a number of townships and counties named in his honour throughout Pennsylvania and the north-west.

SIR JOHN SINCLAIR OF ULBSTER (1754–1835), politician, agricultural reformer and THE FIRST PERSON TO USE THE WORD 'STATISTICS', was born in Thurso Castle. MP for Caithness, he was the first President of William Pitt's Board of Agriculture, which developed into the Department of Agriculture. Between 1791 and 1799 he produced a STATISTICAL ACCOUNT OF SCOTLAND in 21 volumes, which was the FIRST STUDY TO COMPILE ECONOMIC AND SOCIAL STATISTICS FOR THE WHOLE COUNTRY, and provides a unique record of life in late 18th-century Scotland.

CATHERINE SINCLAIR (1800–64), writer and daughter of Sir John Sinclair of Ulbster, was born at THURSO CASTLE. She wrote children's stories and travel books on Scotland and Wales, and was the FIRST PERSON TO GUESS THE TRUE IDENTITY OF THE ANONYMOUS AUTHOR OF THE WAVERLEY NOVELS to be Sir Walter Scott. She also performed philanthropic works and built the FIRST STREET FOUNTAIN IN EDINBURGH, at the end of Princes Street.

HUGH SINCLAIR (1873–1939), Director of Naval Intelligence who founded and

served as the second Director ('C') of the Secret Intelligence Service, which became MI6. In 1938 he purchased Bletchley Park, with his own money, for use as a wartime intelligence-gathering station – it was here that the Enigma code was cracked. His kinsman SIR JOHN SINCLAIR (1897–1977) was head of SIS from 1953 to 1956. Sir John was forced to resign by Prime Minister Anthony Eden for sending a frogman, Commander Lionel Crabb, to investigate the Soviet cruiser *Ordkhonikidze*, which had carried the Russian leader Nikita Khrushchev on a diplomatic mission to Britain. The mission was unauthorised and led to the death of Crabb.

HARRY F. SINCLAIR (1876–1956), founder of Sinclair Oil, the seventh largest oil company in America. He became unintentionally involved in the Tea Pot Dome scandal of 1920–22, when President Warren Harding's Secretary of the Interior leased oil fields in Wyoming to Sinclair without seeking a competitive tender.

MALCOLM ST CLAIR (1897–1952), director of the majority of the Laurel and Hardy films.

DONALD SINCLAIR (1909–81), inspiration for Basil Fawlty of the TV situation comedy *Fawlty Towers*. John Cleese got the idea for *Fawlty Towers* after staying at Donald Sinclair's Gleneagles Hotel in Torquay with the team of *Monty Python's Flying Circus* whilst filming a series in the early 1970s. Much to the amusement of them all, Sinclair hurled Eric Idle's briefcase out of the hotel 'in case it contained a bomb', complained about Terry Gilliam's table manners, and chucked a bus timetable at a guest who dared to ask the time of the next bus into Torquay.

Memorable Quote:
*'He seemed to view us as a colossal inconvenience right from the start.'*
(Michael Palin on Donald Sinclair)

DONALD SINCLAIR (1911–95) and BRIAN SINCLAIR (1915–88), veterinary surgeons who worked with Alf Wight, otherwise known as James Herriot. They were the models for the eccentric Siegfried Farnon and his dissolute younger brother Tristan in Herriot's semi-autobiographical books, adapted into the television series *All Creatures Great and Small.* Donald was played by Robert Hardy, Brian by Peter Davison.

EDWARD SINCLAIR (1914–77), actor, best remembered as Mr Yeatman the verger in the TV situation comedy *Dad's Army.*

SIR CLIVE SINCLAIR, inventor, born 1940. In 1972 he invented the world's first 'slim-line' electronic pocket calculator and later the SINCLAIR ZX80, BRITAIN'S FIRST MASS-MARKET HOME COMPUTER. In 1985 he unveiled the SINCLAIR C5, a battery-powered tricycle, which was not a commercial success but became an icon of the 1980s. His latest invention is the A-bike, a light bicycle that folds up small enough to fit in a rucksack.

JOHN GORDON SINCLAIR, actor, born 1962. He found fame as the lead in Bill Forsyth's 1980 film *Gregory's Girl.*

NIGEL SINCLAIR, Hollywood producer, born 1969. He produced blockbusters such as *Crocodile Dundee,* starring Paul Hogan,

*Braveheart*, starring Mel Gibson as William Wallace, and *Terminator 3*, starring Arnold Schwarzenegger.

ALICE SINCLAIR, fashion model, born 1986. She won Channel Five's *Make Me a Supermodel* in 2005 at the age of 18. Having worked for model agency Select, she decided to leave modelling after two years to continue her studies.

Memorable Quote:
*'There are millions of beautiful women out there, and that isn't enough to succeed.'*

*Well, I never knew this*
*about*
**CAITHNESS FOLK**

RICHARD OSWALD (1705–84), merchant, slave trader and diplomat, born in Dunnet. Having built up huge estates, wealth and knowledge on both sides of the Atlantic, through trading in tobacco, sugar and slaves, and through marriage to a Jamaica plantation heiress, he was chosen by Prime Minister Lord Shelburne to lead the British negotiations with Benjamin Franklin which resulted in the Treaty of Paris in 1783, recognising American independence.

ALEXANDER KEITH (1795–1873), brewer, born in Halkirk. After working as an apprentice brewer for his uncle, he emigrated to Halifax in Nova Scotia at the age of 22, and three years later set up a brewery to produce Alexander Keith's India Pale Ale, created from his own secret recipe. It is still being brewed exclusively in Halifax today.

His nephew, ALEXANDER 'SANDY' KEITH JNR (1827–?), was also born in Halkirk and emigrated to Canada to work in his uncle's brewery. During the American Civil War, Sandy acted as a secret agent and courier for the Confederate States, and was instru-

mental in a plot to send trunks of clothing contaminated with yellow fever to cities in the North, in an early attempt at biological warfare. He later moved on to bombing passenger ships for the insurance money, causing a huge explosion in Halifax harbour in 1857, and finally killing 80 people when his bomb went off prematurely on the dock in Bremerhaven in 1875.

# Alexander Bain
## ◄ 1810–77 ►

ALEXANDER BAIN, clockmaker and inventor, was born in Watten, one of 13 children of a crofter. Apprenticed as a boy to a watchmaker in Wick, he later moved to Clerkenwell, London's clockmaking centre, where, in 1841, he patented THE WORLD'S FIRST ELECTRIC CLOCK, using an electro-magnetic pendulum kept going by an electric current.

In 1843 he patented the FAX MACHINE, which divided a page into strips and broke them into black-and-white sections that could be transmitted by telegraph. He also invented a printing machine to record the messages using an electro-chemical process, and in 1865 his machines were utilised for the world's first commercial fax service between Paris and Lyons in France.

In 1846 he invented the CHEMICAL TELEGRAPH, which hugely increased the speed at which messages could be sent, and later installed the telegraph lines running alongside the railway between Edinburgh and Glasgow.

Between 1943 and 1948 Bain's birthplace, WATTEN, was the site of Britain's most secret prisoner of war facility, CAMP 165, which hosted a number of high-ranking and notorious Nazi officers, known as 'Black POWs'. These included ace U-boat commander Otto Kretschmer, the 'Wolf of the Atlantic', and Gunter d'Alquen, editor of *Das Schwarze Korps*, the official SS paper, and Himmler's top propagandist.

DONALD SWANSON (1848–1924), policeman, born in Thurso, the son of a brewer. He joined the Metropolitan Police at the age of 20 and rose to the rank of superintendent. He was Chief Inspector of CID at Scotland Yard during the Jack the Ripper murders in 1888.

SIR WILLIAM ALEXANDER SMITH (1854–1914), founder of the BOYS' BRIGADE, was born in Pennyland House near Thurso. After schooling in Glasgow, he was commissioned into the 1st Lanarkshire Rifle Volunteers and also joined the Church as a Sunday school teacher. Seeing an opportunity to help boys focus their abilities through an organisation based on Christian principles and army discipline, he formed the Boys' Brigade in 1883 at the Free Church Mission Hall in Glasgow. The Brigade has since grown into a worldwide movement serving millions of children of over 50 different nationalities.

JOHN BARNESON (1862–1941), seaman and oil baron, was born in Wick. Barneson worked his way up to commanding a naval supply ship in the Spanish-American War, and then went into the shipping business in California. Realising the importance of a reliable fuel supply for his ships based in Los Angeles harbour, he put up an oil refinery at Torrance in Los Angeles, and then built CALIFORNIA'S FIRST OIL PIPELINE to feed the refinery with crude oil from the San Joaquin Valley. The oil business he founded, called General Petroleum, was later sold to Standard Oil (ESSO), now Exxon Mobil.

Memorable Quote:
*'Captain John Barneson was one of the choice souls in American life. Honest, courageous, frank, generous and loyal, and with a high quality of humour.'* Herbert Hoover

# Clackmannanshire

MENSTRIE CASTLE ✦ SIR WILLIAM ALEXANDER
✦ BARONETS OF NOVA SCOTIA ✦ EARL OF STIRLING
✦ SIR JAMES HOLBORNE ✦ SIR RALPH ABERCROMBY
✦ NOVA SCOTIA ROOMS

*Menstrie Castle, home of Sir William Alexander, the 1st Earl of Stirling, who established the colony and baronetage of Nova Scotia in the 17th Century.*

◄ CLACKMANNANSHIRE FOLK ►

William Alexander ✦ Archibald Tait ✦ George Brown

# Menstrie Castle

MENSTRIE CASTLE, which is more of a fortified house than a castle, sits in the 'Hillfoot Village' of Menstrie, located at the base of the Ochil Hills.

It was built in about 1560 by a branch of Clan MacAllister who had anglicised their name to Alexander, and in 1567 the castle saw its first birth, that of WILLIAM ALEXANDER.

# Sir William Alexander 1567–1640

As a young man Alexander was appointed as tutor to the Earl of Argyll and accompanied him on the Grand Tour of Europe. He then became tutor to the sons of James VI, Henry and Charles, and moved with them to London when James ascended the English throne.

During this time he gained quite a reputation as a poet, writing a lengthy series of tragedies called *Domesday* and helping King James with his work on the Psalms of David, for which he was knighted in 1614.

Meanwhile Alexander was becoming excited by the new game in town, which was the colonisation of the New World across the Atlantic, and in 1621

he persuaded James that it might be prestigious, as well as profitable, to establish a 'Nova Scotia in America' to rival the colonies of New England, New France and New Spain.

To this end James granted Alexander the charter to a vast tract of land in the north of America, an area larger than Great Britain and France combined, where he could set up his New Scotland and they could all bask in the glory.

At enormous cost Alexander managed to collect together enough hardy folk to fill two ships, and in 1622 he sent them off under the command of his son William to gain a foothold on the new continent.

# Baronets of Nova Scotia

Their mission sadly failed because of a shortage of skilled workmen, and Alexander and the king made a huge financial loss, so in 1624 King

James introduced a new order of baronets for Scottish 'knichts and gentlemen of chiefe respect for the birth, place or fortounes' to be called BARONETS OF NOVA SCOTIA. James died later that year, but his son Charles I eagerly took over the scheme, and by the end of 1625 no fewer than 22 new baronets had been created, the first of which was ROBERT INNES, whose descendants would go on to become Dukes of Roxburghe.

In return for tracts of land in Nova Scotia of 11,520 acres (4,660 ha), the baronets were expected to send out six labourers and craftsmen sufficiently equipped to survive for two years and to pay Sir William Alexander 3,000 Scots merks (166 guineas) for his 'past charges in discoverie of said countrie'.

Unfortunately, those who were not killed off by the harsh climate and conditions were left high and dry when King Charles ceded the colony to the French in 1632, as part of a peace settlement, and ordered the Scottish settlers to be removed.

The Order of Baronets continued, however, since it was far too splendid a way of raising money to be abandoned, and by the time it was wound up in 1707, a total of 329 baronets had been created, of which about one-third still exist.

Nova Scotia was returned to Britain in 1713, and this time the settlers from Scotland succeeded in establishing themselves permanently, no doubt helped in their task by the earlier efforts of Sir William Alexander's hardy pioneers.

# Earl of Stirling

S ir William Alexander became Secretary for Scotland in 1626 and was rewarded in 1633 with the title EARL OF STIRLING. He died virtually penniless, having lost his all when his colony was handed to the French, but his efforts did establish Britain's claim to Nova Scotia and he is commemorated in Halifax by a monument made of stones from his birthplace, Menstrie Castle.

# Sir James Holborne

M enstrie Castle was badly burned by the Marquess of Montrose during the English Civil War, and it was in a somewhat dilapidated state when it was bought in 1649 by SIR JAMES HOLBORNE.

That being the case, Holborne might have been forgiven for being a bit rough with the Marquess of Montrose when he was given the responsibility the following year of escorting Montrose back to Edinburgh from Ardvreck Castle in Sutherland, where the Marquess had been detained.

On the second night of their long journey south, Holborne and his prisoner stopped off at Skibo Castle, near Dornoch, then the home of the Dowager Lady Gray, a well-known Royalist. When she requested that Montrose be seated next to her at the dinner table, Major-General Holborne drew himself up and informed the good lady that strict military protocol would be observed, and Montrose would be placed with an officer either side of him to ensure the safety of the company. A good hostess is not to be denied however, and Lady Gray snatched up a leg of mutton from the table and proceeded to beat the good major-general about the head with such violence that he surrendered straight away, and Montrose was given his rightful place of honour at his hostess's side.

# Sir Ralph Abercromby
## 1734–1801

In 1719 Menstrie Castle was sold to George Abercromby of Tullibody, and in 1734 the castle celebrated another distinguished birth, that of RALPH ABERCROMBY. He went on to study law at the University of Edinburgh and then joined the 3rd Dragoon Guards in 1756 and served in the Seven Years War.

Abercromby disapproved of the war against the American colonies and resigned from the army to become MP for Clackmannanshire, but when France declared war against Britain in 1793 he returned to the military as a major-general and fought with distinction in Flanders and as Commander-in-Chief of British forces in the West Indies. After commanding British troops in Ireland and Scotland, Abercromby was a popular choice to lead the expedition to remove the French from Egypt in 1801, and his brilliant and daring disembarkation of troops at ABOUKIR BAY is regarded as a glorious moment in British military history. He was struck down during the subsequent battle near Alexandria at the moment of victory, and died a week later, acclaimed a hero.

His brother ROBERT ABERCROMBY (1740–1827) also became a general, spending seven years in India as Governor of Bombay and Commander-in-Chief of the Indian forces, and also served as MP for Clackmannanshire.

Ralph's eldest son JOHN (1772–1817) pursued a military career and became Governor of Madras in 1812, while his youngest son ALEXANDER fought with honour in the Peninsular War and at Waterloo, before becoming the third Abercromby MP for Clackmannanshire. Second son JAMES (1776–1858) became Speaker of the House of Commons from 1835 to 1839.

## Nova Scotia Rooms

After the Abercrombys left, Menstrie Castle was abandoned and fell into disrepair, but it was saved from demolition in 1957 when actor MOULTRIE KELSALL (1901–80) mounted a campaign to raise funds for its restoration. By 1964 the castle had been preserved and turned into apartments. Much of the money raised came from descendants of the original Scottish settlers in Nova Scotia, and two rooms are given over to an exhibition about William Alexander and the founding of Nova Scotia, while the walls of one room are decorated with the arms of all the Baronets of Nova Scotia.

*Well, I never knew this*
*about*
CLACKMANNANSHIRE FOLK

## William Alexander
◄ 1726–83 ►

*'The bravest man in America'*

One hundred years after the death of the 1st Earl of Stirling, founder of Nova Scotia, his kinsman WILLIAM ALEXANDER, a descendant of the 1st Earl's grandfather, attempted to resurrect the earldom, which had lapsed with the death of the 5th Earl in 1739.

This William Alexander had fought for the British in the French and Indian Wars that won Canada for Britain – and succeeding to the title Earl of Stirling would have brought him huge land grants in New

England, Nova Scotia and the St Lawrence River valley. Alexander's claim was not dismissed; nor was it accepted, however, as he was unable to provide proof of descent.

Nonetheless, when he returned to America, Alexander styled himself Lord Stirling and that is how he is remembered. He settled down in New Jersey and was one of the founders, as well as THE FIRST GOVERNOR, OF KING'S COLLEGE, later Columbia University. George Washington was a friend, and gave Stirling's daughter away at her wedding.

When the American Revolution began, Stirling was appointed as a brigadier general in the Continental Army, and his defiant stand at the Battle of Long Island, the first major battle of the American Revolution following the Declaration of Independence, undoubtedly saved the Americans from defeat at a time when the Revolution had barely begun. With the Continental Army outnumbered and almost trapped in Manhattan, Alexander led his Maryland Regiment in repeated attacks against the British troops, stalling them long enough for the main body of the Americans to retreat to defensive positions at Brooklyn Heights. Stirling's men were eventually overwhelmed and Stirling himself was captured, but the Continental Army survived to fight another day, and Stirling's courage led to one newspaper

calling him 'the bravest man in America'.

He was later released in a prisoner exchange, perhaps unwisely, and was promoted to major-general, going on to win many more battles for the Americans, although he didn't live to enjoy victory for long, dying of cancer in 1783.

ARCHIBALD TAIT, ARCHBISHOP OF CANTERBURY (1811–82), son of the owner of the Harviestoun estate. For six years he was headmaster of Rugby School, where amongst his pupils was Charles Lutwidge Dodgson (Lewis Carroll). In the spring of 1856 Tait and his wife lost five of their children to scarlet fever, all within five weeks. That same year he was consecrated Bishop of London and in 1868 was translated to Canterbury as 93rd Archbishop. There is a memorial font to him in the church of St James the Great in Dollar.

While on a visit to the Tait family at HARVIESTOUN CASTLE (now demolished) with Miss Charlotte

Hamilton, Robert Burns wrote the following lines:

> How pleasant the banks of the clear-winding Devon
> With green-spreading bushes, and flowers blooming fair,
> But the bonniest flower on the banks of the Devon
> Was once a sweet bud on the braes of the Ayr.

GEORGE BROWN (1818–80), journalist and statesman, born in Alloa. In 1837 he emigrated with his father to New York and then to Toronto, where he founded and became FIRST EDITOR OF THE TORONTO GLOBE, using the paper to promote his ideas for the unity of the Canadian colonies into a single confederation, representation by population and the Abolition of Slavery. As a member of the Canadian Parliament he led the Great Coalition with John Macdonald and George Etienne Carter and is regarded as one of Canada's Founding Fathers. In 1880 he was accidentally shot by a former employee of the *Globe* and subsequently died of an infection.

# Dumfriesshire

*Drumlanrig Castle was built for William Douglas, the 1st
Duke of Queensberry in 1689, and today is one of the
many homes of the Duke of Buccleuch.*

◀ DUMFRIESSHIRE FOLK ▶

Dr James Mounsey ✦ 'Annie Laurie' ✦ Andrew Hallidie
✦ Ian Callum ✦ Allan McNish

# Earl of Dumfries

The title EARL OF DUMFRIES was created in 1633 for WILLIAM CRICHTON, 7TH LORD CRICHTON OF SANQUHAR.

# Sanquhar

The CRICHTON family came to Britain originally from Hungary and took their name from the barony of KREITTON, near Edinburgh. Thomas de Crichton appears on the Ragman Rolls of 1296, and his second son William gained the barony of SANQUHAR through marriage to the heiress Isobel de Ross.

In 1464 their great-grandson Robert was made Sheriff of Dumfries, and in 1487 his son, also Robert, was created 1ST LORD CRICHTON OF SANQUHAR by James III.

The 6TH LORD SANQUHAR was hanged at Westminster in 1612 for being complicit in the murder of his fencing instructor, who seven years earlier had put out one of Sanquhar's eyes in a fencing match. The punishment was a harsh one, but James VI, still securing his position as James I of England, wanted to make an example of a troublesome Scot.

The title of Lord Sanquhar then passed to a cousin, William Crichton, who became the 7th Lord Sanquhar. In 1633 he was created 1ST EARL OF DUMFRIES by Charles I. This title stayed with the Crichtons and then made its way by the female line and by marriage to JOHN, LORD MOUNT STUART, grandson of the 1st Marquess of Bute and future 2nd Marquess of Bute.

Thus did the title Earl of Dumfries descend upon the Stuart family of the MARQUESS OF BUTE, who gave it as a courtesy title to the heir and changed their surname name to CRICHTON-STUART.

# Sanquhar Castle

The Crichton family's main home was SANQUHAR CASTLE, which they built when they obtained the land from the Rosses in the late 13th century. Perched above the River Nith, it was once a noble fortress but is now a melancholy, windswept ruin, occupied only by the White Lady, the ghostly reincarnation of Marion Dalpeddar, one of a number of young local women who 'went in the servants' entrance and came out in the family way'. To ensure her silence she was murdered by someone at the castle in 1580 . . .

When James VI stopped at Sanquhar in 1617, on his way to Glasgow, he was welcomed by the Crichtons with a banquet so extravagant that it almost bankrupted them. Lord Crichton apparently escorted the King to his room by the light of a torch made from £30,000 in bond notes owed to him by James.

In 1639, ironically just after William Crichton was made Earl of Dumfries, the Crichtons sold Sanquhar to Sir William Douglas of Drumlanrig, later 1st Duke of Queensberry (*see* below), and moved to Ayrshire, where they built Dumfries House.

In 1679 Douglas, by then the Duke of Queensberry, began to build himself a new castle down the road at Drumlanrig, but after staying in it for only one night, he decided he didn't like it there and returned to live at Sanquhar. His family eventually moved in to Drumlanrig after the Duke's death, and Sanquhar Castle was abandoned.

## Drumlanrig

The barony of DRUMLANRIG originally belonged to the Earls of Mar but passed by marriage to the Douglas family in the 14th century. The 1ST BARON DRUMLANRIG (d.1427) was William Douglas, elder son of James Douglas, 2nd Earl of Douglas, who was killed at the Battle of Otterburn in 1388.

WILLIAM DOUGLAS, 6TH BARON DRUMLANRIG, died at Flodden Field in 1513. Another William Douglas, 9th Baron Drumlanrig, was created 1ST EARL OF QUEENSBERRY in 1633 by Charles I.

# Queensberry

❦

The Queensberry title is derived from a 2,285 ft (696 m) high mountain to the east of Drumlanrig called Queensberry, from the Anglo-Saxon 'queen berg', meaning 'highest hill'.

WILLIAM DOUGLAS, 3RD EARL OF QUEENSBERRY (1637–95), and builder of the present Drumlanrig Castle, was made MARQUESS OF QUEENSBERRY in 1682 and DUKE OF QUEENSBERRY in 1684.

His son James, the 2nd Marquess and 2nd Duke of Queensberry, was known as the UNION DUKE for his prominent role in carrying through the Act of Union between Scotland and England. When it became apparent that James his heir was insane, the Union Duke split his titles so that James would become 3rd Marquess, while the Dukedom passed to a younger son, Charles.

CHARLES, 3RD DUKE OF QUEENSBERRY, is remembered for his patronage of John Gay, author of the first ballad opera, *The Beggar's Opera*, while his cousin William Douglas, the 4th Duke, was a notorious rake and bounder known as OLD Q, or 'the Goat of Piccadilly' (*see* Peeblesshire).

Despite fathering numerous

---

### The Cannibalistic Idiot

Recognised as unhinged from an early age, JAMES, EARL OF DRUMLANRIG, (1697–1715), heir to the 2nd Marquess, was kept permanently locked away at Queensberry House on Canongate in Edinburgh. In 1707, while his guards were distracted watching the riots caused by his father's Act of Union, the 10-year-old Earl James escaped and took captive a young kitchen boy, whom he despatched, placed on a spit, basted, roasted and then devoured with lip-smacking gusto. Some opponents of the Act of Union saw this gruesome episode as a symbolic punishment for the Union Duke. Known ever after as the 'Cannibalistic Idiot', James became 3rd Marquess of Queensberry on the death of his father in 1711, and died four years later at the age of 17.

The oven before which he cooked the unfortunate lad can still be examined at Queensberry House, which now forms part of the Scottish Parliament complex.

---

children Old Q never married, and after his death the dukedom, along with Drumlanrig Castle, passed to his cousin the Duke of Buccleuch, whose family still possess the title today. The marquessate passed to another cousin, Sir Charles Douglas, who became 6th Marquess of Queensberry and built a new family seat, KINMOUNT HOUSE, near Annan, in 1812.

## Queensberry Rules

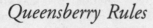

THE 9TH MARQUESS OF QUEENSBERRY, JOHN SHOLTO DOUGLAS (1844–1900), was a keen boxing enthusiast and sponsored the publication of the 12 rules for conducting a boxing match, written by John Graham Chambers. They became known as the 'QUEENSBERRY RULES' – an expression still used today to describe fair play.

The 9th Marquess was also an ardent atheist, and in 1880 he was barred from taking his seat in the House of Lords for refusing to swear allegiance to the Queen, declaring it an act of 'Christian tomfoolery'.

In 1895 Queensberry accused the playwright Oscar Wilde, who was having a relationship with his son Lord Alfred Douglas, or 'Bosie', of being a 'posing sodomite'. Wilde responded by making a libel complaint against the Marquess, which backfired spectacu-

larly and led to Wilde being arrested for gross indecency and imprisoned in Reading Gaol.

Queensberry, a rigid and far from popular man who didn't gain much favour with his family by selling Kinmount House, died at the relatively young age of 55. His younger brother, Lord Francis Douglas, had died in 1865 in a fall during the return from the first successful ascent of the Matterhorn, aged just 18. His body was never found.

The present holder of the title is David Douglas, 12th Marquess of Queensberry, who was born in 1929.

## Annandale

THE 1ST LORD OF ANNANDALE was the Anglo-Norman knight, ROBERT DE BRUS, first of the Bruce dynasty in Scotland. He received Annandale from David I, the brother-in-law of Henry I of England, in 1124.

The de Brus name comes down from an 11th-century Norwegian Earl of Orkney called Brusi, whose descendants settled in Normandy and built themselves a castle there called La Brusée. A younger son, Robert de Brus, came over to England with William the Conqueror and fought at the Battle of Hastings in 1066. His son Robert marched north to help David I in his campaign to reclaim the Scottish crown, and was granted the Lordship of Annandale.

## *Lords of Annandale*

ROBERT BRUCE, 4TH LORD OF ANNANDALE (1195–1233), married Isobel of Huntingdon, second daughter of David, Earl of Huntingdon, who was the grandson of David I and brother of William the Lion, and this blood tie gave their son, ROBERT BRUCE, 5TH LORD OF ANNANDALE, a legitimate claim to the throne when Alexander III, last of the House of Dunkeld, died without an heir in 1286.

In fact, Bruce lost out to John Balliol, who was chosen as King of Scotland by Edward I on account of his being descended from the eldest daughter of David, Earl of Huntingdon, and therefore senior by right of the first-born, or primogeniture.

ROBERT BRUCE, 6TH LORD OF ANNANDALE married Marjorie, the widowed heir to the Earl of Carrick and thus, by marriage, became the Earl of Carrick. Their son, ROBERT THE BRUCE, 7TH LORD OF ANNANDALE, would become King Robert I of Scotland.

## Some Notable Bruces

GEORGE BRUCE OF CARNOCK (1568–1625), merchant and engineer. Bruce operated out of Culross, in Fife, trading with Holland, the Baltic countries and other ports along the Forth River. His interests were mainly in coal-mining and salt, and he devised ingenious ways of draining his mines which enabled him to become the first known person to sink a mine underneath the sea. His finest legacy is the glorious Culross Palace, which he built using imported materials such as glass and tiles from Holland and pinewood from the Baltic.

## *Sir William Bruce*
### *1630–1710*

William Bruce, pioneer of Palladianism and the man who introduced classical architecture into Scotland, was born in Fife, the younger son of the Laird of Blairhall.

created a restrained, classical manor house, which was later dramatically altered by the glorious but showy grandeur of the Adams' vast sweeping facade and colonnades at the front. If you go round to the back of the building you can still see Bruce's superb work.

Bruce's finest creation, KINROSS HOUSE, was built for himself in 1685. It is SCOTLAND'S FIRST CLASSICAL COUNTRY HOUSE.

From boyhood he was a staunch supporter of the Stuart kings, even when it was unwise to be so, and his rise to eminence began when he acted as emissary between General Monck in Edinburgh and Charles II in Holland. At the Restoration, Bruce was showered with rewards, including being given the appointment in 1671 of 'surveyor, contriver and overseer of all the works at the Palace of Holyroodhouse, and of such other castles and palaces in Scotland as the King shall appoint to be repaired'.

The repair and rebuilding of Holyroodhouse was his first major work. His trademark is the emphasis he puts on the setting of the house in a formal and considered relationship to the landcape and gardens.

THIRLESTANE CASTLE in Berwickshire was remodelled between 1670 and 1676 for the Duke of Lauderdale.

At HOPETOUN HOUSE, begun in 1699 for the Earl of Hopetoun, Bruce

## James Bruce
## 1730–94

An explorer and travel writer, James Bruce was an enormous man, both physically and intellectually. He travelled widely in Europe, making sketches and records of the antiquities and artifacts he came across, and in 1762 was appointed British Consul in Algiers, where he became fascinated by the challenge to find the source of the Nile.

After spending two years amongst the people of Ethopia he set out in October 1770 with a party of native porters and reached Lake Tana, source of the Blue Nile, in November. Although not the first European to discover the source he was the first to verify it officially. His adventures were so exotic that Bruce was not believed when he returned to Britain and he was ridiculed, particularly by Dr Johnson and Boswell. He retired to his family home, Kinnaird House in Stirlingshire, to write his memoirs, which were published in 1790 to great acclaim, silencing his critics. He died falling down the front steps of his house while gallantly helping a lady guest to her carriage.

KEN BRUCE, BBC Radio 2 presenter, born in 1951.

FIONA BRUCE, journalist and television news presenter, born in 1964.

*Well, I never knew this about*
## DUMFRIESSHIRE FOLK

## Dr James Mounsey
—◄ 1710–73 ►—

DR JAMES MOUNSEY, 'Chief Director of the Medical Chancery and of the whole Medical Faculty throughout the whole Russian Empire', was born in Skipmyre, birthplace of William Paterson, founder of the Bank of England. Mounsey served as a physician in Russia for 26 years from 1736 to 1762, some of that time as personal physician to the Empress Catherine the Great and her husband Tsar Peter III. Interestingly, three of Catherine's doctors came from the

Lochmaben area of Dumfriesshire, Dr Matthew Halliday and Dr John Rogerson being the other two.

When Tsar Peter was murdered, Mounsey fled from Russia back to Scotland and purchased the ancestral Dumfriesshire estate of the Carruthers family, RAMMERSCALES, near Lockerbie, where he built himself a classical Georgian house of red sandstone overlooking Annandale. Convinced that agents had been sent to kill him by his enemies at the Russian court, Mounsey faked his own death and holed up at Rammerscales, which had been deliberately built with two doors in every room, so that he would have an escape route in the event of trouble. Mounsey's ghost, 'Old Jacobus', is said to haunt the library, and schoolchildren who occupied the house during the Second World War were so spooked they insisted on moving out to the stables.

## 'Annie Laurie'

*Maxwellton braes are bonnie,*
*Where early fa's the dew,*
*And 'twas there that Annie Laurie*
*Gave me her promise true.*
*Gave me her promise true,*
*Which ne'er forgot will be,*
*And for bonnie Annie Laurie,*
*I lay me doon and dee.*

'Annie Laurie', which has been called 'the greatest love song in the world', was written by Annie's sweetheart William Douglas, and later put to music by Lady John Scott, daughter-in-law of the 4th Duke of Buccleuch.

Annie and Douglas never married. Douglas was a Jacobite and had to flee Scotland for a while, although he did marry a Lanarkshire girl, Elizabeth Clerk, in 1706. Annie married a neigh-

*Craigdarroch House*

bour, Alexander Fergusson, Laird of Craigdarroch, seat of the Dumfriesshire Fergussons, and oversaw the building of the new Craigdarroch House by William Adam, in 1729. She lived at Craigdarroch for over 50 years.

## Andrew Hallidie
◄ 1836–1900 ►

ANDREW HALLIDIE, the inventor of STEEL-WIRE ROPE, and creator of the WORLD'S FIRST CABLE-CAR RAILWAY, in San Francisco, was born Andrew Smith, of parents from Dumfriesshire. He later changed his name in honour of his maternal uncle Sir Andrew Hallidie, who had been physician to William IV. In 1852 Hallidie left Liverpool to join the California gold rush and, although he didn't find much gold, he did invent a wire rope to haul cars up the hillside from the mill to the mine.

In 1857 Hallidie settled in San Francisco to concentrate on manufacturing his new wire rope, which was used largely in the construction of suspension bridges. In 1867 he patented the HALLIDIE ROPEWAY, which was a method of transporting heavy materials across difficult terrain by means of an endless elevated cable way, in areas where bridges and roads were impractical.

In 1869 Hallidie witnessed an appalling accident, which drove him to come up with a new system for transporting goods and people up and down the steep hills of San Francisco. It was a damp summer day and the cobblestones were wet and slippery. A heavily laden horse-drawn street car struggling to climb one of the hills suddenly started to slide backwards, and in front of Hallidie's horrified gaze, five terrified horses were dragged downhill to their deaths. Two years later in 1871 he put forward a plan for street cars propelled by underground cables and began to put together finance for the project. On 2 August 1873, in the face of much opposition and ridicule, Andrew Hallidie launched THE WORLD'S FIRST CABLE-CAR RAILWAY, the Clay Street Hill Railroad.

Today the San Francisco cable-car system he pioneered over 130 years ago is still in perfect working order. The LAST PERMANENTLY OPERATIONAL MANUALLY-OPERATED CABLE-CAR SYSTEM IN THE WORLD, it is AMERICA'S ONLY MOVING NATIONAL MONUMENT, and an iconic emblem of the city of San Francisco across the globe.

of Art, and in vehicle design from London's Royal College of Art. He joined Ford in 1979 and cut his teeth on the Fiesta and Mondeo models before being appointed design manager for the Ghia studio in Turin. In 1991 he became chief designer for Tom Walkinshaw's TWR Design, whose clients included Volvo, Nissan, Mazda and Aston Martin. During this period he designed the car for which he is justly famous, the ASTON MARTIN DB7, which won him the Jim Clark Memorial Award in 1995. He is currently design director for Jaguar. His younger brother Moray (b.1958) is also a designer, currently working for Ford in America, and credited with revitalising the Mazda brand for the new millennium.

ALLAN McNISH, racing driver, was born in Dumfries in 1969. He has twice been champion of the American Le Mans series, in 2006 and 2007, and won the Le Mans 24-hour race in 1998 and 2008. In 2002 he drove for the Toyota Formula One team, partnering Mika Salo.

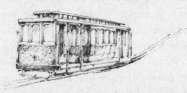

IAN CALLUM, car designer, was born in Dumfries in 1955. He graduated in industrial design from Glasgow School

# Dunbartonshire

*Dumbarton Castle sits on Dumbarton Rock
by the River Clyde and has the largest recorded
history of any fortress in Scotland.*

◄ DUNBARTONSHIRE FOLK ►

John Logie Baird ✦ David Byrne

# Lennox

Loch Lomond was once called Loch Leven, as recalled by the River Leven that runs south from the loch through Strathleven to the Clyde at Dumbarton. The territory around the old Loch Leven was called Levenachs in the Celtic language, which means 'the field of the Leven' and became over time Levenax, Lennax and then Lennox.

This territory formed the old Celtic mormaerdom of Lennox, and the first recognised Mormaer or Earl of Lennox was Arkil, a Saxon noble from Northumbria seeking refuge from William the Conqueror. His descendants appear to have ruled Lennox pretty much undisturbed until 1238, when Alexander II took possession of Dumbarton Castle taking the first tentative steps of the Scottish crown towards the Norse and Celtic west, to which Lennox was the gateway.

The last of this line of earls was Isabella, daughter of Donnchadh, Earl of Lennox. In 1392 she married Murdoch Stewart, who became 2nd Duke of Albany in 1420 but was executed by James I in 1425 for treason. Isabella was allowed to govern Lennox from Loch Lomond until she died in 1458, when the longest surviving Celtic mormaerdom came to an end and the Lennox earldom went to the Stewarts.

# Dukes of Lennox

In 1581 James VI created Esme Stewart 1ST DUKE OF LENNOX. Esme was a cousin of James's father Lord Darnley, and was amongst other things First Gentleman of the Bedchamber, possibly in every sense. Esme was the young James's closest friend and was showered with gifts including Dumbarton Castle, key to Esme's ducal territories. The Presbyterian Scottish nobles disapproved of all this nonsense and in 1582 William Ruthven, Earl of Gowrie, abducted James and imprisoned him in Huntingtower Castle in Perthshire for nearly a year, until he agreed to send Lennox into exile.

Esme died in France the following year, 1583, and his son LUDOVIC, 2ND

DUKE OF LENNOX, married Sophia Ruthven – ironically, the daughter of the man who had forced his own father into exile.

The 6TH DUKE OF LENNOX drowned in the sea off Elsinore in Denmark in 1672, aged just 33, and as he had no children the title became extinct. It was resurrected in 1675 for Charles de Kerouille, an illegitimate son of Charles II who was also made Duke of Richmond. In 1876 the Duke of Richmond and Lennox was made Duke of Gordon, and as he already held the dukedom of Aubigny-sur-Nere he became the proud possessor of four dukedoms, more than any other person in the realm.

## Some Notable Lennoxes

The LENNOX SISTERS, daughters of the Duke of Richmond and Lennox, were immortalised in the BBC television series *Aristocrats*, taken from Stella Tillyard's book of the same name. They were. . .

LADY CAROLINE LENNOX (1723–74) was the wife of Whig politician Henry Fox and mother of Charles James Fox. She became a famous hostess at her home, Holland House in London.

LADY EMILY LENNOX (1731–1814) married the Duke of Leinster.

*Lady Louisa Lennox*

LADY LOUISA LENNOX (1743–1821) married Tom Conolly, grand-nephew of William Conolly, Speaker of the Irish House of Commons, and lived in the biggest house in Ireland, Castletown House in Co. Kildare.

LADY SARAH LENNOX (1745–1826) put forward by her family to be George III's queen, but in the end married Charles Bunbury before eloping with Lord William Gordon, son of the Duke of Gordon and father of her child Louisa. Ostracised by society, she eventually married army officer George Napier, by whom she had eight children.

DAVID LENNOX (1788–1873), stonemason, born in Ayr. He emigrated to Australia in 1832 following the death of his wife, and was hired as a bridgebuilder by the Surveyor-General. His first bridge was the LENNOX BRIDGE at Lapstone Hill in the Blue Mountains of New South Wales, the FIRST PERMANENT BRIDGE and now THE OLDEST SURVIVING BRIDGE ON THE AUSTRALIAN MAINLAND (there is an older bridge in Tasmania).

E.J. LENNOX (1854–1933), architect who designed many of Toronto's most notable landmarks, including Casa Loma, for financier Sir Henry Pellatt, which when completed in 1914 was THE LARGEST PRIVATE HOUSE IN AMERICA.

BOBBY LENNOX, footballer, born in Saltcoats, Ayrshire, in 1943. Lennox was one of the 'Lisbon Lions', the Celtic side that was the first British football team to win the European Cup, beating the Italian club Internazionale in the 1967 final in Lisbon.

ANNIE LENNOX, singer-songwriter born in Aberdeen in 1954. She created the Eurythmics with Dave Stewart in the 1980s, and in 2003 won an Oscar for Best Original Song for 'Into the West', which she co-wrote for the end credits of *The Lord of the Rings: The Return of the King*. She has also won eight Brit awards and four Grammys.

# Luss

LUSS sits on the west bank of Loch Lomond, gazing across the water at the glowering bulk of Ben Lomond, at 3,200 ft (975 m) Scotland's most southerly Munro (a Munro being a mountain over 3,000 ft). Luss is renowned as one of Scotland's prettiest villages and was the outdoor location for the popular Scottish Television drama series *Take the High Road*, in which Luss appeared as 'Glendarroch'.

Luss is the ancestral home of the CLAN COLQUHOUN, and the church in Luss was built in 1875 by Sir James Colquhoun in memory of his father, who had drowned two years earlier in Loch Lomond with four of his ghillies while sailing home from stalking red deer on the Island of Inchlonaig.

# Clan Colquhoun

In the 13th century, the lands of Colquhoun (pronounced 'Cahoon'), in what is now Dunbartonshire, were granted to Humphry de Kilpatrick by the Gaelic Mormaer of Lennox, and Kilpatrick's son Ingelram took to calling himself de Colquhoun. In 1368 Sir Robert Colquhoun married the Fair Maid of Luss, and since then the Clan Chief has been known as COLQUHOUN OF LUSS.

# Rossdhu Castle

The seat of the Colquhouns of Luss was at ROSSDHU (meaning 'black headland'), a wooded peninsula on Loch Lomond near Luss where Sir John Colquhoun, 11th Laird of Luss, Great Chamberlain of Scotland, built a castle in about 1457.

In 1592 Sir Humphrey Colquhoun, 16th Laird of Luss, was caught in a compromising position with the wife of the Macfarlane chief and was chased from Rossdhu to another of his castles at Bannachra. The Macfarlanes set fire to the place to smoke Sir Humphrey out, and he was eventually killed with an arrow fired by his own brother (and heir). Poor Sir Humphrey's genitals were removed, cooked in a rich sauce and served up as a dish for Lady Macfarlane.

# Battle of Glen Fruin
## 7 February 1603

No one is quite sure what really happened, but it is said that two MacGregors were passing by Luss on a cold winter's night and were refused shelter, so they took refuge in an abandoned barn, having slaughtered a sheep, on which they feasted. They were discovered, brought before the Laird of Luss, given a brief trial and executed.

The Chief of Clan Gregor, Alasdair MacGregor of Glenstrae, heard about this and sent 400 of his brawniest fighters to exact revenge. SIR HUMPHREY COLQUHOUN OF LUSS was expecting something of the sort and gathered together a force of twice that number. He then marched to meet the MacGregors at Glen Fruin, a valley running westward from Loch Lomond.

The Colquhouns found themselves trapped in the valley, with a force of MacGregors at the head of the pass blocking them in like a cork in a bottle, and another group stopping their retreat. The Colquhouns' cavalry and men could not manoeuvre in the narrow and boggy terrain and they were cut down almost at will. By the end of the battle some 200 Colquhouns lay dead, while the MacGregors lost no more than a dozen men.

The victorious MacGregors forfeited all sympathy when they went on and plundered the now unguarded Colquhoun lands, helping themselves to some 80 horses, 600 cows and 800 sheep. Soon afterwards James VI outlawed them, proscribed the use of the name MacGregor and prohibited any who bore the name from carrying arms.

Ever since the battle Glen Fruin has been known as the Glen of Sorrow.

## Colquhoun of Luss

In 1625, SIR JOHN COLQUHOUN, THE 19TH LAIRD OF LUSS, a necromancer skilled in black magic, and possibly the last person in Scotland to practise witchcraft openly, conjured up a baronetcy of Nova Scotia, married a sister of the famous Earl of Montrose, eloped with another sister and disappeared to Italy, never to be seen again.

SIR JAMES COLQUHOUN, 25TH OF LUSS, founded the town of HELENSBURGH, which he named after his wife Helen, sister of the Earl of Sutherland. He also built the

present ROSSDHU HOUSE, not far from the old castle, and here entertained Dr Johnson and James Boswell on their way to their tour of the Hebrides. Dr Johnson apparently fell into the loch and came squelching into the new house leaving a trail of water. His irate hostess ordered him out, remarking, 'What a bear!' – at which her husband muttered, 'He is no doubt a bear, but he is Ursus Major!'

*Sir James Colquhoun*

The present Clan Chief is SIR MALCOLM COLQUHOUN, 31ST LAIRD OF LUSS, 9TH BARONET OF LUSS AND 33RD CHIEF OF COLQUHOUN.

Rossdhu House is now the clubhouse for the famous Loch Lomond Golf Club, but nonetheless remains the ancestral seat of the Chief of Clan Colquhoun.

## Notable Colquhouns

PATRICK COLQUHOUN (1745–1820), linen merchant who founded the Glasgow Chamber of Commerce, born in Dumbarton. In 1797 he organised the West India Planters Committees and the West India Merchants to fund THE WORLD'S FIRST REGULAR POLICE FORCE, THE THAMES RIVER POLICE, based on an idea by master mariner John Harriot.

JOE COLQUHOUN (1926–87), artist who first drew the 'Roy of the Rovers' strip cartoon for the *Tiger* comic.

*Well, I never* knew this
*about*
DUNBARTONSHIRE FOLK

## John Logie Baird
◄ 1888–1946 ►

JOHN LOGIE BAIRD, engineer and inventor of THE WORLD'S FIRST WORKING TELEVISION SYSTEM, was born at The Lodge in Helensburgh, a son of the Manse. In 1907 he took up an apprenticeship at the huge Argyll Motor Works in Alexandria and found himself working at a bench with a boy from Belfast named OLIVER HUTCHINSON. The two became firm friends.

This was not the case with a fellow student Baird came across later, when he entered the Royal Technical College in Glasgow and found himself being taught next to John Reith, who would go on to dominate the BBC, the organisation that would pioneer Baird's invention. Reith, even then, was a man intolerant of those he thought fools, which was pretty much everyone.

The lives of all these young men were disrupted by the First World War and they went their separate ways.

After the war Baird found himself in London chasing his dream of

*Argyll Water Works where John Logie Baird met Oliver Hutchinson.*

creating television. He had already succeeded in transmitting shadowy images of a man's hand at his flat in Hastings, and was sure he was on the verge of a breakthrough, when Oliver Hutchinson came back into his life. Meeting by chance while walking down the Strand, they went for a cup of tea and Baird told his old friend all about the progress of his work.

Hutchinson was impressed, and immediately offered Baird his support as a business partner and fundraiser. Within a year Baird had managed to transmit a still image, THE FIRST KNOWN TELEVISION PICTURE, of a young clerk from the office below his laboratory in Soho, William Taynton. The following year, in 1926, Baird gave THE FIRST DEMONSTRATION OF A MOVING PICTURE, and the subject

this time, THE FIRST MAN EVER TO APPEAR ON LIVE, MOVING TELE-VISION, was none other than his business partner and friend from the apprentices' bench back at the Argyll Motor Works in Dunbartonshire, Oliver Hutchinson.

*Oliver Hutchinson*

John Logie Baird went on to demonstrate, in 1928, THE FIRST COLOUR TELEVISION, THE FIRST LONG-DISTANCE TELEVISION PICTURES, from London to Glasgow, THE FIRST BBC TELEVISION PROGRAMME, and THE FIRST TRANSATLANTIC TELEVISION TRANSMISSION FROM LONDON TO NEW YORK. In 1931 he made THE FIRST LIVE TRANSMISSION OF A SPORTING EVENT, televising the Epsom Derby.

In 1926 Baird patented a device that formed images from reflected radio waves, and it is thought that he contributed considerably to the development of radar during the Second World War.

Baird had struggled with ill health all his life, and for his last years he retired to the seaside at Bexhill-on-Sea, where he died after suffering a stroke.

DAVID BYRNE, musician and songwriter with the New Wave band Talking Heads, born in Dumbarton in 1952. He collaborated with Ryuichi Sakamoto and Cong Su on the music for Bernardo Bertolucci's film *The Last Emperor*, which won an Oscar for Best Original Score in 1987, and in 2003 achieved the ultimate accolade when he appeared as himself in an episode of *The Simpsons*.

# East Lothian

---◆◆◆◆---

HADDINGTON ◆ WILLIAM I 'THE LION' ◆ ALEXANDER II
◆ JOHN KNOX ◆ DUNBAR ◆ EARL OF DUNBAR
◆ SOME NOTABLE DUNBARS

*Haddington Town House — the curfew bell in the
steeple rings at 7am and 10pm, maintaining
a tradition observed since 1532.*

◄ EAST LOTHIAN FOLK ►

John Cockburn ◆ Andrew Meikle
◆ Revd Dr John Witherspoon ◆ James Porteous

# Haddington

The capital of East Lothian (formerly Haddingtonshire), Scotland's FIRST ROYAL BURGH and the home of SCOTLAND'S LONGEST PARISH CHURCH, the elegant Georgian town of Haddington has played its part in Scotland's turbulent history, both royal and religious, being the birthplace of William the Lion and his son Alexander and of the Protestant reformer John Knox.

## William I – 'the Lion'
### 1143–1214

Grandson of David I, William was almost certainly born in Haddington, where his mother, Countess Ada, had a home. Redheaded, strong and determined, his reign as the King of Scots, which lasted for 49 years from 1165 until 1214, was the longest in Scottish history until the Union of Crowns in 1603 – James VI of Scotland, who became James I of England, reigned in Scotland for 68 years. Much of William's reign was concerned with winning back Northumbria from Henry II of England, and in 1178 he founded Arbroath Abbey and dedicated it to St Thomas à Becket, in part to irritate Henry, who was being pilloried

for the murder of that 'turbulent priest'. William is buried before the high altar at Arbroath, which was later the scene of the Declaration of Arbroath. William became known as 'the Lion' after the heraldic design of his standard, a red lion on a yellow background, which went on to be adopted as the basis for the Royal Standard of Scotland.

## Alexander II
### 1198–1249

Only son of William the Lion, ALEXANDER II was born in the royal palace at Haddington. In 1215 HE LED HIS ARMY FURTHER SOUTH THAN ANY OTHER KING OF SCOTS BEFORE OR SINCE, reaching Dover in support of the English barons in their quarrel with King John. He sealed his friendship with John's son Henry III by marrying Henry's sister Joan at York Minster, when he was 23 and Joan 11. In 1237 Alexander and Henry negotiated the Treaty of York, which set the boundary between Scotland and England as running from the Solway Firth in the west to the mouth of the River Tweed in the east. With the exception of Berwick, this has remained the border between the two countries to this day. Alexander was the first King of Scots to bring Argyll under his rule, and he was attempting to secure the Western Isles from Norway when he died of fever on the Isle of Kerrera, near Oban.

## *John Knox*
### C.1510—72

JOHN KNOX, Roman Catholic priest turned Protestant preacher, leader of the Scottish Reformation and founder of the Presbyterian Church, was born in Haddington around 1510. In 1558 he published a pamphlet called 'The First Blast of the Trumpet against the Monstrous Regiment of Women', widely seen as an attack on all women but actually directed against the Catholic Mary Tudor and Mary of Guise, mother of Mary Queen of Scots and Queen Regent of Scotland.

The Protestant Reformation in Scotland really began when Knox gave a sermon at St John's Church in Perth in 1559, denouncing the Catholic Church and cementing his image as the archetypal, bushy-browed Scottish preacher, thundering from the pulpit against idolatry and decadence. The listening crowd were whipped up into a frenzy of destruction, looting and sacking the churches in Perth and smashing all the graven images they could find. In 1560, guided by Knox, the Scottish parliament drew up the 'Confession of Faith' establishing the Protestant Church of Scotland, or Kirk, which is still the national church of Scotland today.

Knox's legendary confrontations with Mary Queen of Scots, during which he fiercely admonished the Queen, usually ended with Mary in tears, while Knox looked on unmoved.

In 1564, when he was well over 50, Knox married for the second time. It was a controversial union since not only was the girl, Margaret Stewart, connected to the decadent royal family, but she was only 17 years old. They had three daughters together.

Memorable Quotes:
*'A man with God is always in the majority.'*

*'You cannot antagonise and influence at the same time.'*

# Dunbar

D UNBAR means 'summit fort' in Celtic and it was originally the site of an Iron Age fort of which there is still some evidence. It was later part of Northumbria, and when Northumbria was weakened by assaults from the Vikings, Dunbar was annexed by the growing kingdom of Scotland.

# Earl of Dunbar

T he first man to be styled EARL OF DUNBAR was the Anglo-Saxon noble Gospatric II (d.1138), son of Gospatric, Earl of Northumbria, a kinsman of the Royal House of Dunkeld.

In 1072 Gospatric II was stripped of his Northumbrian earldom by William the Conqueror and fled to Scotland, where he was granted estates in Lothian, including Dunbar, by his kinsman Malcolm III. He attained the status of Earl in 1134, but tended to use the title Earl of Lothian rather than Dunbar.

Gospatric's grandson Waltheof was the first to choose the title Earl of Dunbar rather than Lothian, as Dunbar was the site of his main stronghold.

Waltheof's great-great-grandson Patrick gained control of the Marches along the border with England and hence adopted the title Earl of March. From this time the title Earl of Dunbar tended to be secondary, with Dunbar becoming used as the family name, as in Patrick de Dunbar, Earl of March.

Since the Earls of Dunbar had their own claim to the Scottish throne, the Earl did not support Robert the Bruce at Bannockburn in 1314, and instead sheltered Edward II at Dunbar Castle after his defeat, until Edward could escape back to England by sea. The following year, however, Dunbar and King Robert became allies, and in 1337 Edward III occupied Dunbar's lands at Berwick.

## Some Notable Dunbars

'BLACK AGNES' DUNBAR (1312–69), wife of Patrick Dunbar, 9th Earl of March, and daughter of the Earl of Moray. She was known as Black Agnes because of her olive complexion and dark hair. In 1338, while her husband was absent at Berwick, Black Agnes courageously defended Dunbar Castle for six months while it was besieged by Edward III's men under the Earl of Salisbury. Every time a cannonball struck the castle she would ostentatiously dust away the debris with a brightly coloured handkerchief and then wave to the attackers. Salisbury eventually gave up . . .

*She kept a stir in tower and*
   *trench*
*That brawling, boisterous Scottish*
   *wench.*
*Came I early, came I late,*
*I found Agnes at the gate.*

Agnes inherited the Moray title when her father and brother were killed in battle, but she herself died childless so the title went to her sister Isabella, who was married to her husband Patrick's cousin. Thus the earldoms of Dunbar and March were joined with that of Moray. At the beginning of the 15th century James I became envious of Sir George Dunbar, the hugely powerful 11th Earl of Dunbar, March and Moray, and all the wealth and property the family had accrued over 400 years was annexed to the crown. Dunbar was allowed to keep only the title Earl of Moray.

WILLIAM DUNBAR (1460–1520), 'makar' or poet laureate at the court of James IV. He is credited with being THE FIRST PERSON TO USE THE 'F' WORD IN PRINT, in his poem 'Brash of Wowing' (1503). All his poems can be found in the first books printed in Scotland, 'The Chepman and Myllar Prints', published in 1508.

ADRIAN DUNBAR, actor, born 1958. Appeared in many television programmes and films including *My Left Foot* (1989), *Hear My Song* (1991), which he co-wrote and starred in, and *The Crying Game* (1992).

VICKI NELSON-DUNBAR, tennis player, born 1962. She took part in THE LONGEST WOMEN'S TENNIS MATCH IN HISTORY, which lasted six hours and 31 minutes, during the 'Ginnys of Richmond' tournament in Virginia in 1984. Her opponent was Jean Hepner, and although the match only went to two sets, the second-set tie-break, won 13–11 by Nelson-Dunbar, included a rally of 643 strokes lasting 29 minutes.

*Well, I never knew this*
*about*
## EAST LOTHIAN FOLK

JOHN COCKBURN (1695–1758), 'the Father of Scottish Husbandry', born in Ormiston, maternal grandson of the Earl of Haddington. A supporter of the Union with England, he was a member of the last Scottish parliament and the first representative of East Lothian in the new parliament of Great Britain. When he inherited his estate at Ormiston in 1714 he found it run-down and unproductive, like Scottish agriculture in general, and he determined to introduce all the new agricultural methods he had seen at work in England, such as irrigation, Jethro Tull's seed drill, and the rotation of crops. Such was the success of his operations that landowners came from all over Scotland to study his methods. To promote his views Cockburn instituted the Ormiston Society, inviting noblemen and farmers and all the best intellects of Scotland to meet monthly and discuss the rural economy. Cockburn pronounced his name Co'burn, and this name is still THE ONLY EXAMPLE IN THE ENGLISH LANGUAGE THAT USES A SILENT 'CK'.

ANDREW MEIKLE (1719–1811), agricultural engineer who invented the THRESHING MACHINE, born in Pencaitland. It says on his tombstone that he was descended from 'a line of ingenious mechanics', and he worked as a millwright on the engineer John Rennie's estate at Houston Mill. In 1772 he invented SPRING SAILS for windmills, where the sails were made up of shutters that could be adjusted to take account of the strength of the wind. Later he invented the threshing machine, which Rennie used at Houston and helped Meikle to install at many other mills around East Lothian. Meikle is credited with inspiring John Rennie to become an engineer.

# Revd Dr John Witherspoon
#### ◄ 1723–94 ►

THE REVD DR JOHN WITHERSPOON, the ONLY ACTIVE CLERGYMAN TO SIGN THE AMERICAN DECLARATION OF INDEPENDENCE, was born in Gifford. Through his mother he was descended from John Knox. As a Protestant he was opposed to the Jacobite rebellion of 1745 and was briefly imprisoned at Doune Castle. In 1766, when he was serving as Presbyterian minister at Paisley, he met two of America's founding fathers, Benjamin Rush (the man who reconciled John Adams and Thomas Jefferson) and Richard Stockton, and together they persuaded him to accept the position as president of the Presbyterian College of New Jersey, which would become PRINCETON UNIVERSITY.

While there he became the leader of the Presbyterian Church in America and taught a huge number of students who would become members of the first Congress, including Aaron Burr (Thomas Jefferson's Vice President) and James Madison, 4th US President. Witherspoon's belief in limited government greatly influenced the philosophy and constitution of the new America. In 1773 he part sponsored the famous voyage of the *Hector*, the ship that brought the first Scottish Highlanders to Nova Scotia.

Disillusioned with the British monarchy, he was a strong supporter of the American Revolution from the start and willingly signed the Declaration of Independence which he helped to draft. He almost bankrupted himself rebuilding the iconic Nassau Hall at Princeton after it had been damaged in 1778 during the Revolutionary War.

Memorable Quotes:

*'On the part of America, there was not the most distant thought of subverting the government or of hurting the interest of the people of Great Britain; but of defending their own privileges from unjust encroachment; there was not the least desire of withdrawing their allegiance from the common sovereign till it became absolutely necessary – and indeed, it was his – King George III – own choice.'*

*'Never rise to speak till you have something to say; and when you have said it, cease.'*

## James Porteous
—◄ 1848–1922 ►—

Inventor of the FRESNO SCRAPER, one of the most important pieces of agricultural machinery ever produced, JAMES PORTEOUS was born in Haddington. His father was a wheelwright and blacksmith, and when James emigrated to California in 1873 he was well equipped with the skills needed to build up a successful business manufacturing wagons and machinery. James quickly realised that the farmers of California's San Joaquin valley were struggling to irrigate the dry, sandy soil and needed help in the back-breaking work of levelling the land and constructing the necessary canals and ditches.

So he devised the Fresno Scraper, an ingenious improvement on the basic buckboard they were currently using, whereby soil could be scooped up, fed into a C-shaped bowl and then deposited at the desired low spot. By making it possible for large amounts of soil to be rapidly scraped, moved, dumped and levelled, the Fresno Scraper enabled the development of the San Joaquin valley into the USA's most productive agricultural region, providing up to a quarter of the country's entire agricultural produce.

Between 1884 and the introduction of tractor-drawn machinery, James Porteous built thousands of Fresno Scrapers at his works in Fresno, and they were used all over the world for road and rail making and, most famously, on the digging of the Panama Canal. So brilliant was the invention that modern bulldozers and earth-movers are still designed along the same principles.

# Fife

ANSTRUTHER + BEGGAR'S BENISON
+ SOME NOTABLE ANSTRUTHERS + SECRET ANSTRUTHER
+ SECRET AGENT + BALFOUR + SOME NOTABLE BALFOURS
+ CARDINAL BEATON + ARTHUR BALFOUR

*St Andrews Cathedral was consecrated in 1318 in
front of Robert the Bruce and was the largest
cathedral ever built in Scotland.*

◄ FIFE FOLK ►

Robert Lindsay + Sir Robert Ayton + Alexander Henderson
+ James Wilson + Alexander Berry + James Braid
+ Charles George Hood Kinnear + Jack Vettriano + Ian Rankin

# Anstruther

T he name of the small port of
ANSTRUTHER comes from the
Gaelic 'eanstar', meaning 'little
stream', and the town is indeed split
in two by a stream, the Dreel Burn.

The town gives its name to the
Anstruther family who, over the years,
have picked up a number of baronet-
cies and provided a number of Fife
MPs and Lord Lieutenants.

A Norman knight, William de
Candela, was granted the lands of
Anstruther by Alexander I in the 12th
century, and his son, HENRY DE
AYNSTROTHER, the first to use the
name, made a gift of some land to
the newly founded Balmerino Abbey.

ANDREW ANSTRUTHER OF
ANSTRUTHER fought at Flodden for
James IV, and his great-great-
grandson, a companion for James VI,
was appointed Hereditary Grand
Carver, an office still held by the
family today, the present Master
Carver being Sir Sebastian Anstruther
of Balcluskie.

Philip Anstruther was a fiery cava-
lier who fought valiantly for Charles
I in the English Civil War. He was
captured after the Battle of Worcester,
but released at the Restoration.

# Beggar's Benison

A t some point the Anstruthers
built themselves a small tower to
live in, DREEL CASTLE, the remnants
of which can still be seen. Dreel
Castle, interestingly, was the meeting
place in 1732 of Scotland's, and
possibly Britain's, FIRST OFFICIAL
PRIVATE GENTLEMAN'S CLUB – 'the
Most Ancient and Most Puissant
Order of the Beggar's Benison and
Merryland, Anstruther', or The
Beggar's Benison.

The word 'benison' means blessing,
and refers to a story about James V,
who had a predilection for wandering
about Scotland disguised as a
common person. On one such visit
to Fife, James found himself unable
to cross the Dreel Burn in spate.
Before he could even articulate a Scottish oath a 'fair buxom lassie' lifted
him on to her shoulder and carried
him across the water to the other side.
James was so grateful that he tipped
the damsel with an unexpected gold
coin, and she in return gave him her
benison, or blessing, 'May prick nor
purse ne'er fail you.' That benison
became the club motto.

The club's members included
establishment types who wished to let
their hair down in private, aristocratic
Jacobites, upstanding merchants and
bankers who happened to have a side-
line in smuggling brandy, members of

the customs authorities who wanted to get to know the local pillars of the community, and some who just wanted to get away from the Hanoverian austerity of post-union Scotland. They would meet to feast, sing bawdy songs, read pornography and examine, purely for scientific purposes, naked 'posture girls' – rather like today's lap dancing clubs there appeared to be a policy of 'look but don't touch'.

A popular pastime at the Beggar's Benison in later years was to read out excerpts from John Cleland's *Fanny Hill* – there is a Robert Cleland recorded as a Benison member who may have smuggled copies of his kinsman's manuscript into the club before it was published.

The Beggar's Benison proved so popular that a branch opened in Edinburgh in 1766 and has been considered by some to be a part of the Scottish Enlightenment.

## Some Notable Anstruthers

JOYCE ANSTRUTHER (1901–53), pen name Jan Struther, was an author and hymn-writer and granddaughter of Sir Robert Anstruther, 5th Baronet. She wrote a column for the *Times* newspaper in which she introduced the character MRS MINIVER, who would give an account of her everyday life. In 1939 Struther published the columns in a book that became a bestseller in the United States. She followed this up with a series of letters written by Mrs Miniver, and her running commentary on life in Britain for an ordinary family in the early years of the Second World War is given considerable credit for helping persuade the Americans to enter the conflict. Mrs Miniver was made into a film by MGM in 1942 starring Walter Pidgeon and Greer Garson as the lead character. It won six Academy Awards, including Best Picture, Best Actress, and Best Director. Struther also wrote several hymns, of which the best known is 'Lord of all Hopefulness'.

SIR RALPH ANSTRUTHER, 7th Baronet (1921–2002). He was awarded the Military Cross in 1943 while serving with the Coldstream, Guards. While Hereditary Carver to the

Queen he was also Treasurer to the Queen Mother from 1961 to 1998 and had the unenviable task of trying to curb her spending habits. He eventually suffered a stroke and had to retire to Scotland.

SIR IAN FIFE CAMPBELL ANSTRUTHER, OF THAT ILK, 8TH BARONET OF BALCASKIE AND 13TH BARONET OF ANSTRUTHER (1922–2007), nephew of Joyce Anstruther, took part in the Normandy landings and had a brief diplomatic career before unexpectedly inheriting much of South Kensington from another aunt, a windfall that allowed him to pursue a career as a writer and fund the Anstruther Wing of the London Library. Among his eight books was an account of the Eglinton Tournament (*see* Ayrshire).

## Secret Anstruther

In 1995 Anstruther was revealed as the site of Scotland's Secret Bunker, a refurbished underground radar station from the Second World War, where Scotland's essential governing bodies would have operated in the event of a nuclear strike during the Cold War.

## Secret Agent

Which makes it all the more appropriate that the man often described as 'Britain's first secret agent', SIR ROBERT BRUCE LOCKHART (1887–1970) should have been born in Anstruther. Britain's Foreign Office Vice-Consul, and later unofficial representative in Moscow from 1912 until 1918, he was 'our man in Moscow' during the last years of Tsarist rule, Russia's participation in the First World War, and the Bolshevik Revolution. Although not officially an agent, Lockhart was asked to furnish the Foreign Office with some idea of what was going on, and to try and gauge the intentions of the rapidly changing Russian leadership. Along with his friend and fellow secret agent Sidney Reilly, 'Ace of Spies', Bruce Lockhart was implicated in a plot to murder Lenin and arrested, but was later exchanged for Maxim Litvinov, Lenin's representative in London. In 1932 Lockhart wrote a bestselling book about his time in Russia, *Memoirs of a British Agent*, and during the Second World War was Director-General of the Political Warfare Executive, a secret body set up to create and coordinate propaganda.

# Balfour

The ancient name of BALFOUR is associated with the lands of Markinch, near Glenrothes, and comes from the Bal Orr, or River Orr, that runs through the estate. The first record of a family on the Bal Orr comes in the 11th century, in the days of Duncan I, and there is record of a Michael Balfour from the 12th century.

## Some Notable Balfours

GILBERT BALFOUR (d.1576) was something of a 'gun for hire' and, along with his brothers Robert and Sir James Balfour of Pittendreich, was among the prime instigators behind the murder of Cardinal Beaton in 1546. He later married Margaret Bothwell, whose brother Adam Bothwell, the Bishop of Orkney, gave Balfour some land on Westray, where he built the extraordinary Noltland Castle, its massive circular stone staircase matched in Scotland only by the stair at Fyvie in Aberdeenshire. Appointed Master of Queen Mary's household, he was in a strong position to help the Earl of Bothwell with the murder of Lord Darnley, but after the Queen was deposed he had to flee to Sweden, where he was eventually executed for conspiring against the king of that country.

# Cardinal David Beaton
## 1494–1546

Born at Balfour, the younger son of John Beaton of Balfour, David Beaton was very much a part of the Balfour family, three of whom were implicit in his eventual murder. Educated largely in Paris, and a naturalised Frenchman, Beaton spent his whole life championing the Franco-Scottish alliance against 'the whole pollution and plague of Anglican impiety', and it was his persecution of Protestants that earned him the enmity of John Knox and brought about his downfall.

As Archbishop of St Andrews and THE ONLY OFFICIAL CARDINAL SCOTLAND EVER HAD, he attempted to divert attention from his political machinations over the infant Queen Mary, which resulted in Henry VIII's 'Rough Wooing', by organising the show trial and burning of the itinerant Protestant preacher George Wishart at St Andrews in 1546. Three months later, a posse of Wishart's inflamed sympathisers (somewhat slow burning), which included among its number Beaton's kinsmen Gilbert, Robert and James Balfour, broke into the Cardinal's palace and hanged him out of the window.

SIR ANDREW BALFOUR (1630–94), born in Fife, was the youngest son of Sir Michael Balfour. After studying medicine in St Andrews and France he eventually settled in Edinburgh and was THE FIRST DOCTOR IN SCOTLAND TO PRACTISE DISSECTION OF THE BODY. He set up SCOTLAND'S FIRST PUBLICLY FUNDED HOSPITAL and in 1671 planted a physic garden near Holyrood, which later formed the basis of Edinburgh's Royal Botanic Garden.

## Arthur Balfour
## 1848–1930

*'Nothing matters very much and very few things matter at all.'*

ARTHUR BALFOUR was born in Whittinghame House on his family estate near East Linton in East Lothian. The above quote is thought to reflect Balfour's feelings about life after the tragic death from typhus of his cousin May Lyttelton, whom he had hoped to marry, while they were both in their twenties.

He became Conservative MP for Hertford in 1874, and in 1887 he was appointed to the juicy position of Chief Secretary for Ireland by the Prime Minister, who just happened to be his uncle Robert, Lord Salisbury, giving rise to the phrase 'Bob's your uncle!' meaning, in modern parlance, 'Sorted!'

Balfour was Prime Minister from 1902 to 1905 – he was the only former Scottish Secretary to attain the position. His time in office saw the ending of the Boer War and the introduction of the controversial 1902 Education Act, which abolished school boards and replaced them with Local Education Authorities run by the county councils.

One of nine Prime Ministers to

have sported a moustache, and THE ONLY ONE TO HAVE WORN A PINCE-NEZ, Balfour was known for his dapper appearance, attracting from Irish Nationalists the nickname 'Miss Nancy' or the 'scented poppinjay'.

He has given his name to the 'BALFOURIAN MANNER', meaning an air of cool detachment, remaining above the fray and keeping the vulgar world at arm's length, and, as Foreign Secretary, to the BALFOUR DECLARATION of 1917 supporting the creation of a Jewish homeland in Palestine:

Her Majesty's Government view with favour the establishment in Palestine of a national home for the Jewish people, and will use their best endeavours to facilitate the achievement of this object, it being clearly understood that nothing shall be done which may prejudice the civil and religious rights of existing non-Jewish communities in Palestine, or the rights and political status enjoyed by Jews in any other country.

Memorable Quotes:
*'I never forgive but I always forget.'*

*'I make it a rule never to stare at people when they are in obvious distress.'*

LADY EVE BALFOUR (1899–1990), sister of the Prime Minister. A keen supporter of organic farming, she set up a research centre in her Suffolk garden and published the results in 1943 in *The Living Soil,* which presented the FIRST CASE FOR ORGANIC FARMING. This led to the founding of the SOIL ASSOCIATION in 1946 by 'a group of farmers, scientists and nutritionists who observed a direct connection between farming practice and plant, animal, human and environmental health'. Lady Balfour was the first president.

*Well, I never* **knew this**
*about*
**FIFE FOLK**

ROBERT LINDSAY (1532–80), author of *The Historie and Chronicles of Scotland, 1436–1565,* THE FIRST HISTORY OF SCOTLAND TO BE WRITTEN IN SCOTS rather than Latin, was born in Ceres.

SIR ROBERT AYTON (1570–1628), born in Kincaldie one of the first Scots poets to write in standard English (rather than Scots vernacular). His poem 'Old Long Syne' is believed to have inspired Robert Burns's 'Old Lang Syne'.

ALEXANDER HENDERSON (1583–1646), theologian, born in Criech and credited with composing the final draft of the National Covenant, signed in Greyfriars Kirkyard in 1638.

JAMES WILSON (1742–98), lawyer, born in St Andrews. Wilson emigrated to America in 1766 and settled in Pennsylvania. As a prominent lawyer he was highly regarded at the Constitutional Convention, and it was he who proposed that the executive should consist of a 'single person' – the President. He is thus credited with THE CREATION OF THE AMERICAN PRESIDENCY. In 1775 he made an influential speech advocating the principle of Judicial Review, whereby laws can be referred to and checked for legality against the constitution. This idea evolved into the Supreme Court, and James Wilson was one of the six original justices appointed to that Supreme Court. His signature is on the Declaration of Independence.

ALEXANDER BERRY (1781–1873), entrepreneur, born near Cupar. In partnership with Edward Wollstonecraft (cousin to Mary Shelley, author of *Frankenstein*) he established in 1822 one of the first European settlements in New South Wales, the Coolangatta Estate, on which the town of Berry developed. The estate began as primarily agricultural but later expanded into textiles and shipbuilding. When he died in 1873 Berry left over £1 million, and he is thought to have been AUSTRALIA'S FIRST MILLIONAIRE. He bequeathed some £200,000 to St Andrews University in his home county of Fife.

JAMES BRAID (1795–1860), 'the Father of Modern Hypnotism', was born in Fife. In 1841 he became interested in the subject of mesmerism after attending a demonstration in Manchester given by the French mesmerist Charles Lafontaine. He began to experiment with his wife and found that by getting her to focus on a small, bright object held 8–16 inches (20–40 cm) in front of her eyes he could induce her eyelids to close spontaneously. Concluding that this state was a form of sleep, he named it 'HYPNOSIS' after the Greek god of sleep, Hypnos. Further study persuaded him that 'hypnotherapy' could be beneficial in some medical cases.

CHARLES GEORGE HOOD KINNEAR (1830–94), architect and photographer, born in Kinloch. He established an architectural practice that built many of the Royal Bank of Scotland premises. A keen photographer, he founded the Photographic Society of Scotland and in 1857 invented the BELLOWS CAMERA.

JAMES BRAID (1870–1950), professional golfer, born in Earlsferry. He won five Open Championships, in 1901, 1905, 1906, 1908 and 1910. His retaining of the Open Championship in 1906 was not achieved again by a European player until Pádraig Harrington successfully defended the title in 2008. As a golf course architect Braid designed the King's Course and Queen's Course at Gleneagles, remodelled the championship course at Carnoustie in 1926, and is credited with inventing the 'dog-leg'.

JACK VETTRIANO, painter, born in Methil in 1951. Although dismissed by highbrow art critics, Vettriano's

pictures are hugely sought after and he is one of the most commercially successful living artists. Postcards and posters of his most popular work, THE SINGING BUTLER, outsell all others and the original went at auction for almost £750,000.

*Ian Rankin*

IAN RANKIN, crime writer, was born in Cardenden in 1960. He is especially known for the Inspector Rebus novels, set in Edinburgh, which have been televised on ITV, starring John Hannah, and more recently Ken Stott, in the lead role.

## Musicians from Fife

IAN ANDERSON, singer, instrumentalist and founder member of rock band Jethro Tull, born in Dunfermline in 1947.

BARBARA DICKSON, singer-songwriter, born Dunfermline in 1947.

KT TUNSTALL, singer, songwriter and actress, born St Andrews in 1975.

GUY BERRYMAN, bass player with Coldplay, born Kirkcaldy in 1978.

# Hebrides

---

*Duart Castle on the Isle of Mull,
seat of the Chiefs of the Clan Maclean.*

◀ HEBRIDES FOLK ▶

Alexander McDougall ✦ Mary Macdonald ✦ Alexander McDougall
✦ Donald Caskie ✦ Mary Macleod ✦ Alistair Darling
✦ Robin Ian Evelyn Milne Stuart de la Lanne-Mirrlees of Inchdrewer

# Lord of the Isles

The first to be styled with the romantic title of LORD OF THE ISLES was SOMERLED (1126–64), son of a Gaelic noble from the House of Alpin, Kings of Dalraida, and a Norse mother.

In the 12th century the kings of the fledgeling Scotland were battling to unite the old Pictish and Celtic regions of the country, while the Isles were ruled by the King of Norway.

Somerled began to drive the Norse out of Argyll and the southern Hebrides, winning a great victory off Islay in 1156, and setting himself up on Islay as King, or Lord, of the Isles, nominally subject to both the Kings of Norway and Scotland, but in practice fairly independent. His territory included the Hebrides, Kintyre and the western peninsulas of Argyll, a vast area which made the Lord of the Isles the most powerful territorial Lord in the British Isles, after the Kings of England and Scotland.

When the Isles were finally ceded in perpetuity to Scotland by the Treaty of Perth in 1266, it took another 300 years and much conflict before the Lords of the Isles were fully subject to the Scottish Crown.

In 1540 the title Lord of the Isles was reserved to the crown by James V, and is to this day held by the eldest son of the monarch, which today is Charles, Prince of Wales.

# Three Clans

Somerled, the first Lord of the Isles, was killed in a confrontation with Malcolm IV at Renfrew in 1164, and left three sons, Aonghus, ancestor of Clan McRory, Dughall, progenitor of the Clan MacDougall and Ragnald, whose son Donald fathered the original 'Mac' Donald.

The MacDonalds grew to be one of the largest and most powerful of the Highland clans, with numerous offshoots, not just in Scotland, but throughout the world.

# Some Notable MacDonalds

## Flora MacDonald
## 1722–90

Flora MacDonald was born in Milton on the island of South Uist and brought up on Skye. In 1746, after Culloden, she was asked by her brother to help with a 'fantastical' scheme to smuggle Bonnie Prince Charlie away from the Hebrides. The islands were overrun with government

Memorable Quote:
*'A woman of middle stature, soft features, gentle manners and elegant presence.'*

Dr Johnson

soldiers searching for him, and they were disrupting the daily lives of the island chiefs. So, on the evening of 27 June that year, the Prince stepped into Flora's boat off Benbecula dressed as Betty Burke, an Irish girl, demure in a blue-and-white frock. They rowed across to Skye and, after some adventures, managed to walk to Portree, from where the Prince proceeded on to Rattray and eventually to France. When news of the escape came out, Flora was arrested and put in the Tower of London, but popular opinion demanded she be released, and she returned to Skye to marry Allan MacDonald of Kingsburgh. They emigrated to North Carolina, where Allan fought for the British in the American War of Independence and was captured. Flora travelled back to Skye alone, surviving an attack by a privateer. She was eventually joined by her husband and they settled down to have a large family.

SIR JOHN MACDONALD (1815–91), the FIRST PRIME MINISTER OF CANADA. Born in Glasgow, the son of an evicted Sutherland crofter, MacDonald emigrated to Canada with his family when he was five years old. His passionate crusading for the British North America Act of 1857, which forged the divided colonies into the one nation of Canada, earned him the accolade of CANADA's FOUNDING FATHER. He is the only prime minister to achieve eight majority governments and served in office for a total of 18 years. He was also the leading figure behind the construction of the Canadian Pacific Railway. He was the first of two Canadian prime ministers to die in office.

RANALD MACDONALD (1824–94), the FIRST MAN TO TEACH ENGLISH IN JAPAN. Born in Canada, the son of a Scottish fur trader and a Chinook Indian, he dreamed of going to Japan after meeting a shipwrecked Japanese sailor. He joined a whaling ship to cross the Pacific and took a small boat to the Japanese shore, where he pretended to be shipwrecked, which was the only way to gain entry to Japan, at that time a closed country. He was marched overland to Nagasaki, the only port allowed to do a limited trade, with the Dutch, where he was kept in confinement for ten months. While he was there, a number of important Samurai were sent to learn English from him, including Einosuke Moriyama, who would later be one of the chief interpreters at the negotiations between Commodore Perry and the Tokugawa Shogunate to open up Japan to the outside world. On his return to Canada MacDonald wrote a report urging for closer relations with Japan. His last words, to his niece, were 'Sayonara, my dear, sayonara.'

MAJOR-GENERAL SIR HECTOR ARCHIBALD MACDONALD (1853–1903), known as 'Fighting Mac', was born the son of a crofter. He joined the Gordon Highlanders at the age of 17 and was one of the few ordinary soldiers of that time to rise from the rank of private to commanding officer without the benefit of wealth or class. A hero of the Anglo-Sudanese campaign, he was knighted by Edward VII in 1901 and went on to lead the Gordons in the Boer War. In 1903 he shot himself in a Paris hotel room after allegations about his sexuality from officers who resented the success and popularity of one so common and uncultured. Although his embarrassed family tried to bury him in secret in Edinburgh's Dean Cemetery, a crowd of 30,000 turned out to pay their respects. MacDonald is the soldier depicted on the label for Camp Coffee, which was created for the Gordon Highlanders serving in India who needed a drink they could brew quickly and easily over the campfire.

*Charles B. Macdonald*

CHARLES B. MACDONALD (1855–1939), 'the Father of American golf courses'. Born in Canada to a Scottish father and Canadian Mohawk mother, Macdonald took up golf while studying at St Andrews University in Fife and was tutored by Old

Tom Morris. On returning to America, in 1892 he founded the Chicago Golf Club and the following year built AMERICA'S FIRST 18-HOLE GOLF COURSE there. He was one of the founders of the United States Golf Association in 1894, won the first US Amateur Championship in 1895, beating Charles Sands by 12 and 11 (still a record-winning margin), and went on to found the National Golf Links of America on Long Island in 1908, which hosted the first Walker Cup match in 1922.

# James Ramsay MacDonald
## 1866–1937

'Ramshackle Mac', Britain's first Labour Prime Minister, was born at Lossiemouth, the illegitimate son of a farmer and a maidservant. MacDonald married the daughter of Dr John Gladstone, founder of the YMCA, and was therefore independently wealthy enough to pursue a political career. He was handsome, tall, a powerful speaker, intellectual and a good organiser. He led two administrations, in 1923–4 and 1929–31, and then formed a National Government in 1931–5 to cope with the economic depression. Working with the Tories made MacDonald a

traitor in the Labour Party's eyes. He lost his seat in 1935 and died aboard ship on the Atlantic two years later, THE ONLY PRIME MINISTER TO DIE AT SEA.

In 1929 he appointed THE FIRST-EVER WOMAN CABINET MINISTER, Margaret Bondfield.

A keen golfer, MacDonald was expelled from the Moray Golf Club, who declared that his opposition to the Great War endangered the character of the club. He refused ever to return, even though the expulsion was rescinded in 1929. That year he was also awarded the Freedom of the City of New York.

In 1931 MacDonald entertained Charlie Chaplin at Chequers. They enjoyed a good lunch and then both fell asleep.

MacDonald's wife died tragically young in 1911, after which he regularly received messages from her through a medium. He occasionally replied.

He was THE ONLY PRIME MINISTER TO BE BORN ILLEGITIMATE.

Memorable Quotes:
*'Wars are always popular. Contractors make profits; aristocracy glean honour.'*

*'A terror decreed by a secret committee is child's play compared with a terror instituted by "lawful authority".'*

JAMES MACDONALD (1906–91), sound-effects artist who in 1947 took over from Walt Disney as the voice of Mickey Mouse, was born in Dundee.

DAVID McDONALD, actor, was born in Bathgate in 1971. His stage name David Tennant was inspired by Neil Tennant of the Pet Shop Boys. In 2005 he achieved his childhood dream of playing Doctor Who, becoming the tenth actor to do so.

FIONA MacDONALD, member of the British curling team which took the gold medal at the 2002 Salt Lake City Winter Olympics, born 1974.

KELLY MACDONALD, actress, born 1976. In 2006 she was nominated for a Golden Globe for her performance in *The Girl in the Café* for BBC Television. She is married to Dougie Payne, bass player for the band Travis.

DONALD J. MACDONALD, hotel baron, was born on the Isle of Harris. After working for the Stakis Group for 20 years, in 1990 he founded Macdonald Hotels, starting with two hotels in Aberdeen and Peterhead. Now Scotland's biggest hotel and leisure group, Macdonald Hotels owns more than 100 hotels in Britain and Spain.

*Well, I never knew this about*
**HEBRIDES FOLK**

## Alexander McDougall
### ◄ 1731–86 ►

Alexander McDougall was born on the Isle of Islay, one of five children. In 1738 they all emigrated to America and prospered as tenants on a dairy

farm on Manhattan. Alexander bought himself a cargo sloop, to which he added guns so that he could sail as a privateer during the Seven Years War (1756–63) against the French in North America.

As revolutionary fever grew in

America, inflamed by the Stamp Act of 1765, McDougall became an active leader in the New York Sons of Liberty, a clandestine organisation of American patriots who agitated for independence from Britain. In 1770 McDougall was arrested and gaoled for printing subversive flyers and speaking out against the Quartering Act, which required colonists to provide housing and other support for British troops. He was the FIRST AMERICAN TO BE ARRESTED FOR ADVOCATING AMERICAN INDEPENDENCE.

After the Revolution, during which he rose to be a major-general, McDougall founded and became the FIRST PRESIDENT OF THE BANK OF NEW YORK.

MARY MACDONALD, née MacDougall (1789–1872), crofter's wife, illegal whisky distiller and hymn writer who lived all her life in Bunessan on the Isle of Mull. While sitting at her spinning-wheel she would pass the time by composing hymns. Once such hymn was 'Leanabh an Aigh', meaning 'Child in the Manger', which she wrote in Gaelic and set to a traditional Scottish tune. The words were translated into English in 1888 by the editor of the *Fifeshire Advertiser*, Lachlan Macbean, for his *Songs and Hymns of the Scottish Highlands*, in which he named the tune 'Bunessan' after Mary's home village.

In 1931 children's writer Eleanor Farjeon put some new words to 'Bunessan', and forty years later it became the hit song 'Morning Has Broken', propelled into the top ten by Cat Stevens in 1972.

*Alexander McDougall, inventor of self-raising flour*

ALEXANDER McDOUGALL, inventor of self-raising flour. Born in Dumfriesshire, McDougall worked first as a shoe-maker and then as a schoolteacher in Manchester. All the while he was saving so that he could set up as a manufacturing chemist, and he achieved his ambition in 1845. He brought his two sons into the business, and in 1864 they developed and patented a chemical replacement for yeast. Bakers were sceptical, so the McDougalls bought the flour and mixed in the substitute themselves, producing THE FIRST SELF-RAISING FLOUR IN BRITAIN. By 1869 they needed to expand and so set up the Wheatsheaf Mill by the River Thames at Millwall in London. In 1961

McDougall's became part of Rank Hovis McDougall.

DONALD CASKIE (1902–83), 'the Tartan Pimpernel', was born in Bowmore on Islay, the son of a crofter. Minister of the Scots Kirk in Paris at the outbreak of the Second World War, Caskie was forced to flee to Marseilles, where he refused to take the last ship out to Britain and instead set up a mission to help Allied service personnel escape from occupied France. He was arrested several times and once sentenced to death, but was saved by the intervention of a German army padre. After the war he wrote a book about his experiences, *The Tartan Pimpernel*, to raise funds for the rebuilding of the Scots Kirk in Paris.

MARY MACLEOD (1912–2000), mother of American billionaire business magnate Donald Trump, was born in Tong on the Isle of Lewis.

ALISTAIR DARLING (b.1953), Labour Chancellor of the Exchequer and MP for Edinburgh Central, owns a converted blackhouse in the village of Breacleit on Great Bernera, where his mother's family hail from.

The island of GREAT BERNERA has been owned since 1962 by ROBIN IAN EVELYN MILNE STUART DE LA LANNE-MIRRLEES OF INCH-DREWER, former officer of the College of Arms in London who corresponded with Ian Fleming while the James Bond author was researching *On Her Majesty's Secret Service*, and provided the model for College of Arms representative Sir Hilary Bray, whom Bond impersonates to get close to Blofeld.

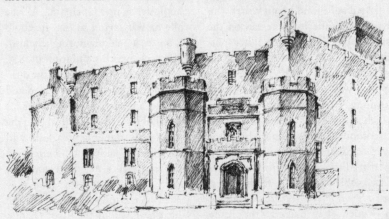

*Dunvegan Castle, seat of the chief of Clan Macleod*

# Inverness-shire

*Inverness Castle, built in 1835 on the site of the castle where Macbeth is said to have murdered King Duncan.*

◄ INVERNESS-SHIRE FOLK ►

Duncan Forbes ✦ James 'Ossian' Macpherson
✦ Jane Waterston ✦ Duncan Grant

# Badenoch

The majestically named BADEN-OCH is a wild and ancient district at the heart of the Highlands which includes the upper reaches of Strathspey and large parts of the Cairngorms and is roughly contained within south-east Inverness-shire. Once part of the Kingdom of Moray and loosely controlled by Clan Chattan, from the time of Alexander II in the early 13th century to the triumph of Robert the Bruce in the early 14th century it was despotically ruled by the Comyns, from their castle at Inverlochy.

## Lords of Badenoch

The first LORD OF BADENOCH was WALTER COMYN (d.1258), son of William Comyn, the Mormaer of Buchan who cleared the descendants of Malcolm Canmore (Bighead) out of Moray and ran Scotland while Alexander III was a boy.

Walter's nephew JOHN I, 2ND LORD OF BADENOCH (1215–75), sneaked into Perthshire while the Earl of Atholl was on crusade and built Blair Castle.

John's son JOHN II, 3RD LORD OF BADENOCH (d.1302), was known as the BLACK COMYN. He was a

Guardian of Scotland, a regent to Margaret, Maid of Norway and one of the 13 'Competitors' for the throne, and he married Princess Elanore, sister to the future King John Balliol of Scotland and daughter of Devorgilla Balliol.

Their son JOHN III, 4TH LORD OF BADENOCH, was known as the RED COMYN, and was killed by Robert the Bruce at Dumfries in 1306.

Thereafter the lordship went to the royals and eventually got subsumed by the Marquess of Huntly in the 15th century. The most notable lord in that time was Alexander Stewart (1343–1405), fourth son of Robert II, the infamous WOLF OF BADENOCH who burned down Elgin Cathedral.

## Frasers of Lovat

The FRASERS originated in Anjou, France, and their name possibly comes from the French word for the strawberry plant, 'fraisier' – silver strawberry flowers appear on the family arms.

The first signs of a Fraser at Lovat appear in documents dated 1367, and probably concern Sir Simon Fraser, brother of Sir Alexander Fraser, Chamberlain of Scotland who fought at Bannockburn with Robert the Bruce. By this time the Frasers had already established their seat at BEAUFORT

CASTLE, then known as Dounie Castle, on the banks of the River Beauly, west of Inverness.

## Beaufort Castle

The present Beaufort is thought to be the 12th or 13th castle on the site and was built in 1882. The original Dounie Castle was besieged by Edward I, damaged in constant clan squabbles, sacked by Oliver Cromwell's men and finally destroyed after Culloden by the Duke of Cumberland. The FRASERS OF LOVAT lived there for 800 years until the castle was sold in the 1990s. In 1995 it became the home of entrepreneur Ann Gloag who, with her brother Brian Souter, founded one of Britain's biggest transport companies, Stagecoach.

## The Old Fox

SIMON FRASER, 11TH LORD LOVAT (1667–1747), was known as 'the Old Fox of the '45' or 'the most devious man in Scotland'. Thwarted in his attempts to get hold of the Lovat lands by wooing his cousin Amelia, daughter of the 9th Lord Lovat, he forcibly married her widowed mother instead, for which outrage he was outlawed. His behaviour was doubly perverse: he did become the 11th Lord Lovat in his early thirties when his father, the 10th Lord Lovat, died in 1699, but as he was outlawed he couldn't inherit the lands.

Instead he went off to France and joined the exiled court of the 'Old Pretender', but returned to side with the Hanoverians in the 1715 Jacobite uprising and was pardoned and given possession of the estate. His downfall came when, in the 1745 rebellion, he took the Jacobite side after their victory at Prestonpans. At the age of

78 he was forced to take to the hills after Culloden, but was captured, taken to London and sentenced to death in 1747. He went to his fate defiantly – 'You'll get that nasty head of yours chopped off, you ugly old Scotch dog!' cried a gentlewoman from the watching crowd; 'I believe I shall, you ugly old English bitch!' he replied, before earning the distinction of BECOMING THE LAST MAN EVER TO BE BEHEADED ON TOWER HILL.

## 17th Lord Lovat

SIMON FRASER, 17TH LORD LOVAT (1911–95), was a highly decorated war hero. At the outbreak of the Second World War he commanded the Lovat Scouts, which had been raised by his father to fight in the Boer War, and which in 1916 became the British Army's first sniper unit, or 'sharpshooters'. He then led THE FIRST COMMANDO UNIT, THE

1ST SPECIAL SERVICE BRIGADE, at the Normandy landings in 1944 accompanied, against orders, by his piper, Bill Millin.

Not long afterwards, Lord Lovat was seriously wounded and retired to concentrate on the family estates, but his last years were saddened by the death of his two sons in accidents and by financial ruin, which caused the sale of Beaufort Castle. Piper Bill Millin played at his funeral in 1995.

The present Lord Lovat is Simon Fraser, 18th Lord Lovat and 25th MacShimidh (Gaelic for 'son of Simon'), Chief of Clan Fraser.

## Clan Mackintosh

The CLAN MACKINTOSH descend from Shaw, the son of Duncan Macduff, Earl of Fife, who was granted lands in Inverness-shire and made Constable of Inverness Castle in reward for helping Malcolm IV suppress a rebellion in Moray in 1160.

The name Mackintosh comes from the name that was adopted by Shaw, 'Mac an Taoiseach', which means 'son of the chieftain', the chieftain here being Duncan Macduff.

# Clan Chattan

In 1291 Angus, Chief of Clan Mackintosh, married Eva, daughter of Gilpatrick, Chief of Clan Chattan, and since then the Mackintosh Chief has always been Chief of Clan Chattan.

The name Chattan is derived from Gillchatan Mor of Ardchattan in Argyll, and after the marriage in 1291 Clan Chattan became the name for a confederation of 16 closely related clans who joined together for mutual defence, and have traditionally been headed by a Mackintosh. The present Chief of Clan Chattan is JOHN MACKINTOSH OF MACKINTOSH who lives in Singapore, the first Mackintosh chief not to live at the ancestral seat of the Mackintoshes, Moy Hall.

# The Rout of Moy

Since 1336 the home of the Mackintosh chiefs has been MOY HALL near Inverness, the scene in 1746 of the 'Rout of Moy'. While the incumbent Mackintosh Chief was off serving with the government army, his Jacobite wife, 'Colonel' Anne Mackintosh, had Bonnie Prince Charlie to stay at Moy, and when she learned that government troops were approaching

to arrest him, she sent four of her men to hide by the roadside. As the troops reached them, the men fired their pistols once in the air and shouted for the Macdonalds and the Camerons to advance. The government soldiers, thinking they were about to be attacked by a whole army, turned tail and ran.

# Some Notable Mackintoshes

CHARLES MACINTOSH (1766–1843), inventor of the MACK or MACKINTOSH (spelt deliberately with a 'k'). A chemist, Macintosh was analysing the by-products of making coal gas when he discovered dissolved india-rubber. He found that if he joined two sheets of fabric together using the india-rubber solution the new material was completely waterproof. After ironing out a few problems he introduced his Mackintosh to the market in 1824. He also worked with Charles

Tennant to invent a revolutionary bleaching powder (*see* Ayrshire), and helped James Neilson devise the hot-blast process for producing high-quality cast iron.

CHARLES RENNIE MACKINTOSH (1868–1928), influential architect and furniture designer whose style blends traditional Scottish architecture with Art Nouveau. His most famous works are the Glasgow School of Art, the Willow Tea Rooms in Glasgow's Sauchiehall Street and Hill House in Helensburgh.

MACKINTOSH'S TOFFEE (c.1890), invented by 'Toffee King' John Mackintosh and his wife to sell in their sweet shop in Halifax, from a blend of American caramel and English brittle butterscotch.

APPLE MACINTOSH (c.1984), the first commercially successful personal computer with a mouse and a graphical user interface, designed by Apple Inc. Chief project manager Jef Raskin decided to name the new computer after his favourite apple the MCINTOSH RED, itself named after Canadian farmer John McIntosh, son of a Scottish immigrant, who grew the original apple tree on his farm in 1801.

# Clan Cameron

CAMERON is a derivation of the Gaelic 'cam-shron', meaning 'crooked nose', and supposedly refers to a prince of Denmark who helped the restoration of Fergus II of Dalraida.

The first known Cameron Chief was DONALD DUBH CAMERON (1400–60), who came to the fore in the district of Lochaber, which includes within its boundaries Ben Nevis.

# Tor Castle

In the early 15th century, Ewen Cameron, 13th Chief, built the powerful stone Tor Castle on a bluff above the River Lochy. This had been the site of the seat of Clan Chattan since the time of Malcolm II, and was the home of the murdered Banquo, Thane of Lochaber, the ghost at Macbeth's feast. Tor Castle remained the seat of the senior Locheil line of Camerons until the 17th Chief, Sir Ewen 'Dubh' Cameron, built himself a more convenient house a little to the north at ACHNACARRY in 1655.

# The Gentle Locheil

In 1745 the 19th Chief, Donald Cameron, known as 'The Gentle Locheil', was planting a line of beech trees near the river bank at Achnacarry when word arrived of Bonnie Prince Charlie's landing. He left his digging and hurried away to join the Jacobite forces. After fighting valiantly at Culloden, the Gentle Locheil fled to France, where he died in 1748. His brother Archibald Cameron was captured and executed in 1753, THE LAST MAN TO DIE FOR THE JACO-BITE CAUSE. Achnacarry House was burned to the ground.

# New Achnacarry

In 1802 Donald Cameron, 22nd Chief, rebuilt Achnacarry in Scottish baronial style.

In 1928 it was chosen as the location for a secret 'peace conference' between leaders of the world's oil industry which resulted in the 'Achnacarry Agreement' on production quotas.

In the Second World War, from 1942 to 1945, Achnacarry Castle served as the headquarters for the men brought in from all the Allied armies to train as the new 'Commando' fighters, and proud wearers of the Green Beret.

Today Achnacarry remains the ancestral seat of the 27th hereditary Chief of Clan Cameron, Donald Cameron of Locheil, born in 1946.

# Some Notable Camerons

RICHARD CAMERON (1648–80), Covenanter. A strict Presbyterian and impassioned field preacher, Cameron was utterly inflexible in his beliefs and condemned ministers who accepted the King's Indulgences. After a brief time of exile in Holland to learn 'to hold in check the ardencies of his heart and tongue', he returned and raised an army of like-minded Covenanters known as CAMERON-IANS. In 1680 they marched on Sanquhar, where Cameron issued the Sanquhar Declaration renouncing allegiance to Charles II and calling for the exclusion of the King's brother James from the succession. Cameron was killed in a skirmish later that year, and in 1689 when William of Orange came to the throne, the Cameronians were pardoned and incorporated into the British army under the same name.

VERNEY LOVETT CAMERON (1844–94), naval officer and explorer, who was THE FIRST EUROPEAN TO CROSS EQUATORIAL AFRICA FROM COAST TO COAST.

DONALD CAMERON, founder of Cameron Balloons, THE WORLD'S BIGGEST MAKER OF HOT-AIR BALLOONS, born 1939. While working for the Bristol Aeroplane Company, he developed the Bristol Belle, EUROPE'S FIRST MODERN HOT-AIR BALLOON, which made its debut flight in 1967. He was THE FIRST

MAN TO CROSS THE SAHARA AND THE ALPS BY HOT-AIR BALLOON, as well as THE FIRST TO FLY FROM BRITAIN TO RUSSIA, and came second in the first-ever transatlantic balloon race in 1992.

JAMES CAMERON, Oscar-winning film director, producer and screen-writer, born 1954. Amongst his blockbusters are the first two *Terminator* films, *Aliens* and *Titanic*, which won 11 Oscars, a record haul equalled only by *Ben Hur* and *The Return of the King*.

RHONA CAMERON, comedian, born 1965.

DAVID CAMERON, born 1966, leader of the Conservative Party since 2005.

*Well, I never* knew this
*about*
INVERNESS-SHIRE FOLK

DUNCAN FORBES (1685–1747), born in Buchrew, was a senior judge who became much admired for advocating leniency for the rebels after the 1715 Jacobite rebellion, and later, as Laird of the Culloden estate, dissuaded many of the local chiefs from joining the Jacobites in 1745, saving them from ruin. A keen golfer, he was a founder of the Gentleman Golfers of Leith, one of Edinburgh's first golf clubs.

# James 'Ossian' Macpherson
## ━━ 1736–96 ━━

JAMES 'OSSIAN' MACPHERSON was a poet, born in Ruthven, near Kingussie. In 1759, while tutoring at Moffat in Dumfriesshire, Macpherson befriended a couple of the worthies who were taking the waters there, and showed them some verses which he claimed to have discovered in the Highlands and translated from the Gaelic. He convinced them the verses were over 1,000 years old and written by Prince Ossian, the son of Fingal, and the good gentlemen told Macpherson they must be published. They were published, in several volumes under the title *The Collected Poems of Ossian* and they caused a sensation, drawing scholars from all over Europe to the Highlands. Even when Dr Johnson pronounced them a fraud, the 'Ossian Verses' were acclaimed everywhere – Napoleon even carried them into battle. To this day no one has been able to prove the verses' provenance, but James Macpherson went on to become an MP. In 1772, at the height of the Ossian mania, Sir Joseph Banks named a cave on the island of Staffa Fingal's Cave.

JANE WATERSTON (1843–1932), the FIRST WOMAN DOCTOR IN SOUTH AFRICA, was born in Inverness. A member of the Free Church of Scotland, she decided to become a missionary in Africa, and obtained an appointment from David Livingstone's expeditionary companion Dr James Stewart at a college in the Eastern Cape. Having observed at first hand the problems faced by African women, she returned to Britain for medical training before establishing her own practice in Cape Town in 1883. In 1888 she became THE FIRST WOMAN TO ACQUIRE THE CERTIFICATE IN PSYCHOLOGICAL MEDICINE OF THE MEDICO-PSYCHOLOGICAL ASSOCIATION OF GREAT BRITAIn. In Cape Town she opened a free dispensary, started THE FIRST MATERNITY SERVICE IN THE CAPE PENINSULA and provided medical and psychological support for refugees during the Boer War.

# Duncan Grant
◄── 1885–1978 ──►

Artist and member of the Bloomsbury Group, Duncan Grant was born in Inverness, the son of an officer in the Indian army. Brought up by his artistic uncle and aunt Sir Richard and Lady Strachey, the parents of Lytton Strachey, he decided to become a painter, much to his father's disgust. In 1905 he spent a year at art school on the Left Bank in Paris, and when he returned to London he fell in love with the future economist John Maynard Keynes. They later travelled around Europe together.

In 1909 Grant moved to Fitzroy Square and was a regular at the Thursday evening gatherings of the Bloomsbury Group. He worked as a designer for Roger Fry's Omega workshops, of which he soon became a director.

His first major commission was for some murals for the refectory of the Borough Polytechnic Institute or 'People's Palace' in South London (now the South Bank University), and he produced two, called *Bathing* and *Football*, which the art critic of *The Times* thought would have a 'degen-erative influence on the children of the working classes'. They are both now in the Tate Gallery.

In 1914, to avoid enlistment, Grant and his latest companion, 'Bunny' Garnett, who were both pacifists, joined Vanessa Bell at Charleston farmhouse in Sussex. In 1918 Vanessa gave birth to Grant's daughter, Angelica, but pretended that the girl's father was her husband Clive Bell. When Angelica learned at the age of 19 that Grant was her father, she married his former lover Bunny Garnett.

Grant and Bell remained together for 50 years and spent some time living in the south of France. After a final fling with the poet Paul Riche, Grant died of pneumonia at the age of 93.

# Kincardineshire

ARBUTHNOTT ✦ SOME NOTABLE ARBUTHNOTS
✦ BARCLAYS OF URIE ✦ BARCLAY'S BANK
✦ THE LAST LAIRD OF URIE ✦ SOME NOTABLE BARCLAYS
✦ BURNETT ✦ SOME NOTABLE BURNETTS

*Arbuthnott House, seat of the Viscount of Arbuthnott,
heriditary Clan Chief of Clan Arbuthnott.*

◄ KINCARDINESHIRE FOLK ►

John of Fordun ✦ William Duthie Kinnear ✦ James Murdoch
✦ Lewis Grassic Gibbon

# Arbuthnott

❧

ARBUTHNOTT is a small village 3 miles (5 km) inland from Inverbervie that stands at the gates of Arbuthnott House, seat of the Viscount of Arbuthnott and the Arbuthnott family.

The name comes from a combination of Celtic words: 'aber', meaning confluence, 'both', meaning a baronial residence, and 'nothea', meaning smaller – thus 'the baronial hall that stands at the place where a smaller river runs into a larger one', which aptly describes the location of Arbuthnott House.

The 'Arbuthnot' lands, originally a Celtic thanage, were owned by the Norman Oliphaunt family until the 12th century, when Hugh of Swinton from Dunbar married the Oliphaunt heiress and took the name Arbuthnot – and it was not until the 19th century that the family began to spell their name with two 't's.

## Some Notable Arbuthnots

ALEXANDER ARBUTHNOT (d.1585), printer of the first printed history of Scotland, Rerum Scoticarum Historia, by George Buchanan, tutor to Mary Queen of Scots and James VI.

JOHN ARBUTHNOT, 'Dr Arbuthnot' (1667–1735), writer, satirist and physician to Queen Anne. In 1692 he published THE FIRST WORK IN ENGLISH ON THE SCIENCE OF PROBABILITY, 'Of the Laws of Chance', in which he applied the laws of probability to ordinary games, a formula that proved a bestseller. In 1712 he created the figure of JOHN BULL as the personification of England, although Bull was originally designed to represent the whole of the United Kingdom. In his 'Treatise of the Art of Political Lying', in which he attempts to teach politicians how to lie effectively, Arbuthnott mischievously foresees the rise of political spin.

THOMAS ARBUTHNOT (1851), sailing ship that carried the first cargo of Australian gold to England. Named after the owner, who was a merchant in Peterhead, Aberdeenshire.

# Barclays of Urie

❧

URIE HOUSE, near Stonehaven, today being restored as a luxury hotel and club house by golfer Jack Nicklaus, was built in 1885 in Elizabethan style by Alexander Baird.

The present building, however, is just the most recent of many houses that have occupied the site. Its predecessor 350 years ago was a Quaker

headquarters and the birthplace of a mighty banking dynasty.

In 1666 Urie was purchased by Colonel David Barclay (1610–86), a descendant of the Barclays of Towie. Colonel Barclay had fought for the King in the English Civil War, but later became a Covenanter. At the Reformation he was briefly imprisoned in Edinburgh Castle, and while incarcerated there he converted to Quakerism. On his release he bought Urie as somewhere to establish a Quaker headquarters for north-east Scotland.

## Robert Barclay
'The Apologist'

❖❖❖

One of the Colonel's first converts was his own son ROBERT BARCLAY, 2ND LAIRD OF URIE (1648–90), known as 'Robert the Apologist'. At the age of 27, Robert wrote

the influential *Apology for the True Christian Divinity*, which set out the principles of Quaker beliefs and brought him the admiration and friendship of the well-known Quakers William Penn and George Fox. Together they formulated the idea for founding a city of brotherly love in America, which came into being in 1701 as Philadelphia. In 1682 James VII (James II of England) granted Robert 5,000 acres (2,000 ha) in East New Jersey and he was elected governor of the state, even though he never went there, preferring to stay at home at Urie, where he implemented a number of far-reaching agricultural improvements on the estate.

## Barclay's Bank

❖❖❖

Robert's second son DAVID BARCLAY (1682–1769), denied the opportunity to run the family estate, took himself off to London where he became a successful merchant. In 1736 he became a partner in a goldsmiths business belonging to John Fream, his second wife's father, whose premises were in Lombard Street in the City of London, at the sign of the Black Spread Eagle. The company diversified into banking and developed into today's Barclays Bank.

The Barclay family ran their business on strict Quaker principles and used some of their wealth to buy land in Jamaica so that they could free the slaves working in the plantations there.

In 1896 Barclay's joined with 19 other banks, mainly run by other family members or fellow Quakers, and formed Barclay and Company Limited.

## *The Last Laird of Urie*

The 6th and last Barclay Laird of Urie was ROBERT BARCLAY ALLARDICE, the 'Father of Pedestrianism', which was an early form of the Olympic sport of race-walking. He became known as 'Captain Barclay the Celebrated Pedestrian'. The Barclay family were renowned for their strength (Colonel Barclay, the 1st Laird, was thought to be the strongest man in Scotland in his time), and the 6th Laird had inher-

ited this strength. He completed numerous record-breaking walks across the Scottish hills, but his greatest exploit took place between 1 June and 12 July in 1809, when he walked 1,000 miles in 1,000 hours over a measured mile at Newmarket Heath, for which he won 1,000 guineas. Five days later he marched off to fight in the Napoleonic Wars.

When Captain Barclay died in 1854, after being kicked by a horse, he was survived only by a daughter who lived in America, and the lairdship of Urie went to a cousin. Urie House was sold to Alexander Baird, who built the present Urie House.

## Some Notable Barclays

SIR DAVID AND SIR FREDERICK, THE BARCLAY BROTHERS (both born 1934). Twins descended from the Barclays of Urie, the Barclay Brothers began to amass their fortune in 1962 by converting run-down properties in

London into hotels. Today they own the Ritz Hotel in Piccadilly. In 1993 they bought the Channel Island of Brecqhou, near Sark, where they live in a mock-Gothic castle designed by Quinlan Terry. In 2004 they bought the Telegraph Group from Conrad Black.

HUMPHREY BARCLAY, television producer, born 1941. Introduced to show business through the Cambridge Footlights, Barclay went into radio and produced a number of comedy shows such as *I'm Sorry, I'll Read That Again*. He then moved to London Weekend Television and for eight years produced the popular *Doctor* series before becoming Head of Comedy. He supervised husband and wife team Judi Dench and Michael Williams in *A Fine Romance*, and in 1983 he commissioned the first black situation comedy on British television, *No Problem!* Also in 1983 he formed Humphrey Barclay Productions, before becoming Head of Comedy Development at Granada and then Celador Productions, known for making *Who Wants to Be a Millionaire?*

ANDREW BARCLAY (1814–1900), engineer. He began by designing telescopes but later founded Andrew Barclay & Sons to build railway steam engines.

FIELD MARSHAL PRINCE MICHAEL ANDREAS BARCLAY DE TOLLY (1761–1818), descendant of the merchant Barclay brothers of Nairn, who settled in Livonia as traders in the 17th century. Barclay de Tolly entered the Imperial Russian Army at an early age and rose through the ranks to command the Russian Army of the West during Napoleon's invasion of Russia in 1812. He proposed the successful 'scorched earth' policy of destroying anything that might be of use to the enemy as you retreat. In 1814 he commanded the capture of Paris when Russia took revenge on France. He was created field marshal and then a prince for his success in the field. Considered one of Imperial Russia's greatest heroes, he is buried in a noble mausoleum in Estonia.

# Burnett

❧

The BURNETTS descend from a Norman family, Bernard or Burnard, who came to England with William the Conqueror in 1066 and then moved north, initially being granted lands in the Borders by King David I.

ALEXANDER BURNARD supported Robert the Bruce at Bannockburn and in 1323 was rewarded with lands in the Royal Forest of Drum in Kincardineshire, and other lands that had been stripped from the Comyns. Burnard was made Royal Forester and as a symbol of office he was given a hunting horn, the HORN OF LEYS. There is a horn on display above the fireplace in Crathes Castle today which family legend says is that very horn.

The Burnards, or Burnetts, made their home on a crannog, or fortified island, in the centre of the Loch of Leys, to the north of Banchory. This served as the family seat for the next 200 years, and they became known as Burnett of Leys.

In the 16th century, Alexander, the 9th Laird, married Janet, an illegitimate daughter of the Abbot of Arbroath, who brought land and money as a dowry, which they decided to spend on building a splendid new home at Crathes, beside the River Dee, a little way downstream.

CRATHES CASTLE was begun in 1560 and was completed 40 years later by Alexander's great-grandson, another Alexander, whose own son was made a baronet of Nova Scotia by Charles I in 1625.

Crathes Castle is one of Scotland's great castles, with magnificent unspoiled interiors and some of the finest Jacobean painted ceilings in Scotland.

The Burnett of Leys family lived at Crathes for nearly 400 years before it was made over to the National Trust for Scotland by Major-General Sir James Burnett of Leys, the 13th

Baronet, in 1952. The Burnett family seat today is the House of Crathes, just down the road from the castle.

## Some Notable Burnetts

### James Burnett, Lord Monboddo 1714–99

A cousin of the Burnetts of Leys, Monboddo was a greatly respected judge at Edinburgh's Court of Sessions. He was very interested in the Ancient Greeks and preferred to live life simply, as they did. Hence he always travelled on horseback, having no truck with such modern contraptions as a coach.

born in Manchester, who married Dr Swan Burnett of Washington DC in 1873. She is remembered for her much-loved children's novels such as *Little Lord Fauntleroy* (1886) – Fauntleroy's attire, long curls, velvet suit and lace collar, was based on Oscar Wilde's mode of dress – *A Little Princess* (1905) and *The Secret Garden* (1911).

In 1773 Monboddo published a book called *Of the Origin and Progress of Man and Language*, in which he conjectures that man may be descended from apes and discusses many of the evolutionary theories later put forward by Charles Darwin. Erasmus Darwin, Charles's grandfather, acknowledges Monboddo's work in his own publications on the subject.

Lord Monboddo had many distinguished visitors to his home, Monboddo House, near Fordoun. Dr Johnson visited with James Boswell, who described Monboddo as 'a wretched place, wild and naked with a poor old house'. Another visitor, Robert Burns, on the other hand, was much taken with Monboddo's youngest daughter, Eliza, a celebrated beauty. When she died at the age of 25, Burns wrote a poem, 'Elegy on the late Miss Burnet of Monboddo'.

FRANCES HODGSON BURNETT (1849–1924), playwright and author

LEO BURNETT (1891–1971), American advertising executive whose many creations included the Marlboro Man, the Jolly Green Giant, and Tony the Frosties Tiger. He was named by *Time* magazine as one of the 100 most influential people of the 20th century.

HENRY JOHN BURNETT (1941–63), the last man to be hanged in Scotland, for the murder of his rival in love, Thomas Guyan. Burnett had kept his girlfriend Margaret Guyan, the estranged wife of Thomas, under lock and key, and when she escaped back into the arms of her husband, Burnett went round and blasted Guyan in the face with a shotgun. Eleven weeks later, on 15 August 1963, he was hanged in Craiginches Prison in Aberdeen.

SIR ALASTAIR BURNETT, born 1928, newsreader for ITN from 1963 to 1991. He also edited the *Economist* and the *Daily Express*.

*Well, I never knew this*
*about*
## KINCARDINESHIRE FOLK

JOHN OF FORDUN (d.1384) was born in Fordoun. Very little is known about his life except that he served for some time as a chaplain at St Machar's Cathedral in Old Aberdeen. His claim to fame is as the author of THE FIRST KNOWN HISTORY OF SCOTLAND, CHRONICA GENTIS SCOTORUM. Written in Latin, it was first printed in 1691.

WILLIAM DUTHIE KINNEAR (1880–1974), better known to his friends as

'Wally', was born in Laurencekirk. A world-class rower, he won the gold medal for the single sculls at the 1912 Olympics in Stockholm.

JAMES MURDOCH (1856–1921), scholar and journalist who worked as a teacher in Japan and Australia, was born in Stonehaven. His life's work was a three-volume *History of Japan*, which took him 14 years to write, from 1903 until 1917. It was THE FIRST

COMPREHENSIVE HISTORY OF JAPAN EVER WRITTEN IN THE ENGLISH LANGUAGE.

## Lewis Grassic Gibbon
──◄ 1901–35 ►──

Lewis Grassic Gibbon, writer and leading figure of the Scottish Renaissance movement, was born James Leslie Mitchell in Aberdeenshire, but grew up in Arbuthnott, and it was the distinctive mellow Kincardineshire landscape that influenced his writing in later life. After an unsuccessful stint as a journalist on the *Scottish Farmer*, he enlisted and travelled through India and the Middle East, first with the army and then the Royal Air Force, before getting married and settling down in Hertfordshire.

In 1929 he began writing full time, and between 1928 and 1934 produced 17 full-length books under his pen name, which was derived from his mother's maiden name. His best-known book is *Sunset Song*, published in 1932, and the first of a trilogy, *Scottish Quair*, which tells the story of one woman's life in the Mearns in the early part of the 20th century.

At the age of 33, on the brink of a brilliant career, Lewis Grassic Gibbon died of peritonitis brought on by a perforated ulcer. In 1991 the Lewis Grassic Gibbon Centre was opened in Arbuthnott to commemorate the author's life.

# Kinross-shire

THE ADAM FAMILY ✦ WILLIAM ADAM
✦ JOHN ADAM ✦ ROBERT ADAM ✦ JAMES ADAM

*William Adam, patriarch of Scotland's great architectural
family, who founded Blairadam estate near Kinross,
still owned by his descendants.*

◄ KINROSS-SHIRE FOLK ►

William Blairadam ✦ Sir William Bruce

# The Adam Family

In 1730 WILLIAM ADAM, the patriarch of Scotland's great architectural family, bought the estate of Blair Crambeth, 2 miles (3.2 km) south of Kinross, as somewhere to create a country home for his growing family. He renamed the property BLAIRADAM, laid out gardens and parkland, and in 1733 built Blairadam House in woodlands on the south of the estate – which is still owned by the Adam family today.

## William Adam
## 1689–1748

William Adam was born near Kirkcaldy, where his father was a mason and ran a small building outfit, which William eventually turned into the biggest construction company in Scotland. William's maternal grandfather was Lord Cranstoun, whose own maternal grandfather was Francis Stewart, the Earl of Bothwell.

While in his twenties, William travelled widely in France and Holland visiting country houses, an experience which greatly influenced his style in later life. In 1714 he entered into a partnership with a local laird, William Robertson of Gladney, to set

up a brickworks, which became THE FIRST BRICKWORKS IN SCOTLAND ABLE TO MAKE DUTCH PANTILES. In 1716 William married Robertson's daughter Mary.

William Adam's style is reminiscent of baroque, and his main influences are known to have been James Gibbs and John Vanbrugh.

# William Adam's
# Major Works

FLOORS CASTLE, in Roxburghshire, was William's first great commission. In 1721 he was asked by the 1st Duke of Roxburgh to redesign and extend their existing tower house at Floors into a modest country house.

HOPETOUN HOUSE, in West Lothian. In that same year, 1721, William was asked by the Earl of Hopetoun to add to William Bruce's work at Hopetoun House. Adam put on an imposing new façade, colonnades and pavilions and began the grand state apartments. His work at Hopetoun was not finished by the time of his death in 1748, but was completed by his sons.

MELLERSTAIN HOUSE, in Berwickshire. In 1725, George Baillie of Jerviswood and his wife Lady Grisel Baillie commissioned William to attach two wings to an existing, rather tumbledown, tower house.

ARNISTON HOUSE, in Midlothian, was begun in 1726 for Robert Dundas, 2nd Lord Arniston. William completed the first phase, at which point the money ran out and it fell to son John to complete Arniston.

THE HOUSE OF DUN, a small 'villa' overlooking the Montrose Basin in Angus, was designed and built for a leading lawyer, David Erskine, Lord Dun, in 1730. The house is a somewhat more ornamental version of the Château d'Issy, near Paris.

HADDO HOUSE, in Aberdeenshire, was built on the site of an earlier house between 1732 and 1735 for William Gordon, 2nd Earl of Aberdeen.

CHATELHERAULT HUNTING LODGE, outside Hamilton in Lanarkshire, was built in 1734 to provide stabling and other estate offices for Hamilton Palace. Intended partly as a folly to be seen from the palace, the building consists of four tall, shallow pavilions connected by walls. Although the west pavilion leans a little, the lodge outlasted the palace, which was demolished in 1921 because of subsidence due to mining underneath.

DUFF HOUSE, in Banffshire, perhaps William Adam's masterpiece, was built in 1735 for William Duff of Braco, later 1st Earl Fife. However, it cost over £70,000 to build and disputes with the Earl over the cost almost bankrupted William and certainly hastened his death.

The commission for FORT GEORGE, opposite Channonry Point, at the mouth of the inner Moray Firth in Inverness-shire, was awarded to William Adam in his role as Master Mason to the Board of Ordnance in North Britain. Begun in 1748, it was built as a garrison for the government troops charged with keeping order in the Highlands after the Jacobite rebellion in 1745 and was the largest construction project ever attempted in the Highlands up to that time. Fort George took 21 years to complete and was finished off by son John.

# John Adam
## 1721–92

JOHN ADAM was born in Kirkcaldy, and when he was seven the family moved to a house on the Cowgate in Edinburgh, as his father's career as a country house architect blossomed. The Adam home became something of a social centre in the early days of the Scottish Enlightenment, much visited by the Edinburgh 'glitterati', which greatly benefited the standing of the family and increased their social contacts.

From an early age John was groomed to take over the running of the business, which not only involved the design and construction of country houses but took in associated activities such as mining and quarrying as well. John also eventually became Laird of Blairadam, with responsibility for running the estate, and took over from his father as Master Mason to the Board of Ordnance in north Britain. All this left him little time for creating his own designs and is, perhaps, why he is less known as an architect than his two younger brothers, who joined him in the partnership.

## John Adam's Major Works

B RAEMAR CASTLE, in Aberdeenshire, which had been left in ruins since being attacked and gutted in 1689 by John Farquharson, known as the 'Black Colonel' for his dark, swarthy looks and fierce nature. In 1748 John Adam was commissioned by the Hanoverian government to restore the castle and make it habitable as a barracks for government troops.

PAXTON HOUSE, which sits on a ridge overlooking the River Tweed in Berwickshire, built in 1758 for Patrick Home, to impress the love he had met in Berlin, 18-year-old Sophie de Brandt, lady-in-waiting to Queen Elizabeth Christina of Prussia.

MOFFAT HOUSE, in the centre of Moffat, in Dumfriesshire, built in 1761 for the 2nd Earl of Hopetoun, as somewhere for him to stay when partaking of the waters at the Moffat spa.

## Robert Adam
### 1728–92

R OBERT ADAM was born in Kirkcaldy and grew to become Scotland's most renowned 18th-century architect and interior designer – it is perhaps for his interiors that he is best remembered. His work had a major influence on architecture not just in Britain but across Europe and America as well, and he is considered the leading figure of the classical revival in England and Scotland.

Somewhat poorly as a child, Robert had his education disrupted by the Jacobite occupation of Edinburgh and he learned his craft by helping on his father's projects, such as at Hopetoun House, where the splendid courtyard pavilions with their extraordinary towers are amongst his first works and an early indication of his promise.

After William's death Robert went into partnership with his older brother John, and their first grand project together was DUMFRIES HOUSE in Ayrshire, the new home of William Dalrymple, 5th Earl of Dumfries.

In 1754 Robert went off on the Grand Tour of Europe, at the suggestion of the Earl of Hopetoun, who was impressed by Robert's work on the state rooms at Hopetoun. He spent much of the time in Rome studying the classical and Palladian designers, and improving his drawing skills.

On his return, Robert set up a practice in London with younger brother James and began to build up a portfolio of works, some of Palladian design, but also many incorporating Greek, Roman, and baroque influences – and everything he worked on, both interior and exterior, was noted for its attention to detail.

Robert did not neglect his Scottish roots, however, and between 1768 and 1774 he served as MP for Kinross-shire, living in the small house his father had built for him on the edge of the Blairadam estate.

He died suddenly in London of a burst blood vessel and is buried in Westminster Abbey.

## Robert Adam's Major Works in Scotland

MELLERSTAIN, an old tower house in Berwickshire, which had been extended by Adam's father in 1725 with two new wings. In 1770 Adam built a large central block to connect them. Inside, the library is one of Adam's finest rooms, with a brilliantly coloured ceiling of green and pink, and wonderfully detailed plaster work framing depictions of 'Minerva', 'Teaching' and 'Learning' by Zucci.

CULZEAN CASTLE in Ayrshire, perhaps Robert's masterpiece in Scotland, sits on a dramatic cliff-top site overlooking the Firth of Clyde. Between 1772 and 1790 the original tower house of the early 15th century was transformed into a neo-classical mansion for the Earl of Cassilis, Robert's leading Scottish patron.

Interiors of PAXTON HOUSE and WEDDERBURN CASTLE, both in

Berwickshire, and both for Patrick Home. Robert and James worked on these commissions together, between 1773 and 1775.

Robert Adam's Saloon at YESTER HOUSE, in East Lothian, created in 1789 for John Hay, 2nd Marquess of Tweeddale, has been described as 'THE FINEST ROOM IN SCOTLAND'.

GOSFORD HOUSE, in East Lothian, was built to Robert's design between 1790 and 1800 for the 7th Earl of Wemyss as a golfing pavilion. Later it was radically, and somewhat unsympathetically, altered by William Young.

CHARLOTTE SQUARE, the finest square in Edinburgh's New Town, and the last part of the initial phase of the New Town to be finished, was designed by Robert, but he died just before building began in 1792.

## *James Adam*
## *1732–94*

Youngest of the Adam brothers, and often overshadowed by his father and particularly brother Robert, James was born in Edinburgh and went off on his own Grand Tour in 1760. Most of his work was done in conjunction with Robert, and so it is difficult to pinpoint his contribution, but the fact that they worked together for so long and with such magnificent results indicates that James was an indispensable part of the Adam team.

*Well, I never knew this about*
## KINROSS-SHIRE FOLK

## Blairadam Club

The 3rd Laird of Blairadam was John's only surviving son William (1751–1839), who practised as a lawyer and carried on the family tradition of being MP for Kinross-shire. He was a close friend of Sir Walter Scott, and they, along with seven others, formed the Blairadam Club, which met for the first time in 1816.

The members would ride out to Blairadam from Edinburgh on a Friday afternoon, spend Saturday visiting some place of historical interest such as a castle or abbey ruins, enjoy a quiet Sunday with church service at Cleish, lunch and an afternoon nap, make another excursion to somewhere with antiquarian value on the Monday and then ride back to town on Tuesday in time for court. Most civilised.

Of William's children, John served as acting Governor-General of India in 1823, Charles achieved the rank of admiral in the Royal Navy and Frederick became Governor of Madras.

KINROSS HOUSE, masterpiece of architect Sir William Bruce (*see* Dumfriesshire), is the finest building in the county. This magnificent house was built in 1685 on an estate Bruce had bought off the impoverished 8th Earl of Morton in 1675. There is a theory that Bruce had intended the house for James, Duke of York, later James VII, had he been prevented from ascending the throne, but in the event Bruce lived there himself, ending up, it must be said, in financial difficulties.

Kinross House is SCOTLAND'S FIRST CLASSICAL COUNTRY HOUSE, built for comfort rather than defence, and is surrounded by one of Scotland's first formal gardens, which were also designed and laid out by Bruce.

*Fish Gates, Kinross House*

# Kirkcudbrightshire

THE STEWARTRY ✦ LORDS OF GALLOWAY
✦ SOME NOTABLE FERGUSONS
✦ BALLIOL LORDS OF GALLOWAY ✦ KING JOHN (BALLIOL)

*MacLellan's Castle in Birkcudbrightshire, built in the late
16th century by Provost Sir Thomas MacLellan and a fine
example of the transition between castle and home.*

◄ KIRCUDBRIGHTSHIRE FOLK ►

Elspeth McEwen ✦ John Johnston ✦ James Clerk Maxwell
✦ Dr Hamish MacInnes ✦ Barbara Armstrong

# The Stewartry

Kirkcudbrightshire forms the eastern part of the old kingdom of Galloway, which was annexed to the Crown of Scotland in 1455, and was from then on administered by a steward on behalf of the King. For this reason the county is known as the Stewartry.

# Lords of Galloway

The province of GALLOWAY used to consist of the area now occupied by Wigtownshire and Kirkcudbrightshire as well as the southern portion of Ayrshire known as Carrick and a part of western Dumfriesshire. The name means 'land of the stranger Gaels' and was settled in the 8th and 9th centuries by Gaelic people from Ireland, later joined by Anglo-Saxons from Northumbria and also Viking invaders. In early times the province looked far more to the lands of the Irish Sea, Dublin, Man and the lower Hebrides, than to the Scottish kingdoms and has, even today, maintained a distinctive character.

The first Lord of Galloway we really know much about is FERGUS OF GALLOWAY, who ruled the province for some 50 years, much like a king, from around 1110 until his death in 1161. He is thought to have been a native of Galloway with Norse origins, descended from the ancient kings of Dalraida through his mother. He was the first ruler to give Galloway a strong identity, managing to preserve the semi-independence of his fiefdom by maintaining good relations with both David I of Scotland and Henry I of England.

Fergus – from whom many Fergusons claim descent – eventually retired to live as a monk at Holyrood Abbey. He left Galloway to be jointly ruled by his sons Uchtred and Gilbert, who fought for dominance, with Gilbert eventually emerging the winner. Fergus's great-great-granddaughter was Devorguilla of Galloway, the mother of King John of Scotland.

# Some Notable Fergusons

JAMES FERGUSON (1710–76) astronomer, inventor and lecturer, was born near Rothiemay, the son of a farm labourer. He taught himself to read and write, and by watching his father at work he learned how to make mechanical appliances to use for scientific research. His genius was in being able to explain science to others in simple terms; he became hugely popular as a lecturer and was invited to become a fellow of the Royal Society in 1763. He built a number of astronomical instruments including an orrery (a clockwork model of the solar system), which is in the Royal Museum in Edinburgh, a tide dial and a device called an eclipsarion which he used to explain solar eclipses.

PATRICK FERGUSON (1744–80), born in Pitfour, Aberdeenshire, invented the breech-loading rifle, which was capable of firing seven shots per minute. With the help of this weapon, the British were able to defeat the Americans at the Battle of Brandywine in 1777. Ferguson was killed at the Battle of King's Mountain in South Carolina, USA, in 1780.

SIR ALEX FERGUSON, football manager, was born in 1941 in Govan, the son of a ship worker. He became manager of Manchester United in

1986 and has won more trophies than any other manager in the history of English football.

SARAH FERGUSON, Duchess of York, born 1959. Perhaps the most famous 'Fergie'. She is descended from Charles II and the Scott family.

NIALL FERGUSON, financial historian, was born in 1964 in Glasgow. He is a contributing editor to the *Financial Times* and his latest book, *The Ascent of Money: A Financial*

*History of the World*, was made into a Channel 4 television series, with Ferguson as presenter.

# Balliol Lords of Galloway

T he story of the Norse-Gaelic Lords of Galloway ends with Alan, who died without a male heir and left the kingdom divided between his three daughters. The most prominent of these was Devorguilla (1210–90) who married the Norman knight John de Balliol (c.1208–68) in 1233.

John was named in honour of King John of England. His family came originally from Bailleul in France and had come over to England with William the Conqueror and been granted lands in the North East.

John and Devorguilla's marriage combined two great estates and made the family both wealthy and influential. John de Balliol became to all intents and purposes Lord of Galloway and was appointed as one of the regents of Scotland during the minority of Alexander III, while Devorguilla was descended through her mother from King David of Scotland and was hence of royal blood.

In 1263 John endowed funds to set up a hostel for poor students at Oxford. Devorguilla later made further generous donations and the hostel grew to be Balliol College.

After John's death in 1268 Devorguilla had his heart embalmed and placed in an ivory casket banded with silver. At mealtimes she would put the casket beside her and hand out her husband's share of the food to the poor.

When Devorguilla herself died in 1290 she was buried, clutching the casket to her breast, in the New Abbey that she had founded in 1273 in her husband's memory for monks from Dundrennan. New Abbey became known as 'dulce cour', or Sweetheart Abbey, and that is how it is known today. Thus did Devorguilla provide us not only with one of Oxford's oldest and most prestigious colleges but also a new expression for the English language.

# King John (Balliol)

John and Devorguilla had four sons, only one of whom, John, survived them both. When Alexander III unexpectedly died by falling off his horse in Fife and his heir Margaret, 'the Maid of Norway', was drowned off Orkney, John, de facto Lord of Galloway, became one of the 13 'Competitors' for the Scottish throne.

Edward I of England, who was asked by the Guardians of Scotland to arbitrate between the Competitors, chose John Balliol, who thus became King John of Scotland, and was crowned at Scone on St Andrew's Day, 1292.

It seems that Edward chose John Balliol for a purpose, perceiving him as the weaker man and more likely to submit to being a 'puppet' king than Bruce or any of the other likely contenders. John soon became known as 'Toom Tabard', or 'Empty Coat', owing to his lack of real authority, and the Guardians decided to take matters into their own hands by agreeing an alliance with France against Edward – this became known as the Auld Alliance and would remain active on and off for the next 250 years.

John was eventually forced to abdicate and ended his days in the family home at Bailleul in France. Not all Scots recognised the abdication, however, since it was executed under duress, and the rebellion led by William Wallace against the English in 1297 was fought in King John Balliol's name.

*Well, I never knew this*
*about*
## KIRKCUDBRIGHTSHIRE FOLK

ELSPETH McEWEN, the last witch to be tried and executed in Scotland, was born in Dalry and lived alone in a hovel in the village of Bogha. In 1698 she was accused of drawing off milk from her neighbour's cows with a magical wooden pin that she kept hidden in the roof, and of making her neighbour's hens lay the wrong number of eggs. Her fate was sealed when the horse which conveyed her to court was seen trembling and sweating blood. On this evidence she was imprisoned and tortured before being burned to death on a hillside overlooking Kirkcudbright.

# John Johnston
———◄ 1791–1880 ►———

JOHN JOHNSTON, 'the Father of American Tile Drainage', was born near Dalry. In 1821 he emigrated to the United States and bought a farm in Seneca County, New York, calling it Viewfields. Although the soil was rich and fertile, it was often waterlogged beneath the surface, due to an abundance of natural springs. From his experience working on the land back in Kirkcudbrightshire, Johnson knew how much the yield from wet soil could be increased by tile drainage – a system of underground plumbing using long pipes made from curved tiles to drain water into nearby streams. He therefore sent to Scotland for two pattern tiles, from which Benjamin F. Whartenby, a local crockmaker in nearby Waterloo, made up 3,000 drain tiles. In 1838 Johnston began to lay them down on the farm until eventually he had laid 72 miles (116 km) of tiles across 320 acres (130 ha), increasing his yield fivefold.

This was the first example of tile drainage in America and it transformed agriculture across the Midwest, enabling the pioneers to cultivate millions of acres of otherwise unproductive land. By 1849 Whartenby was making over one million tiles a year and Waterloo had become the tile capital of America.

# James Clerk Maxwell
———◄ 1831–79 ►———

*'One scientific epoch ended and another began with James Clerk Maxwell.'*
Albert Einstein

Although born in Edinburgh, JAMES CLERK MAXWELL grew up, studied and spent much of his life in Kirkcudbrightshire, on his family's Middlebie estate, not far from Castle Douglas. His father, born John Clerk, had added Maxwell to his name upon inheriting Middlebie from Maxwell cousins, and built a rambling house there which he called Glenlair.

Ferociously inquisitive from a very early age, James was educated for a while at home before being sent to Edinburgh Academy to study mathematics and then, at 16, to Edinburgh University, where one of his tutors was James Forbes (*see* Aberdeenshire). He later graduated from Trinity College, Cambridge, with a maths degree, and at the age of 25 he was appointed to the Chair of Natural Philosophy at King's College, Aberdeen, from where he moved to occupy the same chair at King's College, London. His final position was as the first Professor of Experimental Physics at Cambridge and Director of the new Cavendish Laboratory there – under Maxwell's leadership it developed into the world's leading research laboratory.

Between working at these posts

Maxwell spent many of his most productive years in experimentation and research at Glenlair. Although he died young, from cancer at the age of 48, his contributions to science are considered to be as important as those of Sir Isaac Newton and Einstein. His earlier studies looked at the nature of colour, and he was able to show for the first time that all the colours seen in nature are combinations of the three primary colours, red, blue and yellow. In 1861 he created THE WORLD'S FIRST-EVER COLOUR PHOTOGRAPH, which is still preserved at Cambridge.

His most significant work was in the field of electromagnetic theory. He was able to demonstrate that electric and magnetic fields travel through space in the form of waves and at the speed of light. His theory of the nature of light as a form of wave motion explained the phenomena of light and other optical properties and formed the basis for modern radio communications, broadcasting and television, radar and navigational aids, and radio-controlled rockets and satellites. Einstein believed that Maxwell's theories built upon and improved those of Newton and made possible his own Theory of Relativity.

James Clerk Maxwell is buried in Parton churchyard, next door

to Glenlair, and is remembered by, amongst many other memorials, the Maxwell, a unit measuring magnetic flux, Maxwell's Equations, which describe the properties of electric and magnetic fields, numerous Maxwell laws and theorems, as well as the Maxwell Montes, a mountain range on Venus, the Maxwell Gap in the Rings of Saturn, the James Clerk Maxwell Telescope at the Mauna Kea Observatory in Hawaii, which is THE LARGEST SUBMILLIMETRE ASTRONOMICAL TELESCOPE IN THE WORLD, several university buildings in Edinburgh and London, a statue in Edinburgh's George Street, and by James Clerk Maxwell Street in Cambridge.

Glenlair burned down in 1929, but it was largely restored and modernised by the Ferguson family in 1993, and a charitable trust was formed to preserve Glenlair as a museum and monument to James Clerk Maxwell.

DR HAMISH MACINNES, Scotland's finest living mountaineer, born in Gatehouse-of-Fleet in 1930. He pioneered modern mountain rescue in Scotland and, as founder of the Glencoe Mountain Rescue Team, gained the nickname the 'Fox of Glencoe'. He has many winter climbing 'firsts' to his name, including the first winter traverse of the Cuillin Ridge on Skye in 1965, and has three times climbed Mount Everest. He invented the short 'Terrordactyl' ice axe and the MacInnes stretcher, used by mountain rescue teams all over the world. MacInnes has been a mountain safety officer and climbing 'double' on a number of feature films including *The Eiger Sanction* (1975) and *The Mission* (1986).

BARBARA ARMSTRONG, rally driver, born at Clarebrand, near Castle Douglas, in 1966. She was a works driver for the SEAT UK team from 1996 until 2000 and was the British Ladies Rally Champion in 1998 and 1999.

# Lanarkshire

---

House of Hamilton ✦ Bothwell Castle ✦ Cadzow
✦ Hamilton and Douglas ✦ Earls of Arran
✦ Marquess of Hamilton ✦ Dukes of Hamilton
✦ Some Notable Hamiltons ✦ House of Douglas
✦ The Douglas Larder ✦ The Good Sir James
✦ Some Notable Douglases

*Hamilton Palace, demolished in 1921 because of
subsidence due to coal mining, was the largest
private home in Europe.*

◀ Lanarkshire Folk ▶

Robert Dinwiddie ✦ William Cullen ✦ Robert Dale Owen
✦ John Scott Russell ✦ Sir Dugald Clerk

# House of Hamilton

The story of the HOUSE OF HAMILTON begins in 1271 with the signature of a Norman knight, GILBERT DE HAMELDUN, which is recorded on a charter of Paisley Abbey.

There are many Hamelduns (Hambledons) in England, but it is thought that this Gilbert may have been the grandson of the Earl of Leicester, and so it is possible that Gibert's Hambledun is the one in Leicestershire.

# Bothwell Castle

Gilbert's heir WALTER FITZ GILBERT DE HAMELDUN held the castle of BOTHWELL, in South Lanarkshire, for Edward I at the start of the First War of Scottish Independence, and after the Battle of Bannockburn in 1314 he gave shelter to a number of English nobles who were fleeing

back to England, among them the Earl of Hertford.

This was a crucial moment for the House of Hamilton. Walter Fitz Gilbert de Hameldun was in a position to decide whether to stay loyal to the English king and remain English or throw his lot in with the victor of Bannockburn, Robert the Bruce, and commit to the Scots. In the end he chose a Scottish future for his family and handed his guests over to the pursuing Edmund Bruce.

# Cadzow

For this gesture Walter was given confiscated Comyn lands in Renfrewshire, the Lothians and, most pertinently, the barony of CADZOW, which today bears the name HAMILTON. CADZOW CASTLE, built in the 12th century as a summer residence for David I before passing to the Comyns, became the Hameldun family seat.

Walter's son DAVID, 2ND LAIRD OF CADZOW (d.1378), remained loyal to the Bruces and was captured, along with David II, at the Battle of Neville's Cross in 1346. The two were released together in exchange for a huge ransom fee.

David's son, another DAVID, 3RD LAIRD OF CADZOW (1333–92), was the first to use the surname Hamilton, appearing in 1381 as DAVID HAMILTON, LORD OF CADZOW.

## Hamilton and Douglas

JAMES HAMILTON, 6TH LAIRD OF CADZOW (1415–79), was raised to LORD HAMILTON, and in 1445 James II gave him permission to change the name of his lands from Cadzow to Hamilton. At this time the Hamilton family began to get entwined with the Douglas family: Lord Hamilton's mother was a Douglas, and his own

first marriage was to the widow of the 5th Earl of Douglas, which made him stepfather to the young 6th Earl of Douglas and his brother, who would both be murdered at the infamous 'Black Dinner' (see below).

Hamilton's second marriage was to Princess Mary, daughter of James II, by whom he had James, 2nd Lord Hamilton.

## Earls of Arran

JAMES, 2ND LORD HAMILTON (1475–1529), negotiated the marriage of his cousin James IV to Henry VIII's sister Margaret Tudor and in 1503 was made Earl of Arran. In 1510 he rebuilt Brodick Castle as his home on the island of Arran. His nephew PATRICK HAMILTON (1504–

---

### The Black Dinner

Archibald, the 5th Earl of Douglas, was Regent to the infant James II and had two sons, William and David. When Archibald died, William became 6th Earl of Douglas for just one year before his life was cut short through the treachery of his great uncle, James Douglas, Earl of Avondale, who along with William Crichton, Chancellor of Scotland, wanted to break the alarming power of the Black Douglases as they were known. The young William and his brother David were invited to dine with the young James II at Edinburgh Castle for what became known as the 'Black Dinner', and there they were charged with treason and beheaded in front of the King. James Douglas then made himself 7th Earl of Douglas.

---

28) became SCOTLAND'S FIRST PROTESTANT MARTYR when he was burned at the stake at St Andrews on the orders of Cardinal Beaton. It took Hamilton six hours to die, and his agonising martyrdom ignited the first flames of the Scottish Reformation.

JAMES HAMILTON, 2ND EARL OF ARRAN (1516–75), as great-grandson of James II, was second in line to the throne behind the infant Mary (later Queen of Scots), to whom he was regent. In 1543 he signed the Treaty of Greenwich, by which Mary was promised to Henry VIII's son Edward, but later changed his mind, enraging Henry and bringing about the 'Rough Wooing'. Hamilton then negotiated the marriage of Mary to the Dauphin of France, for which he was made Duke of Châtellerault – a title he lost when he opposed the regency of Mary's mother, Mary of Guise.

## Marquess of Hamilton

JAMES HAMILTON, 3RD EARL OF ARRAN, was proposed by his father and John Knox as a husband for Elizabeth I and later for Mary Queen of Scots, but the pressure got to him and he went quite mad, so his brother took over his affairs and was made 1ST MARQUESS OF HAMILTON for his efforts in 1599.

## Dukes of Hamilton

The 3RD MARQUESS OF HAMILTON (1606–49) carried the Sword of State at Charles I's coronation in London in 1625. The King later raised him to 1ST DUKE OF HAMILTON as a reward for trying to dissuade the Scottish Covenanters from supporting the English Parliamentarians. In 1646 Charles conferred on him the office of KEEPER OF HOLYROODHOUSE, a position still held by the Hamiltons, who maintain private apartments there.

The Duke managed to secure the support of the Scottish Parliament for Charles and led a Scottish army into England to confront Oliver Cromwell, but he was captured by Cromwell's forces after the Battle of Preston in 1648. He was tried and executed by decapitation in March 1649. His brother William, Earl of Lanark, became the

2nd Duke, but he died from his wounds after fighting courageously for Charles II at the Battle of Worcester in 1651, and the title went to his niece Anne, who became Duchess of Hamilton (1631–1716) in her own right.

In 1656 Anne married William Douglas, 1st Earl of Selkirk (1634–94), who was created Duke of Hamilton at his wife's request and who adopted the surname Douglas-Hamilton.

This couple laid the foundations of what would become Hamilton Palace, when they commissioned James Smith to remodel their court-yard-style house at Hamilton.

duel with Lord Mohun over an inheritance. The Duke ran Lord Mohun through with his sword, but was then himself killed by Mohun's second.

Memorable Quote:

*'Are none of the descendants here of those worthy patriots who defended the liberty of their country against all invaders, who assisted the great King Robert Bruce to restore the constitution, and avenge the falsehood of England and usurpation of Balliol? Where are the Douglases and the Campbells? Where are their peers?'*

Speech opposing Union with England, 1706

# 4th Duke of Hamilton

Their son, the 4TH DUKE OF HAMILTON (1658–1712), lost a fortune in the ill-fated Darien Scheme to set up a Scottish trading colony in Panama, which almost bankrupted Scotland and strengthened the hand of those advocating the union of Scotland with England. Anti-unionists looked to Hamilton to lead the protests, but he was ambivalent, and during the vote remained confined to his quarters in Holyroodhouse with that famous political get-out, the 'toothache'. A few years later, in 1712, he died in a notorious

# 5th Duke of Hamilton

The 5th Duke commissioned William Adam to design a grand extension for Hamilton Palace, but died at the age of 40 of jaundice before the building could begin. Adam did, however, complete the splendid CHATELHERAULT HUNTING LODGE,

named after the dukedom received by the 2nd Earl of Arran for negotiating the marriage of Queen Mary to the Dauphin of France. The hunting lodge still stands, at the heart of the Chatelherault Country Park.

## 6th Duke of Hamilton

T he 6TH DUKE OF HAMILTON (1724–58) married Elizabeth, one of the 'beautiful Miss Gunnings', daughters of an impecunious squire from Hemingford Grey, whose complexions had been nurtured by the springs of Holywell in Ireland, and who were considered the loveliest women of their day.

## 10th Duke of Hamilton

T he 10TH DUKE OF HAMILTON (1767–1852) was something of a snappy dresser, always attired in a laced military greatcoat, with tights and Hessian boots, and his fingers covered with gold rings. He could certainly afford the gold rings – in 1810 he married the daughter of the richest man in England, plantation owner William Beckford.

In 1835 the Duke set about transforming Hamilton Palace into a

residence befitting a man of his pretensions, and to this purpose he dusted off the designs William Adam had drawn up for the 5th Duke and asked his kinsman, the architect David Hamilton, to build something along those lines. By the time the rebuilding was complete in 1842 Hamilton Palace was THE LARGEST PRIVATE RESIDENCE IN EUROPE.

Amongst the many treasures the 10th Duke inherited from his father-in-law was a magnificent sarcophagus from Memphis, in Egypt, and the Duke let it be known that when he died he wanted his body to be mummified and entombed in the sarcophagus. This was then placed on a black marble plinth in the centre of the grand mausoleum the Duke had ordered to be built on the family estate in Hamilton.

*Hamilton Mausoleum*

## 11th Duke of Hamilton

❡❡❡

His son, the 11TH DUKE OF HAMILTON, married Princess Marie of Baden, granddaughter of the Emperor Napoleon. Their daughter Mary married Prince Albert I of Monaco, and their son Louis introduced the first Monaco Grand Prix in 1929. Mary Hamilton is the direct ancestor of the present Prince Albert of Monaco.

## 13th Duke of Hamilton

❡❡❡

The 13TH DUKE OF HAMILTON (1862–1940) was forced to have Hamilton Palace demolished in 1921 when it started to collapse into the coal-mines driven underneath it. The Hamilton Mausoleum also began to subside, and the bodies within it, including the 10th Duke in his great sarcophagus, were removed to the nearby Bent Cemetery.

The 13th Duke moved into his shooting lodge on the moors in South Lanarkshire, DUNGAVEL HOUSE.

## 14th Duke of Hamilton

❡❡❡

DOUGLAS DOUGLAS-HAMILTON, THE 14TH DUKE OF HAMILTON (1903–73), was one of four brothers, all of whom were in the Royal Air Force at the rank of squadron leader or above at the outbreak of the Second World War, a unique family achievement.

Before he became Duke, Douglas was the youngest squadron leader of his day, commander of the famous 602 Glasgow Squadron, the first squadron to be issued with Spitfires. In 1933, in an open-cockpit biplane, Douglas made THE FIRST FLIGHT OVER MOUNT EVEREST, FLYING HIGHER THAN ANY MAN HAD EVER FLOWN BEFORE.

In 1936 Douglas flew to Germany to attend the Berlin Olympics, and it has been suggested that while he was there he met with a number of academics who would later become advisers to Rudolf Hess. Douglas became 14th Duke of Hamilton in 1940, and in 1941 Hess parachuted into a field in Eaglesham, in Renfrewshire, apparently to meet with the Duke to discuss a possible peace treaty between Britain and Germany.

Hess was arrested by a local farmer, and assuming a false name, asked to be taken to the Duke, who recognised Hess immediately and informed Winston Churchill. Hess was imprisoned for the rest of his life.

In 1946 the Duke purchased Lennoxlove House in East Lothian and sold Dungavel House, which is now run by the government as a holding centre for asylum-seekers. The 13th Duke remains buried there.

The present incumbent is ANGUS DOUGLAS-HAMILTON, 15TH DUKE OF HAMILTON, who is head of the House of Hamilton and lives at Lennoxlove House.

## Some Notable Hamiltons

## Sir William Hamilton
### 1730–1803

G randson of the 3rd Duke of Hamilton, SIR WILLIAM HAMILTON was an antiquarian and a diplomat. While Britain's ambassador to the court of Naples from 1764 to 1800 he studied earthquakes and volcanoes and gathered together an impressive collection of Greek vases and other antiquities, some of which he sold to the British Museum. The

Duchess of Portland paid Hamilton 1,800 guineas for an antique glass vase from the Barberini collection, now known as the Portland Vase.

In return for having his debts settled, Hamilton's nephew Charles Greville sent his uncle a young lady friend who earned the approbation of the ambassador and his male guests by performing dances inspired by classical scenes while wearing, and this is key, no undergarments. In 1791 Hamilton, at the age of 61, persuaded the 26-year-old Emma Lyon to marry him, and thus was the scene set for one of the great romances of history, that of Lord Nelson and Emma Hamilton.

## Alexander Hamilton
### 1755–1804

G randson of Alexander Hamilton of Grange (who laid the foundation stone of Eglinton Castle in Ayrshire), young Alexander fought in the American Revolutionary War as aide-de-camp to George Washington and commanded three battalions at Yorktown.

Elected after the war to the Continental Congress, he soon resigned to concentrate on law and business and in 1784 founded the New York Bank. As New York delegate to the Constitutional Congress he was the only

New Yorker to sign the American Constitution, and he also wrote the majority of the 'Federalist Essays' (along with James Madison), which were instrumental in the forming of that Constitution.

In 1789 Hamilton was appointed by Washington as the first Secretary of the Treasury. He constructed a sound financial policy that gave the fledgling nation credibility throughout the world, and co-founded the first National Bank, the US Mint and the US Coast Guard. Hamilton also helped to draft Washington's farewell address in 1796.

In 1801 he founded what is now the USA's oldest daily newspaper, the *New York Post*. He named his New York house The Grange, after his family's home in Scotland. It is now a national monument.

In 1804 Hamilton fought a duel

with Vice-President Aaron Burr after refusing to apologise for making derogatory remarks about Burr at a New York dinner party. Hamilton received a fatal gunshot wound from which he died the next day.

PROFESSOR JAMES HAMILTON (1767–1839), Professor of Midwifery at Edinburgh University in succession to his father Alexander Hamilton (1739–1802). James was THE LAST PERSON TO BE CARRIED ABOUT EDINBURGH IN A SEDAN CHAIR.

IAN ROBERTSON HAMILTON, born in Paisley in 1925, was the leader of the group who removed the Stone of Scone, the ancient coronation stone of the Scots, from Westminster Abbey in 1950 and placed it under the altar at Arbroath Abbey.

# *House of Douglas*

D ouglas comes from the Gaelic 'dubh ghlas', meaning 'black water', and the House of Douglas descends from William de Douglas, a knight of Flemish origin who is recorded as owning the castle and lands of Douglas Water in South Lanarkshire in 1161.

The Douglas descendants fought with Alexander III against the Norwegians at the Battle of Largs in 1263.

Sir William Douglas 'Le Hardi' joined the rebellion of William Wallace, but was captured at the Battle of Falkirk in 1298 and taken to London, where he died a prisoner in the Tower, his lands forfeit to Edward I.

## The Douglas Larder

William Le Hardi's dispossessed son James Douglas (1286–1330) joined Robert the Bruce in his campaign for the Scottish Crown and soon proved himself an able and courageous soldier.

In 1308, in an episode that became know as the Douglas Larder, he led a small band of men to his family's estate at Douglas and hid in the village church to ambush the English soldiers who were occupying Douglas Castle when they came to attend Sunday service.

The ambush was a success. Many of the English soldiers were killed and the rest were taken up to the castle, put in the cellar with all the stores, beheaded and then set alight. The castle went up in flames and Douglas's reputation with the English as 'Black Douglas' was assured.

*Hush ye, hush ye, little pet ye.*
*Hush ye, hush ye, do not fret ye.*
*The Black Douglas shall not get ye.*
English Lullaby

## The Good Sir James

While to the English Douglas may have appeared 'Black', to the Scots he will always be 'Good Douglas'. He was knighted for his brilliantly conceived capture of Roxburgh Castle and then distinguished himself at the Battle of Bannockburn.

When Robert the Bruce died in 1329, Douglas took his King's heart, sealed in a casket, to fight the Moors in Spain, fulfilling Bruce's wish to go on crusade as atonement for his murder of John Comyn in 1306. At the Battle of Teba in 1330 Douglas fell while leading a cavalry charge, and as he lay dying he flung Bruce's heart into the air crying, 'Forward, brave heart!'

The heart was recovered and brought back to Scotland to be buried in Melrose Abbey, and it appears on the Douglas crest as a winged heart surmounted by a crown.

The Good Douglas's younger brother Archibald, Guardian of Scotland, died at the Battle of Halidon Hill in 1333 while trying to relieve Berwick-on-Tweed, as did the Good's son William. Hence, Archibald's son, also William, eventually became the next Lord Douglas.

# Some Notable Douglases

DAVID DOUGLAS (1799–1834), botanist who worked as a gardener at Scone Palace and then went plant hunting in the Pacific North West. THE DOUGLAS FIR is named after him, and the first Douglas fir in Britain, grown from a seed sent back by Douglas from America in 1826, is still growing at Scone.

SIR JAMES DOUGLAS (1803–77), colonial governor known as 'the Father of British Columbia'. Schooled in Lanark, Douglas joined the North West Company and later the Hudson's Bay Company as a fur trader. In 1841 he was ordered to set up a trading post on the southern tip of Vancouver Island and founded Fort Victoria, on the site of the present-day city of Victoria. From 1851 Douglas was Governor of Vancouver Island, and in 1858 he became THE FIRST GOVERNOR OF BRITISH COLUMBIA, holding both posts until he retired in 1864.

DONALD DOUGLAS (1892–1981), founder of the DOUGLAS AIRCRAFT COMPANY in 1921. In 1924 Douglas planes were used to achieve THE FIRST AERIAL CIRCUMNAVIGATION OF THE WORLD. The iconic Douglas DC 3 (DC stands for Douglas Commercial) is regarded as one of the most influential aeroplanes in aviation history. In 1967 Douglas merged with McDonnell to become McDonnell Douglas and is now part of Boeing.

*Well, I never* knew this
*about*
LANARKSHIRE FOLK

ROBERT DINWIDDIE (1693–1770), colonial governor, born in Glasgow. Lieutenant-Governor of Virginia from 1751 to 1758, Dinwiddie had the firm belief that the colonies should raise money for their own protection rather than relying on help from the British government. To this end, on spotting the talents of a young George Washington, he gave Washington his first command, an expedition to confront the French. As discoverer and patron of George Washington, Dinwiddie is sometimes described as 'GRANDFATHER OF THE UNITED STATES'.

WILLIAM CULLEN (1710–90), doctor and chemist, born in Hamilton. Amongst many positions he held were those of doctor to the 5th Duke of Hamilton and Professor of Chemistry and Medicine at Edinburgh University. In 1756 he gave THE FIRST-EVER PUBLIC DEMONSTRATION OF ARTIFICIAL REFRIGERATION.

ROBERT DALE OWEN (1801–77), born in Glasgow, the son of reformer Robert Owen and grandson of David Dale, founders of the New Lanark industrial and social complex. In 1825 he emigrated to America with his father and, using the ideals behind New Lanark, founded the Utopian settlement of New Harmony in Indiana, which introduced THE FIRST PUBLIC KINDERGARTEN AND THE FIRST FREE PUBLIC LIBRARY IN AMERICA. A passionate anti-slavery campaigner, he was influential in Abraham Lincoln's Emancipation Proclamation of 1862.

JOHN SCOTT RUSSELL (1808–82), naval engineer, born in Parkhead, Glasgow. He built the biggest ship in the world at the time, Isambard Kingdom Brunel's *Great Eastern*. In 1834, while conducting practical research for the design of canal boats, he discovered what he called the wave of translation and is now called a SOLITON. Today soliton waves are used to carry information along fibre-optic cables for the internet.

SIR DUGALD CLERK (1854–1932), designer of THE FIRST TWO-STROKE ENGINE in 1878, born in Glasgow.

# Midlothian
## (Edinburghshire)

❖❖❖❖❖

DUNDAS OF ARNISTON ✦ VISCOUNT MELVILLE
✦ MELVILLE CASTLE ✦ DALHOUSIE
✦ SOME NOTABLE RAMSAYS ✦ ST CLAIRS OF ROSLIN
✦ ROSLIN CHAPEL ✦ ROSLIN CASTLE

*Arniston House, ancestral home of the great legal
family of Dundas, designed and built by the great
architectural family of Adam.*

◀ MIDLOTHIAN FOLK ▶

George Cleghorn ✦ Robert Smith ✦ James Hutton ✦ Joseph Black
✦ Robert Aitken ✦ Henry Brougham ✦ James Pillans
✦ Alexander Gordon Laing ✦ John Lawson Johnston
✦ Cargill Gilson Knott ✦ James Arnott Hamilton
✦ Richard Noble ✦ Derek Dick

# Dundas of Arniston

In 1571 the Arniston estate, 10 miles (16 km) south of Edinburgh city centre, beneath the Moorfoot Hills, was acquired by GEORGE DUNDAS, 16TH LAIRD OF DUNDAS, for his new-born son JAMES DUNDAS (1570–1628), who later built himself a fine courtyard tower house there and set about founding Scotland's most distinguished legal family. Throughout the 17th and 18th centuries no fewer than five Dundas lairds of Arniston sat in the Supreme Court of Scotland.

The FIRST LORD ARNISTON (1620–79) was James's son. He was appointed a Lord of Session as Lord Arniston in 1662 but resigned his seat rather than renounce the National Covenant he had signed in 1639.

In 1725 ROBERT, 2ND LORD ARNISTON, commissioned William Adam to build a new house at Arniston, incorporating some of the original tower house, a project that was inherited on his death the following year by his son ROBERT, 3RD LORD ARNISTON (1685–1753), who was already Lord Advocate and would become Lord President of the Court of Session, the highest office in the judiciary, in 1748.

ROBERT, 4TH LORD ARNISTON (1713–87), Solicitor-General for Scot-land from 1742 to 1746, inherited Arniston in 1753 and brought in William Adam's son John to complete Arniston House, making it what we see today, one of the finest Palladian houses in Scotland.

ROBERT, 5TH LORD ARNISTON (1758–1819), served as Solicitor-General from 1790 to 1796 and as Lord Advocate from 1789 to 1801.

Arniston House remains in the Dundas family and is open for guided tours during the summer.

Perhaps the most colourful member of this celebrated family was Henry Dundas, Viscount Melville, younger brother of the 4th Lord Arniston.

# Henry Dundas, 1st Viscount Melville 1742–1811

HENRY DUNDAS, known as Henry the Ninth or the Uncrowned King of Scotland, pretty much ran Scotland on behalf of William Pitt. From 1775 until 1805 he held the offices of Lord Advocate and Keeper of the Privy Seal, and wielded unprecedented power over the affairs of Scotland, powers which he used largely for the benefit of Scotland. He negotiated the restoration of many of the estates forfeited after Culloden and lifted the ban on wearing tartan. As chairman of the Committee for Indian Affairs he relieved the East India Company of its political responsibilities for India, transferring power to the government in Westminster, and at the same time increased the influence of Scots in India. He rose to be War Secretary from 1794 to 1801 under William Pitt, and briefly First Lord of the Admiralty. In 1806, while Treasurer at the Admiralty, Dundas was accused (possibly for political reasons) of financial mismanagement and became THE LAST PERSON TO BE IMPEACHED IN BRITAIN, but after THE LAST IMPEACHMENT TRIAL TO BE HELD IN THE HOUSE OF LORDS, he was acquitted and restored to the Privy Council.

Henry Dundas and other members of his family feature in Patrick O'Brien's Jack Aubrey novels.

## Melville Castle

When Henry Dundas was elevated to the peerage in 1802 he chose the title Viscount Melville from his home, Melville Castle near Dalkeith, which he had inherited from his father-in-law. He is commemorated by the Melville Monument, which is based on Trajan's Column in Rome, and stands in St Andrew Square in Edinburgh's New Town.

## Dalhousie

The title EARL OF DALHOUSIE was created in 1633 by Charles I for William Ramsay, son of Sir John Ramsay of Dalhousie, 1st Lord Ramsay.

The Ramsay name is thought to have come from the village of Ramsey in Huntingdonshire. Simon de Ramsay, a Norman knight, came north with David I and was granted lands in Lothian, which included Dalhousie. The family became known as the Ramsays of Dalhousie.

WILLIAM RAMSAY OF DALHOUSIE was a supporter of Robert the Bruce, fought at Bannockburn and signed the Declaration of Arbroath in 1320.

SIR ALEXANDER RAMSAY OF DALHOUSIE was one of the most courageous men of the age, rescuing Black Agnes, the Countess of Dunbar, at the siege of Dunbar Castle in 1338 and capturing Roxburgh Castle from the English for David II in 1342. However, Ramsay's reputation threatened the dominance of the Douglases in the Borders, and they seized him and incarcerated him in Hermitage Castle, where he was starved to death.

ALEXANDER RAMSAY OF DALHOUSIE fell at Flodden in 1513, and his son Nicholas fought for Mary Queen of Scots at the Battle of Langside, but eventually made peace with James VI.

JOHN RAMSAY, a grandson of Nicholas, gained great favour with James VI in 1600 when he rescued the King from kidnap by the Earl of Gowrie, who was run through by Ramsay's sword and killed.

John's son William became the 1ST EARL OF DALHOUSIE in 1633.

In 1831 the 8TH EARL OF DALHOUSIE received the lands of his uncle William Maule, the Earl of Panmure, which included Brechin Castle and the largest estate in Angus, and his youngest son was made Baron Panmure.

GEORGE RAMSAY, 9TH EARL OF DALHOUSIE, was Governor of Nova Scotia from 1816 to 1820 and began the Ramsays' connection with India, becoming Commander-in-Chief in India.

His son James, 10th Earl, became THE YOUNGEST EVER GOVERNOR-GENERAL OF INDIA in 1847, in recognition of which he was created MARQUESS OF DALHOUSIE.

He annexed the Punjab in 1849, and Burma in 1852, followed by a range of independent Indian states, creating the basis for the British Raj. While criticised for causing resentment with his expansionist policy, which is blamed by some for the Indian Mutiny of 1857, Ramsay built up a strong infrastructure of roads and railways, communications, irrigation and modern government and his legacy survives in India to this day.

The Marquess left India in 1856, the year before the mutiny, after his beloved wife fell ill. She died on the journey home and Ramsay, broken-hearted, died at Dalhousie Castle not long after his return. He died child-less and the marquessate became extinct.

The title of Earl of Dalhousie was inherited by James's first cousin Fox Maule-Ramsay, grandson of the 8th Earl, who was christened Fox in honour of the Whig politician Charles James Fox.

The 15th Earl (1914–99) was appointed Governor-General of Rhodesia and Nyasaland in 1957, serving until 1963 when the federa-tion was dissolved and Nyasaland subsequently gained independence as Malawi, Northern Rhodesia as Zambia and Southern Rhodesia as Zimbabwe.

The present incumbent, and Chief of Clan Ramsay, is JAMES RAMSAY, 17TH EARL OF DALHOUSIE, who was born in 1948.

## Some Notable Ramsays

ALLAN RAMSAY THE ELDER (1686–1758), poet and bookseller who opened the first circulating library in Scotland. One of Scotland's first naturalist poets, he is considered the 'link' between the old-style 'makars', or bards, of the royal court and the new free-style poets such as Robert Burns.

ALLAN RAMSAY THE YOUNGER (1713–1784), artist and eldest son of Allan Ramsay the poet. Considered the greatest portrait painter of his day, later an arch rival of Joshua Reynolds, he was court painter to George III and has left a legacy of royal and aristocratic portraits second to none. The novelist Laurence Sterne once said to him, 'Mr Ramsay, you paint only the Court cards, the King, the Queen, and the Knave.' Ramsay also painted many of the great figures of the Scottish Enlightenment. Two particularly fine portraits of David Hume and Jean-Jacques Rousseau are amongst the most important works of the 18th century. Like his kinsman James, Allan was an influential abolitionist.

JAMES RAMSAY (1733–89), naval surgeon and Anglican priest. When his ship the *Arundel* intercepted a British slave ship in the Caribbean, Ramsay was appalled by the inhumane condi-tions he encountered. Invalided out of the navy, he became a priest on St Kitts, where he ministered and acted as surgeon to the plantation slaves. On his return to England he wrote about his experiences in 'Essay on the Treatment and Conversion of African Slaves in the British Sugar Colonies', which was published in 1784. This was the first personal account of the horrors of slavery and had a profound effect on such influential figures as the Bishop of London, the Prime Minister William Pitt the Younger, William Wilberforce and, particularly, Thomas Clarkson. It has been said that the abolition of the slave trade owed more to James Ramsay's arguments, proposals and personal integrity than to any other influence.

SIR WILLIAM RAMSAY (1852–1916), chemist who discovered the gases argon, helium, neon, krypton, xenon and radon. He was awarded the Nobel Prize for Chemistry in 1904.

WILLIAM RAMSAY (1868–1914), inventor of Kiwi shoe polish. Born in Glasgow, he emigrated to Melbourne, Australia, with his family at the age of ten. He became a partner in his father's estate agency John Ramsay & Son, and on a sales trip to New Zealand he met and married Annie Meek. On his return to Melbourne he set up a company to produce polishes and creams, and in 1906 began producing a new shoe polish which he called Kiwi, named in honour of his wife's New Zealand heritage. In 1912 Ramsay's father established the firm in London, and Kiwi is now the best-selling shoe polish in the English-speaking world.

MICHAEL RAMSAY (1904–88), 100th Archbishop of Canterbury.

DENNIS RAMSAY, artist, born 1925. Descended from the artistic Ramsays, Dennis is a still-life and religious painter as well as a portrait artist. He studied under Pietro Annigoni, who became godfather to his youngest child, Julian. Amongst his many royal paintings is a portrait of the Duke of Edinburgh commissioned in 2001 for the Duke's 80th birthday.

GORDON RAMSAY, chef, born 1966. Ramsay started out as a professional footballer at Glasgow Rangers, but at 19 his career was halted by a bad knee injury, and he turned to cookery.

He was THE FIRST SCOTTISH CHEF TO GAIN THREE MICHELIN STARS, for his first restaurant, Gordon Ramsay in Chelsea. In 2001 his restaurant Petrus gained notoriety when six bankers spent £44,000 on wine during a single meal.

He has starred in two television series, *Ramsay's Kitchen Nightmares*, in which he played a kitchen troubleshooter, and *Hell's Kitchen*, where he attempted to train British celebrities to be chefs. He has gained a reputation for foul language, and his latest series is called *The F Word*.

# St Clairs of Roslin

The St Clair family originated from St-Clair-sur-Epte in Normandy and came across to England with their cousin William the Conqueror in 1066, eventually moving north to Scotland, where they were granted the lands of Roslin by David I in the 12th century.

Over the next hundred years the St Clairs fought courageously for the Scottish kings, particularly at the Battle of Largs, in Ayrshire in 1263, when Sir William St Clair led the forces of Alexander III to victory over the Viking Norwegians.

Fourteen-year-old Sir William St Clair (1300–30) fought for Robert the Bruce at Bannockburn and later accompanied Sir James Douglas on his mission to take Bruce's heart to the Holy Land. He was killed in Spain along with Douglas fighting the Moors at the Battle of Teba in 1330.

Both were buried in the old Roslin Chapel.

# Roslin Chapel

Since 2003 thousands of disciples have trekked to Roslin to see the famous chapel mentioned in Dan Brown's novel *The Da Vinci Code*, in search of clues about the mysterious Knights Templar, the European order of Knights dedicated to protecting the Temple of Solomon in Jerusalem. Largely associated with the Crusades, the Templars' popularity waned once the Holy City was lost and they were officially disbanded in 1312, although the organisation is said to have carried on in secret.

It is believed by some that the Sinclairs were themselves Knights Templar. Legend has it that Sir William Sinclair led the surviving Templars at the Battle of Bannockburn, and that those who died that day were buried in the old chapel at Roslin. In 1398 Sir William's son Henry, 1st Earl of Orkney (1345–1400), is said to have undertaken a remarkable voyage to Greenland with the Venetian sailor Antonio Zeno, possibly on behalf of the Knights Templar, and discovered what are now Nova Scotia and Massachusetts.

Henry's grandson William, the last

Sinclair Earl of Orkney (1410–84), rebuilt Roslin Chapel in a grand style, above the original chapel, between 1447 and 1486. In the crypt there is a grave slab that could belong to one of the Templars buried in the old chapel after Bannockburn, and the chapel itself is full of fantastical stone carvings of what is said to be Templar imagery. Some of the carvings appear to be of plants found only in America, such as aloe vera and maize, and since they were carved several years before Columbus's discovery of America in 1492, this gives some credence to the accounts of Henry Sinclair's voyage of 1398.

## Roslin Castle

S ir William's grandson Henry St Clair, who in 1379 became Earl of Orkney (*see* Orkney) through his mother, began the first stone castle at Roslin, which was continuously added to and developed over the next 300 years.

In 1452 Roslin Castle was badly damaged by a fire, during which the family's valuable papers, including the earliest extant work in Scots prose, the Roslin-Hay manuscript, were passed to safety out of a window. They now reside in the National Library of Scotland.

The castle was refurbished, but much of it was destroyed again during the 'Rough Wooing' in 1544.

A new castle was built into the cliffs above Roslin Glen, accessed only by a drawbridge, and part of this remains habitable. The Earl of Rosslyn now leases it out as a holiday home through the Landmark Trust.

*Well, I never knew this*
*about*
# MIDLOTHIAN FOLK

GEORGE CLEGHORN (1716–94), medical pioneer, born in Edinburgh. As an army surgeon in Minorca he discovered that quinine bark acted as a cure for malaria, endemic in Britain at the time and a severe threat to the British in India. The discovery led to the invention of TONIC WATER and, indirectly, to 'gin and tonic'.

ROBERT SMITH (1722–77), architect, born in Dalkeith. Smith designed and built three of America's most iconic buildings: Princeton University's NASSAU HALL, the largest stone

*Carpenter's Hall, Philadelphia*

building in America on its completion in 1756, CARPENTER'S HALL in Philadelphia, home of America's oldest trade guild, and site of the First Continental Congress of the United Colonies of North America, from 5 September to 26 October 1774, and Philadelphia's eye-catching CHRIST CHURCH STEEPLE. He also built Benjamin Franklin's house in Philadelphia.

JAMES HUTTON (1726–97), known as the 'Father of Modern Geology', was born in Edinburgh. A member of the Scottish Enlightenment and particular friends with David Hume, Adam Smith and Joseph Black, he developed the theory of Uniformitarianism as a basis for the geological formation of the earth – proposing that the natural processes that operated in the past are the same as those that can be observed at work in the present, with 'no vestige of a beginning, no concept of an end'.

JOSEPH BLACK (1728–99), chemist, who discovered latent (or hidden) heat and specific heat. He also discovered CARBON DIOXIDE, $CO_2$. A mentor

---

of James Watt and an associate of David Hume, Adam Smith and others of the Scottish Enlightenment, he is buried in Greyfriars Kirkyard.

ROBERT AITKEN (1734–1802), printer born in Dalkeith. He emigrated to Philadelphia and set up as a bookseller in 1769. When the American War of Independence cut off the supply of bibles from Britain, Aitken sought and received the endorsement of Congress to print 10,000 certified bibles, which became THE FIRST BIBLES EVER TO BE PRINTED IN THE UNITED STATES.

# Henry Brougham
## 1778–1868

HENRY BROUGHAM, lawyer, politician, inventor and nephew by marriage of William Adam, was born at No. 21, St Andrew Square, in Edinburgh.

Educated at Edinburgh University, he became a lawyer in London and gained immense popularity by successfully defending Queen Caroline against divorce proceedings brought by George IV.

In 1826 he narrowly avoided embarrassment when he paid off the notorious courtesan Harriette Wilson and her publisher, who were threatening to name him in her memoirs. (The Duke of Wellington, when confronted with the same threat, cried 'Publish and be damned!')

Brougham survived to become Lord Chancellor in 1830 and was responsible for promoting the Reform Act of 1832, which began the dismantling of the 'rotten boroughs', and the 1833 Slavery Abolition Act, which abolished slavery throughout most of the British Empire.

Henry Brougham holds the record for the longest speech ever given in the House of Commons. He left his audience in the chamber 'thin and exhausted' after holding forth for six hours.

He was also the designer of the Brougham carriage, a light four-wheeled, horse-drawn, enclosed carriage with a glazed front window and steering front wheels.

In 1835 Henry Brougham discovered and fell in love with a small fishing village on the French Côte d'Azur and bought some land there on which he built a sanitorium. This soon attracted the wealthy from all over Europe and began the rise of Cannes as an international resort.

There is a statue of Brougham on the waterfront at Cannes opposite the Palais des Festivals et des Congrès, which hosts the annual Cannes Film Festival.

JAMES PILLANS (1778–1864), academic and headmaster of the Old High School in Edinburgh. As class sizes got bigger, Pillans began to find it increasingly difficult to teach effectively while each pupil was working on his own individual hand-held slate, so he took the biggest slate he could find and put it up on the wall of the classroom so that everyone could see it. This meant that the teacher could have the attention of the whole class. He also came up with the idea of writing on the slate board with chalks. Teaching was transformed.

ALEXANDER GORDON LAING (1793–1826), army officer and African explorer, born in Edinburgh. In 1822 he was sent by the army to West Africa to promote commerce and to help suppress the slave trade. On his journey he was able to locate the source of the Niger, although he was prevented from reaching it by hostile natives. In 1825 he returned to Africa to continue his exploration of the Niger basin by crossing the Sahara Desert. His letters to the British consul in Tripoli show that he was the FIRST EUROPEAN TO REACH TIMBUKTU, in 1826. He was murdered there some days later.

# John Lawson Johnston
## ◂ 1839–1900 ▸

JOHN LAWSON JOHNSTON, the inventor of BOVRIL, was born in Roslin. In 1870 Napoleon III was desperate to find sustenance for his troops fighting the Prussians and made an order for a million cans of beef. This was logistically almost impossible to supply, and the canny Johnston reckoned that beef in some liquid form would be less expensive, easier to transport and more warming for the troops in winter conditions. And so he developed Johnston's Fluid Beef, a thick salty beef extract that could be diluted with water. It proved an instant hit, was given the more catchy name Bovril in 1886, and has sustained soldiers and sports fans out in the cold all over the world ever since.

The name Bovril comes from the Latin 'bovis', meaning cow, and 'vril', a powerful energy fluid dreamed up by the popular author Edward Bulwer-Lytton for his novel *The Coming Race*.

By 1968 Bovril owned enough beef ranches in Argentina to cover an area equivalent to half the size of England.

CARGILL GILSON KNOTT (1856–1922), seismologist, born in Penicuik. In 1883 Knott was invited out to Japan to help Richard Henry Brunton, 'the Father of Japanese Lighthouses', construct lighthouses that would be proof against the frequent earthquakes experienced by Japan. Knott established the first network of seismological observatories in Japan, which are still working today.

JAMES ARNOTT HAMILTON, designer of the ultra-slim delta wing on Concorde, born in Penicuik in 1923.

RICHARD NOBLE, holder of the world land speed record between 1983 and 1997, born in Edinburgh in 1946. His car, *Thrust 2*, reached 633 mph (1,019 kph) at the Black Rock Desert in Nevada, USA. This record was broken in 1997 by Andy Green in *Thrust SSC*, for which Noble was project manager and chief designer. *Thrust SSC* today holds THE WORLD LAND SPEED RECORD of 763 mph (1,227 kph) and was THE FIRST-EVER LAND VEHICLE OFFICIALLY TO BREAK THE SOUND BARRIER. Richard Noble is currently project manager for *Bloodhound SSC*, which is being developed to set a new land speed record – it is designed to reach 1,000 mph (1,600 kph).

DEREK DICK, 'FISH', musician and lyricist, former lead singer for rock band Marillion, born 1958. His nickname apparently comes from the amount of time he spent reading in the bath when he was a boy.

# Morayshire

(Elginshire)

---

+ EARL OF MORAY + EARLS OF ELGIN + ELGIN MARBLES
+ GORDON CASTLE + GORDON HIGHLANDERS
+ THE GAY GORDONS + GORDON SETTER
+ GORDON RIOTS + 5TH DUKE OF GORDON

*Elgin town centre. Elgin is one of Scotland's oldest royal burghs, given its charter by King David I in 1151 and described by Edward I as 'bon chastell et bonne vill' — a good castle and a good town.*

◄ MORAYSHIRE FOLK ►

William Dunbar + Ethel Bedford-Fenwick + David West
+ John Garden + Meg Farquhar + Roy Williamson
+ Peter Kerr + Kevin McKidd

MORAYSHIRE recalls the days of the great kingdom of Moray, one of the original seven Celtic kingdoms, once overseen by a mormaer, and comprising a vast area stretching from Buchan in the east, through Ross, to the Atlantic coast. Moray formed the heartland of Macbeth's kingdom, and here in Morayshire can be found his 'blasted heath' and the site of Duncan's castle, at Forres.

## Earl of Moray

Robert the Bruce understood the historic and symbolic significance of Moray to Scotland and in 1312 created the earldom of Moray for his nephew Thomas Randolph, who later recaptured Edinburgh Castle from the English in 1314 by scaling the walls at night. Randolph also fought for Bruce at Bannockburn and signed the Declaration of Arbroath in 1320.

*Brodie Castle, Forres, near Macbeth's 'blasted heath'.*

When Randolph's second son, the 3rd Earl of Moray, died at the Battle of Neville's Cross in 1346, his sister Black Agnes, married to the Earl of Dunbar, became Countess and so the title passed to the Dunbars.

In 1372 the earldom estates were divided, with the Dunbars being given the coastal regions and Alexander Stewart, favourite son of Robert II, being made Lord of the upland area of Badenoch. This was always going to lead to trouble, and when the Bishop of Moray turned to the Dunbar Earl of Moray for protection against the arrogant and wilful Stewart, the Lord of Badenoch descended on Elgin and burned both the town and the cathedral to the ground, fully earning his epithet 'the Wolf of Badenoch'.

The title descended finally to Elizabeth Dunbar, 8th Countess of Moray, and was conferred on her husband James Crichton, but he was killed fighting James II in 1455 and the title became dormant.

George Gordon, 4th Earl of Huntly, who pretty much ruled the north east of Scotland, helped himself to the earldom in 1549, but Mary Queen of Scots snatched it back and bestowed it on her bastard brother James Stewart in 1562. Gordon flew into a sulk and barred the

*Elgin cathedral – 'Lantern of the North'.*

Queen from Inverness Castle when she came to visit (*see* Nairnshire). The whole affair turned nasty and Gordon confronted the new Earl of Moray at the Battle of Corrichie, but was defeated and died of apoplexy not long afterwards.

The Earl of Moray's daughter and heir married Lord Doune, and their son became 2nd Earl of Moray, of the fifth creation, in 1592, only to be murdered by Gordon's vengeful heir the new 5th Earl of Huntly, and descend into folklore and song as 'The Bonny Earl of Moray'.

His descendants, the owners of Castle Doune, still possess the title Earl of Moray, the present holder being Douglas Stuart, 20th Earl of Moray.

## Earls of Elgin

The title EARL OF ELGIN was created in 1633 for a branch of the Bruce family, and was first conferred on Thomas Bruce, 3rd Lord Kinloss.

The 3RD EARL OF ELGIN (1656–1741) remained loyal to James VII and helped James to escape from London in 1688, during the Glorious Revolution. After a spell in the Tower of London Elgin was exiled to Brussels, where he died in 1741.

JAMES BRUCE, 8TH EARL OF ELGIN (1811–63), was a colonial diplomat who served as Governor of Jamaica 1842–7, Governor-General of Canada 1847–54, High Commissioner to China 1857–61, and Viceroy of India

1861–3. While Commissioner to China he oversaw the end of the Second Opium War, and in 1860 ordered the destruction of Qing Dynasty's Old Summer Palace outside Beijing.

The present holder of the title is ANDREW BRUCE, 11TH EARL OF ELGIN. He is hereditary Chief of Clan Bruce and the family seat is Broomhall House, near Dunfermline in Fife.

*8th Earl of Elgin*

## Gordon Castle

S tanding on the edge of Fochabers is what remains of GORDON CASTLE, once the home of the Dukes of Gordon, and once the largest country house in Scotland.

The original castle was built in 1470 by George Gordon, the 2nd Earl of Huntly, and enlarged by his grandson

into a Renaissance palace known as the BOG O' GIGHT, which was so magnificent that the 1ST DUKE OF GORDON (1649–1716) made it his main home.

In 1769 ALEXANDER GORDON, 4TH DUKE OF GORDON (1743–1827), commissioned John Baxter to rebuild the castle into a grand stately home. Baxter kept the six-storey 84 ft (26 m) high medieval tower from the Bog o' Gight, enfolded it in a new four-storey block and added wings, creating THE LONGEST FAÇADE IN SCOTLAND, 568 ft (173 m) long.

A smart new town was laid out about one mile (1.6 km) to the south to replace the run down village that had to be swept away to make room for the huge new palace.

In 1775 the 4th Duke also built the Highlands' highest village at Tomintoul, in Banffshire, as a formal settlement for all his tenants scattered across his vast estates.

## Gordon Highlanders

I n 1794 the 4th Duke was asked to raise an infantry regiment to fight in the French Revolutionary Wars, and he threw himself into the business of recruiting men from his estates throughout Aberdeenshire, Moray, Banff and Kincardine. In this endeavour he was greatly helped by his wife JANE MAXWELL, FLOWER

## Elgin Marbles

THOMAS BRUCE, 7TH EARL OF ELGIN (1766–1841), served as the British Ambassador to the Ottoman Empire between 1799 and 1803. During this time he obtained permission from the Ottoman authorities, who at the time ruled Greece, to remove a number of marble sculptures from the Parthenon in Athens and ship them back to Britain. Some, like Lord Byron, said it was an act of vandalism, while Elgin claimed that he was saving the marbles from being further damaged by the fighting of the Greek War of Independence, during which the Acropolis was besieged twice.

Dull is the eye that will not weep to see
Thy walls defaced, thy mouldering shrines removed
By British hands, which it had best behoved
To guard those relics ne'er to be restored.

From *Childe Harold's Pilgrimage*, by Lord Byron

In 1816 the sculptures, which became known as THE ELGIN MARBLES, were purchased by the British Government and put on display in the British Museum. The argument continues over whether they should now be returned to Greece or left undisturbed in London.

OF GALLOWAY, one of the most beautiful women of her day. She rode out to all the country fairs and town markets, dressed in regimental jacket and Highland bonnet, and placing a guinea between her lips gave each new recruit a kiss.

Christened the GORDON HIGHLANDERS, the regiment was officially designated the 100th Regiment of Foot before becoming the 92nd Regiment of Foot in 1799. Their tartan was devised by Forsythe of Huntley, who wove a yellow stripe into the standard government plaid, which he thought would appear 'very lively'.

The Gordon Highlanders swiftly gained a reputation for courage and discipline. They fought with distinction throughout the Napoleonic Wars, particularly at Corunna (their black buttons are worn in honour of their brave commander Sir John Moore who died in the battle) and Waterloo, where the Duke of Wellington was heard to say, 'I like the cut of your men, Gordon.'

They served during the Indian Mutiny and on the North West Frontier, through both world wars and in Northern Ireland, the Gulf War and Bosnia, and have won 20 Victoria Crosses to date. In 1994 the regiment was amalgamated with the Queen's Own Highlanders to form the Highlanders.

## The Gay Gordons

The GAY GORDONS is a popular Scottish folk dance associated with the Gordon Highlanders and possibly developed from a tune composed by fiddler William Marshall (1748–1833), who was steward of the Gordon household under the 4th Duke.

## Gordon Setter

The 4th Duke of Gordon is credited with developing the black and tan GORDON SETTER dog, and it was two dogs from the Duke's kennels that established the Gordon Setter line in America.

# Gordon Riots

◆►◆◄◆

The GORDON RIOTS of 1780 get their name from Lord George Gordon (1751–93), younger brother of the 4th Duke of Gordon. In 1779, while an MP, he organised a number of Protestant associations to agitate for the repeal of the Papist Act of 1778, which marked the beginnings of the movement for Catholic Emancipation.

On 2 June 1780, Gordon marched on Parliament at the head of a crowd some 60,000 strong, carrying banners proclaiming 'No Popery!' While Gordon was in the House of Commons presenting his petition, the mob outside rioted and then rampaged through London, attacking Newgate Prison, the Bank of England and even Kenwood house, home of the Lord Chief Justice, the Earl of Mansfield.

In the riots 285 people were shot dead by the army, and Gordon, a charismatic and popular figure, was arrested and charged with treason, but found not guilty. He nonetheless refused to conform and was excommunicated and imprisoned in Newgate for defaming a number of influential Catholics, including Marie Antoinette. At the end of his life he converted to Judaism, for which he was shunned, and died in prison of typhoid fever.

# 5th Duke of Gordon

◆►◆◄◆

GEORGE GORDON, 5TH DUKE GORDON (1770–1836), died childless, leaving his wife Elizabeth Brodie as the last Duchess of Gordon, and the dukedom and estates passed to their nephew the Duke of Richmond.

The greater part of Gordon Castle has been demolished, with just the medieval Bog o' Gight tower and a detached, self-contained portion of the house surviving.

*Well, I never knew this*
*about*
## MORAYSHIRE FOLK

WILLIAM DUNBAR (1750–1810), explorer and astronomer. Born in Duffus House, near Elgin, the younger son of Sir Archibald Dunbar (by his second wife, and therefore denied any inheritance), William emigrated to America to continue his studies of the natural sciences after graduating from King's College in Aberdeen. He became a merchant and cotton planter in Natchez, Mississippi, and made the first meteorological observations in the Mississippi valley in 1799. He built himself an astronomical observatory at Natchez, which became a place for many of the American scholars and scientists of the time to meet. In 1804 he was asked by Thomas Jefferson to lead an expedition to explore the southwestern boundaries of the Louisiana Purchase and made some of the earliest records of the flora and fauna of the Ouachita Mountains, as well as the first detailed chemical analysis of the Hot Springs of Arkansas.

ETHEL BEDFORD-FENWICK (1856–1947), 'NURSE No. 1', born in Elgin. One time matron of St Bartholomew's Hospital in London, she founded the Florence Nightingale International Foundation and campaigned for a proper certificate for nursing, for the recognition of the title of nurse and for the registration of nurses. She achieved the latter with the Nurses Registration Act of 1919, and when the register opened in 1923, Ethel appeared as 'Nurse No. 1'.

DAVID WEST (1868–1936), watercolour artist, born in Lossiemouth. Known mainly for his watercolours of Morayshire scenery, West was the first British artist to hold a one-man exhibition of his work in Argentina. He also painted a miniature watercolour for Queen Mary's doll's house, designed by Edwin Lutyens in 1923 and on display at Windsor Castle.

JOHN GARDEN (1882–1968), founder in 1920 of the Communist Party of Australia, born in Lossiemouth.

MEG FARQUHAR, born 1910 and appointed as assistant professional at Moray Golf Club in 1929, was the FIRST WOMAN PROFESSIONAL GOLFER.

ROY WILLIAMSON (1936–90), musician and songwriter with folk group the Corries, born in Edinburgh but educated at Gordonstoun and lived much of his life in Morayshire. He wrote the Scottish anthem 'FLOWER OF SCOTLAND', which commemorates Robert the Bruce's victory over Edward II at Bannockburn and is sung at international sporting occasions.

PETER KERR, writer, jazz musician and record producer, born in Lossiemouth in 1940. After touring with the top Scottish jazz band the Clyde Valley Stompers, in 1972 he produced the world's best-selling instrumental record, the Royal Scots Dragoon Guards' version of 'Amazing Grace', which sold 13 million copies worldwide.

KEVIN McKIDD, actor, born in Elgin in 1973. Known for his roles as Tommy in the film *Trainspotting*, as the Earl of Bothwell in the BBC TV mini-series *Gunpowder, Treason and Plot* and as Lucius Vorenus in the BBC TV series *Rome*.

# Nairnshire

---

*Bandstand on the seafront in Nairn, county town, resort town and fishing town where the north east meets the Highlands.*

### NAIRNSHIRE FOLK

James Augustus Grant + 'Willie' Whitelaw

# Roses of Kilravock

The name ROSE is derived from that of a Norman knight called de Ros, who came north in the 12th century, and was granted the lands of Geddes, in the county of Nairn. In 1219 Hugh Rose of Geddes appears as witness to the foundation of the Priory at Beauly in Inverness-shire. Hugh's son married the daughter of his neighbour, de Bisset of Kilravock, and came into the Kilravock estate in 1293. It has remained in the Rose family ever since.

The first few generations of Roses lived in a small house made of wood and stone built on the hilltop above the flood plain. However, the 14th and 15th centuries were times of lawlessness, with great families fighting over the Scottish throne and clans squabbling amongst each other for lands and titles. Strong, defensive stone castles began to spring up all across Nairnshire, notably at Cawdor and Rait, and in 1460 Hugh Rose, the 7th Laird of Kilravock, joined the club by erecting a large stone tower on his land, designed by James III's architect Cochran, who had recently added to the keep at Cawdor. As an indication of how dangerous the times were, and how urgently the Roses needed a safe haven, KILRAVOCK TOWER was finished in under a year.

# Muriel of Cawdor

It was around this time that the Rose family, which throughout most of its history has lived a blameless and quiet life, became embroiled in one of the great romantic stories of Scotland. It began quietly enough with the marriage of Isabella, daughter of the 7th Laird, to John, second son of their close neighbour William de Calder (Cawdor). Some while after the ceremony John's older brother William went mad and had to be shut away, so John became the heir to Cawdor. John died in 1498, leaving his wife pregnant, and she in due course gave birth to a red-haired baby girl, MURIEL, who was the sole heir to the great estate of Cawdor.

*Kilravock Castle*

Muriel was in a perilous position, because her grandfather William and his brothers were determined that a mere girl should not inherit Cawdor and take it away from the Calder family when she married. However, owing to an arrangement that William had previously come to with James IV, Cawdor was actually leased from the Crown under a charter, and so Muriel came under the King's protection. James arranged for ARCHIBALD CAMPBELL, 2ND EARL OF ARGYLL, a distant kinsman of the Thane of Cawdor and the most powerful man in Scotland at that time, to become Muriel's guardian, and Campbell sent his cousin, Campbell of Inverliver, with a strong guard, to collect his valuable prize, no doubt with a mind to securing the inheritance for himself.

In the meantime, Muriel's grandmother, the redoubtable Lady Kilravock, dubious of the Earl of Argyll's intentions, branded her young granddaughter on the hip with a red-hot key and bit off the top of her little finger, so that she could be recognised and Argyll could not substitute his own daughter should anything bad happen to Muriel . . .

Inverliver collected Muriel and started for home, but had not gone far before he was overtaken by William de Calder and his four brothers, determined to take possession of Muriel. Inverliver sent Muriel on ahead with a small guard, then

dressed up a stook of corn to look like a little girl and fought to protect it with all his vigour. Seven of his own sons died before Inverliver withdrew, satisfied that Muriel was beyond capture. When asked if the sacrifice had been worth it, particularly as Muriel might die before she came into her inheritance, the Earl of Argyll replied, 'Muriel of Cawdor will never die as long as there's a red-haired lassie on the shores of Loch Awe.'

As it turned out, Muriel did live to collect her inheritance, indeed she survived into a ripe old age, and married the Earl of Argyll's second son Sir John Campbell. The Earls of Cawdor of the present day are directly descended from this couple.

# Black Baron

Life at Kilravock settled back into its normal torpor until the 10th Laird, who was known as the Black Baron, was captured at the Battle of Pinkie Cleugh in 1547, during the 'Rough Wooing'. He had to pay a mighty ransom for his freedom – and on top of that, in 1553, he somehow had to find the money to build a comfortable manor house beside the old keep, in which to accommodate his 17 sisters and daughters. They obviously looked after him well because he reigned as Laird for 50 years. It was during the Black Baron's time, in 1562, that Mary Queen of Scots stayed at Kilravock after she had been refused entry to Inverness Castle by George Gordon, the Earl of Huntly (see Morayshire).

## Jacobite Rebellions

The 15th Laird, although against the Act of Union, was one of the Scottish members of the first Parliament of Great Britain. He supported the Hanoverians and kept Kilravock open as a refuge for those fleeing from the Jacobites in 1715.

In 1745, during the time of the 16th Laird, and two days before the Battle of Culloden, Bonnie Prince Charlie stopped by while rounding up his men in preparation for the coming showdown. He walked around the estate, took some refreshment and told Rose how he envied the peace and quiet of Kilravock, surrounded as it was by war and strife. The next day, to the alarm of all concerned, the Duke of Cumberland dropped in to spend the night and casually enquired, 'You have had my cousin here?' Rose could not deny it and mumbled something about not really being in a position to refuse the Prince. Cumberland reassured the Laird that he had done right to show hospitality.

## Kilravock Today

From that time on Kilravock has enjoyed a restful existence and remains the seat of the Clan Rose today. The present chief is Anna Rose, 25th of Kilravock, a direct descendant of the first chief, the Rose family being one of the few in Scotland where the chiefship has been passed down in an unbroken line.

In 1967 Anna Rose gave Kilravock to the Kilravock Castle Christian Trust, which runs the house as a Christian retreat.

## Some Notable Roses

HUGH ROSE, 1ST BARON STRATHNAIRN (1801–85), army officer, who in 1841 was appointed as British Consul General in Syria. He showed conspicuous courage in stopping Maronite and Druze militias shooting at each other by riding in between their lines. He also rescued 600 hostages being held by the Druze at

the American Christian mission at Abaye. Later he served as commander-in-chief of the army in Central India during the Indian Mutiny in 1857.

SIR ALEC ROSE (1908–91), yachtsman. In 1968, at the age of 59, he became one of the first people to sail around the world single-handed, in his ketch *Lively Lady*. In December the previous year the Australian Prime Minister Harold Holt had travelled to Melbourne to see Rose complete that leg of his voyage. After doing so, Holt went for a swim off the nearby Cheviot Beach and was never seen again, presumed drowned.

SIR MICHAEL ROSE, SAS army officer, born 1940. Rose led the SAS team that rescued the hostages being held in the Iranian embassy in London in 1980. During the Falklands War in 1982 he commanded the operation that regained Mount Kent, overlooking the capital Port Stanley, and negotiated the surrender of the Argentine forces. In 1994 he was appointed commander of UN troops in Bosnia. In 2006 he courted controversy by calling for Prime Minister Tony Blair to be impeached for taking Britain to war with Iraq in 2003 on false pretences.

Memorable Quote:
*'To go to war on what turns out to be false grounds is something that no one should be allowed to walk away from.'*

JUSTIN ROSE, golfer, born 1980. He came to prominence aged 17 when, as an amateur, he came fourth in the Open Championship at Royal Birkdale in 1998. He was the top-ranked British golfer in 2007, finishing fifth in the US Masters that year and 12th in the world rankings.

## Cawdor

Cawdor was originally Calder, which in turn came from the French name de Cadella. Hugo de Cadella was an influential supporter of Malcolm Canmore, and his son Gilbert de Cadella was rewarded with lands in the county of Nairn, to which he gave the name Calder. Over the years Calder morphed into Cawdor.

## Cawdor Castle

At the end of the 14th century, the 3RD THANE OF CALDER, who lived in a small tower on a hillock about half a mile (0.8 km) away from the site of the present castle, decided he needed somewhere bigger and more secure for his family. In this aim he was aided by a vivid dream, in which he was advised to follow his donkey and build a new home wherever the animal lay down to sleep. The wretched creature chose to settle beneath a thorn tree and so the obedient Thane constructed his tower house around the tree, which is still there, in the ground-floor dungeon known as the Thorn Tree Room. The tree, which is actually a holly, has been dated to about 1372, which would indicate that the tower was built not long after that.

## Campbell Thanes

At the end of the 14th century, through a combination of marriage, bad luck and treachery, Cawdor passed out of the Calder family to the Campbells.

Sir John Campbell, 9th Thane of Cawdor, and his wife Muriel, the heiress, returned from Argyll when she had come of age, and after disposing of any remaining Calders who might have been minded to cause trouble, they settled down to consolidate their dynasty.

The Thanes of Cawdor grew rich and powerful, despite the occasional setback. The 11th Thane got into a clan feud and was dispatched with a blunderbuss; the 12th Thane bought the island of Islay and went bust; and the 13th Thane went insane, poisoned by his wife, who liked to experiment with new herbs from the garden – after one of her dinner parties three guests were found dead in their beds the next morning.

The 15th Thane lived in more peaceful times, and decided he could allow himself to greet visitors with mulled wine rather than boiling oil, and began the transformation of Cawdor Castle into the civilised abode it is today.

## Earls of Cawdor

A subsequent Thane, John Campbell (1768–1821), was made Baron Cawdor in 1797 after forcing the surrender of Napoleon's expeditionary force at Fishguard, during the last invasion of mainland Britain. His son was made 1ST EARL OF CAWDOR in 1827.

The 6TH EARL OF CAWDOR (1932–93) caused something of a stir by leaving Cawdor Castle to his second wife, Angelika Lazanky von Bukowa, who lives there today, rather than his son and heir, the present 7TH EARL OF CAWDOR.

There have been some 50 male Campbells of Cawdor since the days of Muriel, and between them they have garnered three VCs and 16 DSOs.

*Well, I never knew this*
*about*
**NAIRNSHIRE FOLK**

## James Augustus Grant
◄ 1827–92 ►

JAMES AUGUSTUS GRANT, soldier and explorer, was born in Nairn. Educated at Nairn Grammar School and Marischal College, Aberdeen,

Grant joined the Indian Army in 1846 and took part in the Sikh War of 1848–9, served through the Indian Mutiny of 1857 and was wounded at the Relief of Lucknow.

He returned to England in 1858, and in 1860 accompanied his Indian Army chum John Hanning Speke on his controversial expedition to find the source of the Nile – Speke's claim to have found the source of the White Nile in Lake Victoria was disputed by Richard Burton. Grant's record of their journey, *A Walk Across Africa*, gives an account of the lives of the natives they met, and a vivid description of the illness he contracted when they reached the western side of Lake Victoria.

For the last 20 years of his life Grant lived at his family home in Nairn. Grant's gazelle is named in his honour.

a template for the Good Friday Agreement of 1998. He acted as Margaret Thatcher's deputy prime minister for the first ten years of her premiership from 1979 to 1988.

## 'Willie' Whitelaw
◄ 1918–99 ►

*'Every prime minister needs a Willie'*
Margaret Thatcher

WILLIAM WHITELAW, soldier and politician, was born in Nairn. He served in the (Scots) Guards Tank Brigade during the Second World War, and in 1944 won a Military Cross at the Battle of Caumont for taking command of his tank unit and continuing the advance after his commanding officer had been killed. In 1972 he became the FIRST SECRETARY OF STATE FOR NORTHERN IRELAND, after the imposition of direct rule, and was one of those who contributed to the Sunningdale Agreement, which formed

Memorable Quotes:
*'It is never wise to appear to be more clever than you are. It is sometimes wise to appear slightly less so.'*

*'The Labour Party is going around stirring up apathy.'*

# Orkney and Shetland

Norse Earls of Orkney ✦ Sigurd and Maelbrigte
✦ St Magnus ✦ Scottish Earls of Orkney
✦ Sinclair Earls ✦ Duke of Orkney
✦ Stewart Earls of Orkney and Lords of Shetland
✦ Earls of Zetland ✦ Marquess of Zetland

*Skara Brae, in Orkney, Europe's
most complete Neolithic Village*

◄ Orkney and Shetland Folk ►

Thomas Stewart Traill ✦ Washington Irving ✦ Arthur Anderson
✦ Dr John Rae ✦ Edwin Muir ✦ George MacKay Brown
✦ James Isbister ✦ Norman Lamont ✦ Magnus Linklater ✦ Ian Bairnson

ORKNEY AND SHETLAND are Scotland's northern outposts, each with its own distinctive culture and identity.

The first settlers arrived on the islands sometime before 3,000 BC and built themselves stone houses and communities such as those found at Skara Brae on Orkney and Jarlshof on Shetland. The islands were subsequently occupied through the Bronze and Iron Ages, but by Picts and by Celts – never by Gaelic peoples.

For much of their history the islands all belonged to Norway, and the easternmost Shetlands are as near to Bergen as to Aberdeen.

The Norse heritage is evident in place names such as Stromness ('strong tide place') and in rituals such as Lerwick's 'Up Helly Aa'.

Orkney's flag, the St Magnus cross, uses the red and yellow colours of Scotland's lion rampant and the Norwegian royal coat of arms with the blue of the sea and a Nordic cross. The flag of Shetland, a white cross on a blue background, recalls the colours of the Scottish saltire, with the Nordic cross design.

## Norse Earls of Orkney

In 876 Harald Harfager, or Fairhair, the first king of a united Norway, conquered Orkney and Shetland and granted them to his companion-in-arms Rognvald 'the Wise' Eysteinsson, who became the first known Earl, or Jarl, of Orkney, ruling over not just Orkney but also Shetland and parts of Caithness and Sutherland. Rognvald himself returned to Norway and passed control to his brother Sigurd, making him the 2nd Earl. All subsequent Earls of Orkney until the 13th century were descended from these two brothers.

Rognvald's son Rollo became the first Earl of Normandy and his direct descendant was William the Conqueror, Duke of Normandy.

The Earls of Orkney were in effect independent Princes of Norway, subject to Norwegian Kings, and as the earldom also included parts of Caithness and Sutherland on the mainland, they were occasionally subject to the Kings of Alba as well.

## Sigurd and Maelbrigte

The story goes that Sigurd, 2nd Earl of Orkney, who mounted numerous raids on the mainland of what is now Scotland, on one of these occasions killed the Mormaer of Moray, Maelbrigte Tusk, known as such because of his protruding teeth. Following tradition, Sigurd cut off Maelbrigte's head and strapped it to his saddle, but as he was riding home Maelbrigte's teeth gouged a wound in the Earl's leg, which became infected, and before long Earl Sigurd was dead too.

## St Magnus

Throughout its history, the earldom was often shared between brothers and cousins, each of whom would look after a different part of their far-flung territory. Such was the case at the beginning of the 12th century when Haakon and his cousin Magnus, who was renowned as a pious and scholarly man, ruled jointly as Earls of Orkney.

At some point their respective followers began to squabble, and in 1116 the two Earls agreed to meet on the island of Egilsay to thrash things out. Treachery was afoot. While Magnus turned up alone, as had been agreed, Haakon brought a force of armed men and proceeded to stove in his gentle cousin's head with an axe. Magnus was buried where he lay and Haakon became the sole Earl.

Strange things began to happen. The bare ground where Magnus was buried suddenly sprouted grass and turned green, and there were reports of miraculous happenings and healings on the spot. Magnus's mother was permitted to bury her son's remains in the church on the island of Birsay, and the wonders continued, until the authorities thought there must be something in this and, in 1135, made Magnus a saint.

St Magnus's nephew Rognvald swore that if ever he became Earl of Orkney he would raise a great church in his uncle's memory, and when he did come to power Rognvald kept his promise. In 1137 he began the magnificent ST MAGNUS'S CATHEDRAL, in Kirkwall, which still stands today in tribute to the saintly Earl of Orkney.

Rognvald was himself murdered by relatives in 1158 and was likewise made a saint, by Pope Celestine 30 years later. He is also buried in the cathedral he built.

## Scottish Earls of Orkney

In 1232 the Norse earldom of Orkney passed through the female line to the Mormaers of Angus, and after that the now Scottish earldom worked its way down to Maol Iosa, Mormaer of Strathearn, all the while remaining subject to the Kings of Norway.

## Sinclair Earls

Maol Iosa's closest heir as Earl of Orkney was HENRY SINCLAIR (1345–1400), Maol's grandson by his daughter Isobel. Henry was the Norman baron of Roslin in Midlothian, and he was confirmed as Earl of Orkney by King Haakon VI of Norway in 1379.

Henry is best remembered for his epic voyage to Greenland with the Venetian sailor Antonio Zeno in 1398, during which he is rumoured to have discovered America.

In 1468 Princess Margaret, daughter of Christian I, King of Norway, was betrothed to James III of Scotland, and the Norwegian king pledged Orkney and Shetland as surety for her dowry. The money was never paid, and the islands have belonged to Scotland ever since – although the Norwegians, and plenty of islanders, prefer to think otherwise.

In 1470 King James persuaded the 3rd Earl of Orkney, William Sinclair, to give up his earldom to the Crown, in return for lands in Fife, and from that time it became a Stewart bauble.

# Duke of Orkney
## 1567

---

The first recipient of the bauble was JAMES HEPBURN, 4TH EARL OF BOTHWELL, who happened to be William Sinclair's great-great-grandson and could therefore claim to be legitimate heir to the last Earl of Orkney. When he married Mary Queen of Scots in 1567 as her third husband, he requested that she grant him the earldom, but she went one better and created him DUKE OF ORKNEY. His reign was brief, however. He had to give up the title later that year when Mary was forced to abdicate.

# Stewart Earls of Orkney and Lords of Shetland
## 1581–1614

---

In 1564 Mary awarded her half-brother Robert Stewart (1533–93), illegitimate son of James V, the royal estates in Orkney and Shetland. He proceeded to run them in a ruthless and tyrannical fashion, using the islanders as slave labour for his various construction projects, including a sumptuous palace at Birsay, on Orkney.

Stewart was eventually imprisoned in Edinburgh by the Earl of Morton, regent for the young James VI, when it turned out that he had committed treason by trying to sell Orkney to the King of Denmark.

When James came of age, however, he released Robert, and in 1581 created his rotten uncle the new Earl of Orkney and Lord of Shetland.

Robert's son PATRICK STEWART (1569–1615), the next Earl of Orkney, was even worse, forcing the islanders to 'all sorts of servile and painful labour, without either meat, drink or hire'. The results of all their labours were the huge castle at Scalloway, on Shetland, and the incredible Earl's Palace beside the cathedral in Kirkwall which, even in ruins, is regarded as THE FINEST RENAISSANCE BUILDING IN THE WHOLE OF SCOTLAND.

Earl Patrick was finally executed for treason in 1615, along with his own son Robert, and the earldom was forfeit. James VI finally swept away all the islanders' Norwegian laws and customs and replaced the Norwegian 'udal' tenure, by which farmers and individuals held the rights to the lands on which they worked and lived, with a feudal system of large estates occupied by tenant farmers.

The earldom of Orkney thereafter became more a ceremonial title, without the same rights of ownership

*Earls Palace, Kirkwall, Orkney*

as before, and it was this Scottish-style earldom that was bestowed upon Lord George Hamilton, 5th son of the Duke of Hamilton, when he was created Earl of Orkney in 1696.

The title has passed down through his family, sometimes through the female line, and the present incumbent is OLIVER PETER ST JOHN, 9TH EARL OF ORKNEY, born in 1938, who lives in Canada.

# Earls of Zetland

Z etland is a Norse name for Shetland. THE 1ST EARL OF ZETLAND WAS LAWRENCE DUNDAS (1766–1839), grandson of Sir Lawrence Dundas (1710–81).

Sir Lawrence was a businessman who had made his fortune by supplying the government army during the campaigns against the Jacobites and also during the Seven Years War in Flanders. He founded Grangemouth in Stirlingshire in 1769, and sponsored the construction of the Forth and Clyde Canal, which went through his estate at Kerse, near Falkland. His house in St Andrew Square in Edinburgh became the headquarters of the Royal Bank of Scotland (*see* Midlothian). Sir Lawrence bought many properties, including an estate with lands on both Orkney and Shetland.

Sir Lawrence's son THOMAS DUNDAS (1741–1820) was responsible for commissioning the *Charlotte Dundas*, the world's first practical

## Marquess of Zetland

The 2nd Earl's nephew, LAWRENCE DUNDAS, 3RD EARL OF ZETLAND (1844–1929), was created MARQUESS OF ZETLAND in 1892 at the end of his three-year term as Lord Lieutenant of Ireland.

His son LAWRENCE, 2ND MARQUESS OF ZETLAND (1876–1961), was Governor of Bengal and Secretary of State for India, as well as president of the Royal Geographical Society and the first chairman of the National Trust.

The 3rd Marquess was a fine tennis player who played in the Wimbledon championships in the 1940s, and the present incumbent is MARK DUNDAS, 4TH MARQUESS OF ZETLAND, who was born in 1937 and lives in Aske Hall in Yorkshire, bought by Sir Lawrence Dundas in 1763.

The present Marquess's younger brother LORD DAVID DUNDAS (b.1945) is a musician and composer who wrote the Channel 4 jingle that was heard before every programme for the first ten years of the channel. He also wrote the original score for the 1987 film *Withnail and I* and had a UK hit with 'Jeans On' (as in 'I pull my old blue jeans on'), which reached No. 3 in the UK charts in 1976 – he had originally written it as a jingle for the Brutus Jeans television advertisement.

steamboat, for use on the Forth and Clyde canal. The boat was named after his daughter. Thomas served as Lord Lieutenant of Orkney and Shetland.

Thomas's son Lawrence, who also served as Lord Lieutenant of Orkney and Shetland, was created an Earl in 1838 by Queen Victoria, as a reward for giving financial assistance to her parents, the Duke and Duchess of Kent. He chose to use Zetland as the name for his title since it was the favourite of all his estates.

His son THOMAS, 2ND EARL OF ZETLAND (1795–1873), owned a famous racehorse, VOLTIGEUR, who won the Derby and the St Leger in 1850. The following year Voltigeur and the winner of that year's Derby, The Flying Dutchman, owned by the Earl of Eglinton, raced each other at York for 1,000 guineas. The Flying Dutchman won what became known as the Great Match.

*Well, I never knew this about*

## ORKNEY AND SHETLAND FOLK

THOMAS STEWART TRAILL (1781–1862), medical professor, was born in Kirkwall, Orkney. He befriended the Arctic explorer William Scoresby, who named Traill Island in Greenland in his honour. In 1826 Traill found a publisher for John James Audubon's celebrated book *The Birds of America*, and Audubon subsequently named the Traill's Flycatcher after him. Traill also edited the eighth edition of the *Encyclopaedia Britannica*.

*Washington Irving*

WASHINGTON IRVING (1783–1859), American writer, whose parents moved to New York from Orkney. He is best remembered for his short stories, 'The Legend of Sleepy Hollow' and 'Rip Van Winkle'.

## Arthur Anderson
### ◄ 1792–1868 ►

ARTHUR ANDERSON, co-founder of P&O, was born in Bod of Gremista near Lerwick, Shetland, and worked as a boy with the local fishermen, gutting and cleaning fish. At the age of 16 he was pressed, like many other Shetlanders, into the Royal Navy, which was desperate for men to fight in the Napoleonic Wars.

In 1815, when the war was over and he was no longer needed, Anderson was cast out in London, 600 miles (965 km) from home, with no money and nowhere to live. He eventually found a job as a clerk for a dour shipbroker called Brodie McGhie Willcox, and by 1822 they had become partners. In 1826 they took over as London agents for the hugely successful City of Dublin Steam Packet Co., and this led to the partners developing a steamship business for freight and passengers between Britain and the Iberian peninsula, under the name of the Peninsular Steam Navigation Company.

In 1837 the British government awarded them the contract to carry mail to Spain and Portugal, the first time such a contract had been given to a commercial shipping company, and their reputation for reliability led in 1840 to another contract to carry mail to Britain's empire in the east, under their new name, the Peninsular and Oriental Steam Navigation Co., or P&O.

Passengers were always P&O's most important business, and in 1844 they introduced the world's first pleasure cruise, on which they gave free passage to the distinguished writer William Makepeace Thackeray on the condition that he gave them favourable publicity.

Anderson was not too busy to remember his Shetland roots. From 1847 to 1852 he served as MP for Orkney and Shetland, and he founded the *Shetland Journal*, the Shetland Fishery Company and a home for Shetland fishermen's widows.

By the time of Arthur Anderson's death in 1868, P&O owned the largest commercial fleet of steamships in the world.

# Dr John Rae
## ◄ 1813–93 ►

DR JOHN RAE, arctic explorer, was born in the Hall of Clestrain in Orphir, Orkney. He studied medicine in Edinburgh and then, like so many Orcadians, joined the Hudson's Bay Company, in his case as a doctor. While serving at the fur-trading post at Moose Factory, the first English-

speaking settlement in Ontario, he made a study of the local Inuits, learning how to use snowshoes, live off the land and travel great distances with little equipment.

In 1848 he joined Sir John Richardson's expedition to find the Northwest Passage, and in 1853 he was able to put his skills to good use in search of the two missing ships from the Franklin Expedition. While exploring King William Island he received reports from the local Inuit suggesting that the last survivors of the expedition had resorted to cannibalism. When he informed the Admiralty of his findings, Franklin's widow was outraged and Rae was condemned. For a while he was written out of history, despite the fact that he had discovered the last link in the Northwest Passage.

Dr Rae was buried quietly in the kirkyard of St Magnus's Cathedral and there is a fine memorial to him inside. His reputation has been restored somewhat in recent years, and his research into the Inuits and their cold survival techniques has won him many admirers.

EDWIN MUIR (1887–1959), the poet and novelist, born on a farm in Deerness, Orkney. His idyllic childhood among the islands inspired a clear poetic style that was simple and uncluttered; his unhappy time as a young adult in Glasgow, when his whole family died within two years of each other, added a darker depth and tension to his work. An important figure in the Scottish literary renaissance, he wrote in English, rather than Scots, so as not to restrict his audience, a decision which caused frequent clashes with the Scottish nationalist writer Hugh MacDiarmid.

GEORGE MACKAY BROWN (1921–96), poet, born in Stromness, Orkney, and spent all his life in the islands, apart from a brief spell as a mature student at the University of Edinburgh. Orkney was the inspiration for his work, which included poems and novels drawn from Orkney's history and legends. In 1987 he won the James Tait Black Memorial Prize for *The Golden Bird: Two Orkney Stories*, and in 1994 he was nominated for the Booker Prize. Many of his works were put to music by PETER MAXWELL DAVIES (b.1934), Master of the Queen's Music, who has lived in Orkney since 1971 and founded the St Magnus Arts Festival in 1977.

JAMES ISBISTER (1913–40), farm labourer, was the first civilian to lose his life in the Second World War, when a stray bomb fell on his cottage near the Brig o' Waithe, Stenness, Orkney, on 16 March 1940, during an air raid on Scapa Flow.

NORMAN LAMONT, politician, born in Shetland in 1942. He ran John Major's campaign to replace Margaret Thatcher as leader of the Conservative Party and Prime Minister in 1991 and was Chancellor of the Exchequer during 'Black Wednesday' in 1992.

Memorable Quote:
*'Je ne regrette rien.'*

MAGNUS LINKLATER, freelance writer, journalist and newspaper editor, born in Harray, Orkney, in 1942, the son of Eric Linklater, who was also a writer. (Linklater is a Norse name.) Currently a columnist for *The*

*Times*, Magnus was editor of *The Scotsman* from 1988 until 1994 and chairman of the Scottish Arts Council from 1996 to 2001. He has written a number of books on politics and Scottish history.

IAN BAIRNSON, musician, was born in 1953 in Levenwick, Shetland. Guitarist and producer for the band Pilot, he was a core member of the Alan Parsons Project and is renowned for his guitar solo on Kate Bush's 1978 No. 1 hit 'Wuthering Heights'.

# Peeblesshire

---◆◆◆◆---

NEIDPATH CASTLE ✦ OLD Q ✦ TRAQUAIR
✦ EARL OF TRAQUAIR

*Neidpath Castle, set above the River Tweed,
built by the Frasers, refurbished by the Hays and
childhood home of the Duke of Queensberry.*

◄ PEEBLESSHIRE FOLK ►

John Porteous ✦ Sir John Elliot ✦ William and Robert Chambers
✦ Robert Smail ✦ Margot Asquith

# Neidpath Castle

—•◄••►•—

The first NEIDPATH CASTLE was built on a bluff high above the River Tweed in the 13th century by the Fraser family, when they were Sheriffs of Tweeddale. Tweeddale is the name given to the upper reaches of the River Tweed from its source to where it is joined by the Lyne Water, west of Peebles.

John Hay, the 2nd Earl of Tweeddale, remodelled Neidpath and planted an avenue of yew trees, some of which survive. He was later declared bankrupt and sold Neidpath to WILLIAM DOUGLAS, 1ST MARQUESS OF QUEENSBERRY, in 1686.

# Old Q

—•◄••►•—

When the Marquess of Queensberry bought Neidpath off John Hay, he gave it to his second son Lord William Douglas, who was created Viscount of Peebles by William III, as well as 1st Earl of March. His descendant, WILLIAM DOUGLAS, 3RD VISCOUNT PEEBLES AND 3RD EARL OF MARCH, later 4th Duke of Queensberry and known as OLD Q, was born in 1725 in his family's town house in Peebles. In his younger years he used Neidpath Castle as his main home.

Made fatherless when he was only six, Old Q grew up without an education, but instead dedicated his life to pleasure and to the Turf. By the time he was 21 he was a successful jockey and had built up a widely admired stud. As an owner he was the first to have his jockeys 'ride to order' – the order usually being that the horses of his deadly enemy the Duke of Bedford should, at all costs, be prevented from winning.

A keen betting man, Douglas devised countless unusual wagers to enable him to clean up, including one where he bet that he could have a letter transported from A to B at 50 miles per hour (80 kph), twice as fast as anyone was capable of travelling at that time. He then lined up a team of cricketers and had them throw to each other a cricket ball into which the letter was sewn. The letter reached its destination with time to spare and Douglas raked in the loot. One of his unsuccessful bets was that George III would not recover from his first bout of insanity – the King did get better and unceremoniously sacked Douglas as Lord of the Bedchamber.

Douglas became 4th Duke of Queensberry rather unexpectedly in 1778 after the rightful heir, Henry, Lord Drumlanrig, accidentally shot himself dead while riding through Yorkshire, and the next heir, Henry's younger brother Charles, finally expired of a nervous disposition caused long before when he was

caught up in the Lisbon earthquake of 1755.

Along with his other passions, Old Q was most fond of the ladies, especially young prima donnas, and in pursuit of this high calling he became a great patron of the Italian opera, showing a kindly concern for a 15-year-old singer called La Zamparini, and later for two others, La Rena and La Tondino.

Such qualities made Old Q a shoe-in for Sir Francis Dashwood's Hellfire Club, at whose gatherings he was able fully to indulge his healthy appetites. A more personal obsession, however, was a young woman called Maria Fagniani, over whom he disputed paternity with the MP George Selwyn. Maria married the Earl of Yarmouth in 1798, and in order to raise money for her dowry, Old Q cut down vast swathes of the woodland at Neidpath, denuding the banks of the Tweed of their beautiful timber and provoking an indignant sonnet from William Wordsworth.

*Degenerate Douglas! Oh, the
    unworthy Lord,
Whom mere despite of heart could
    so far please,
And love of havock, (for with such
    disease
Fame taxes him,) that he could
    send forth word
To level with the dust a noble
    horde,
A brotherhood, of venerable trees*
. . .

Old Q also decimated the woods around his Dumfriesshire home at Drumlanrig, earning the wrath of Robert Burns, who wrote a searing poem about it on the window of a nearby inn – 'Verses on the Destruction of the Woods near Drumlanrig'.

In his later years Old Q retired to the house he had built for himself in London's Piccadilly, where he spent many fruitful hours sitting at his bow window admiring the girls passing by outside, while his butler called out their names. His Grace's horse was kept tethered in readiness at the door, in case the master should spot some particularly fine young lady and need to ride out after her. Eventually, however, despite sustaining his libido by partaking of hot buttered muffins plucked from the mouths of dairymaids, while bathing in asses' milk scented with almonds, the Duke reached a stage in life where he found his window seat so restful that he no longer felt the need to move from it. An acquaintance who went out to India to make his fortune returned ten years later to find Old Q sitting in exactly the same spot as when he had left.

When Old Q died childless at the age of 85, of a 'severe flux', possibly brought on by the frisky charms of his latest companion, a beauty known as the Hottentot Venus, his various titles were dissipated, and the Viscountcy of Peebles (along with the Earldom of March) was picked up by Francis Charteris, 8th Earl of Wemyss, who was a descendant of the 1st Viscount Peebles's sister Lady Anne Douglas.

The title has remained as a subsidiary title of the Earls of Wemyss and March to this day.

There is a Neidpath in Saskatchewan, which was named after Neidpath Castle in Peeblesshire by the Canadian settlement's first postmaster, John Mitchell, whose family emigrated to Canada from Peebles in the 19th century.

# Traquair

The 1st Earl of Traquair was John Stewart, 7th Laird, who was created Earl in 1633 by Charles I.

Traquair is possibly THE OLDEST INHABITED HOUSE IN SCOTLAND, and certainly one of the most romantic.

Hidden away in the glorious Tweed valley near Innerleithen, the present building, once described as a 'grey forlorn-looking mansion, stricken all over with eld', clusters around a 12th-century peel tower and seems to have been there longer than the very hills that surround it. Traquair began life as a royal hunting lodge, possibly built by Alexander I, and was said to be the favourite residence of William the Lion.

Gifted to Sir James Douglas by Robert the Bruce in the 14th century, the estate passed through a number of hands before being returned to the Crown. In 1469 James III gave Traquair to his unpopular favourite, Dr William Rogers, described as a 'Master of Music'.

James III's uncle, the Earl of Buchan, known as Hearty James, decided that he would like Traquair as a home for one of his sons and persuaded the unfortunate doctor to sell up on favourable terms by having him strung up by his feet from a bridge over the Tweed. In this way the estate came to James Stewart, the Earl's natural son, who was named 1ST LAIRD OF TRAQUAIR and whose descendants still live there today.

The 1st Laird fell at Flodden in 1513, leaving a son, William, who made considerable additions to the house. The 4th Laird, John Stewart, was knighted by his kinswoman Mary Queen of Scots, becoming Sir John

Stuart. (He took the new French spelling of the family name, which Mary had adopted as Queen of France – there being no 'w' in the French alphabet.) Mary appointed him captain of the Queen's Guard, in which role he helped her escape from Holyrood after the murder of her favourite Rizzio, which had been organised by her jealous husband Lord Darnley. Mary and Darnley came to stay at Traquair not long afterwards on a hunting trip, and Sir John made plain his disapproval of Darnley's manners and attitude, rebuking him over dinner for calling the Queen his 'mare'.

## Earl of Traquair

It was his son, Sir John Stuart, the 7th Laird, who was made EARL OF TRAQUAIR in 1633 and became Lord High Treasurer, in effect the most powerful man in Scotland after the King. Stuart was undone by attempting to steer a middle path between Charles I and the Covenanters, and in 1641 he was dismissed from office and forced to retire to Traquair, where he spent his time improving the house and environs, including diverting the River Tweed until it ran 'so conveniently near that the laird could fish for salmon from his bedroom window . . .'

The Earl's only involvement in the subsequent Civil War was to refuse shelter to the Marquess of Montrose after his defeat at the Battle of Philiphaugh in 1645, but the following year Charles I once more sought Traquair's support, which resulted in the Earl being captured at the Battle of Preston and imprisoned at Warwick Castle for four years. Evicted from Traquair by his enemies and left with nothing, he was reduced to begging in the streets of Edinburgh and died in 1659 under the unflattering title of the 'Beggar Earl' – just one year before the Restoration of Charles II, which belatedly restored Traquair and the family fortunes to the Beggar Earl's son John.

John was a staunch Catholic and married two staunchly Catholic wives. These were dangerous times to be a Catholic and John had a secret staircase built, hidden behind a cupboard in the upstairs room where they celebrated Mass, as a means of escape should the house be searched by the Puritans.

Charles, the 4th Earl, was not only a Catholic but a Jacobite, and was imprisoned in Edinburgh Castle during the 1715 Jacobite uprising. His wife was sister to the 5th Earl of Nithsdale, who was rescued by his own wife from the Tower of London where he had been sent for his Jacobite sympathies. Letters kept at Traquair written between Lady Traquair and Lady Nithsdale paint a vivid picture of those perilous times.

In 1745 Bonnie Prince Charlie stayed at Traquair as a guest of the 5th Earl, a stay that by all accounts was full of carefree partying and jollity – the calm before the gathering storm that would reach its climax at Culloden. As the Prince bade his farewell on that golden autumn morning, the Earl shut the Bear Gates, at the top of the driveway, behind his

rightful King and made a vow that never again would they be opened until a Stuart king was crowned in London. They have remained closed ever since.

The earldom of Traquair became extinct in 1681 with the death of the 8th Earl, who died childless. He had resisted the efforts of his relatives to find him a bride by putting stinging nettles and dead wasps in the beds of lady visitors seeking matrimony, and so the Traquair estate passed to his sister Lady Louisa Stuart, who lived to be 100.

On her death Traquair was inherited by William Maxwell, a younger son of the 9th Lord Herries and descendant of the 5th Earl of Nithsdale and the 4th Earl of Traquair. He added Stuart to his name and Traquair today is home to the widow and daughter of Peter Maxwell-Stuart, the 20th Laird, who died in 1990 having, amongst other achievements, restored the famous Traquair Brew House, which continues to produce much-praised traditional real ale.

*Well, I never knew this*
*about*
**PEEBLESSHIRE FOLK**

## John Porteous
━━● 1695–1736 ●━━

Captain of the Edinburgh city guard and cause of the Porteous Riots of 1736, JOHN PORTEOUS was born at The Glen, near Traquair. On 14 April 1736, convicted smuggler Andrew Wilson was hanged in the Grassmarket in Edinburgh for the crime of robbing a customs officer who had reduced him to penury. The sympathy of the crowd was with Wilson, and they expressed their outrage by throwing things and threatening the hangman. Captain Porteous was ordered to quell the mob and attempted to do so by ordering his troops to fire over their heads, which unfortunately resulted in the death or wounding of some 30 people who had been viewing the scene from upstairs windows.

Porteous was arrested and sentenced to be hanged, but he appealed to the King in London and his sentence was deferred. This enraged the crowd, who did not like seeing an official spared where one of their own had been condemned, and

they stormed the Tolbooth where Porteous was being held, dragged him out, beat him and strung him up in the Grassmarket. Honour satisfied, they dispersed. Porteous was buried in Greyfriars churchyard the following morning, and fearful of further inflaming the situation, the authorities never convicted anyone of his murder.

The PORTEOUS RIOTS, as they became known, are depicted in the early chapters of Sir Walter Scott's 1818 novel *The Heart of Midlothian*.

John Porteous was one of the contestants in THE FIRST GOLF MATCH EVER RECORDED IN A NEWSPAPER, in 1724. The 'solemn match of golf' between Porteous and the Hon. Alexander Elphinstone was played out in front of the Duke of Hamilton and a large audience, with Elphinstone the winner of the 20 guineas prize money.

SIR JOHN ELLIOT (1736–86), physician to George, Prince of Wales, later George IV, was born in Peebles. In 1771 he married GRACE DALRYMPLE, born in Edinburgh, the daughter of an advocate, who became a celebrated courtesan known as Dolly the Tall and was mistress to, amongst many others, Lord Valentia, Lord Cholmondeley, Charles Windham, George Selwyn, the Duke of Orleans and the Prince of Wales himself – possibly but not probably all at the same time. She and Sir John were divorced in 1774. There is a noted portrait of her by Thomas Gainsborough that belongs to the Frick Collection in New York.

# Chambers Brothers

WILLIAM CHAMBERS (1800–83) and ROBERT CHAMBERS (1802–71) were both born in a house built by their grandfather in Peebles Old Town, sons of a wealthy mill-owning family. Inspired by the discovery of an *Encyclopaedia Britannica* hidden away in a chest in their attic, they set up together as publishers, and in 1832 began producing *Chambers's Journal,* a weekly newspaper covering science, literature, religion and a comprehen-

sive list of other subjects.

William Chambers also wrote numerous travel books, did good works in Peebles, rescuing the tower of old St Andrew's Church and deeding the Chambers Institute to the town as an art gallery and museum. In 1865 he became Provost of Edinburgh, set about improving the Old Town and, at his own expense, arranged for the restoration of St Giles's Cathedral, or the High Kirk of St Giles. He died three days before the work was completed, and the first service held in the newly refurbished church was his own funeral. He is remembered in Edinburgh by Chambers Street.

Robert wrote books on history, including *Traditions of Edinburgh* (1824), *Popular Rhymes of Scotland* (1826), *Dictionary of Eminent Scotchmen* (1835), *Romantic Scottish Ballads* (1859) and *Domestic Annals of Scotland* (1856–61), and composed songs and ballads.

The Chambers Brothers' most famous legacies are the CHAMBERS ENCYCLOPAEDIA and the CHAMBERS DICTIONARY, which contains a larger selection of words and definitions than any other single-volume dictionary and is a favourite with crossword and Scrabble enthusiasts.

Chambers is still based in Edinburgh today. In 1990 they purchased the independent Harrap, publisher of bilingual dictionaries, and in 2008 acquired the Brewer's list from Orion, which includes *Brewer's Dictionary of Phrase and Fable.*

ROBERT SMAIL, printer, who in 1847 established a stationery shop and printers in Innerleithen, which remained in the Smail family until 1985, when Cowan Smail retired and the property was acquired by the National Trust for Scotland. R. Smail & Sons is one of the few operational letterpress printers left in Scotland, and much of the printing equipment dates back to Victorian days. The works is now run as a museum.

MARGOT ASQUITH (1864–1945), wife of Prime Minister Henry Herbert Asquith, was born Margot Tennant on the Tennant family estate in Peeblesshire. The Tennants were wealthy industrialists (*see* Ayrshire). Margot Asquith was noted for her glittering social life, acerbic wit and outspokenness.

Memorable Quotes:
*'Lord Kitchener – if not a great man he was, at least, a great poster.'*

*'Lord Birkenhead is very clever but sometimes his brains go to his head.'*

*'What a pity, when Christopher Columbus discovered America, that he ever mentioned it.'*

*'He could not see a belt without hitting below it.'* (Of Lloyd George)

*'He has a brilliant mind until he makes it up.'* (Of Sir Stafford Cripps)

# Perthshire

---

CLAN MURRAY ✦ MARQUESS OF ATHOLL
✦ DUKES OF ATHOLL ✦ LORD GEORGE MURRAY
✦ BLAIR CASTLE ✦ SOME NOTABLE MURRAYS
✦ GLENEAGLES ✦ HALDANES ✦ UNION JACK
✦ COLOURS AND LIMES ✦ BRODRICK CHINNERY-HALDANE
✦ SOME NOTABLE HALDANES

*Scone Palace, home of the largest room in Scotland
and site of the last coronation in Scotland,
that of Charles II in 1651.*

---

◄ PERTHSHIRE FOLK ►

---

Adam Ferguson ✦ Carolina Oliphant ✦ Helen Duncan
✦ Colonel David Stirling ✦ Denis Lawson ✦ Ewan McGregor

# Clan Murray

The Murrays are descended from an early 12th-century Flemish nobleman called FRESKIN. As a thank-you for his help in driving the Norse out of Sutherland, Freskin was granted lands in the old mormaerdom of Moray by David I. Freskin's family intermarried with the line of Celtic mormaers and began to call themselves de Moravia, de Moray and then just Murray.

A famous ANDREW MURRAY, the builder of the mighty Bothwell Castle in Lanarkshire, was leader of the Murrays at the Battle of Stirling Bridge in 1297 and was mortally wounded there. His son SIR ANDREW MURRAY married Robert the Bruce's sister Christian and led the Murrays at the Battle of Halidon Hill in 1333.

Around that time, the son of MALCOLM DE MORAVIA married Ada, heiress to the lands of Tullibardine in the Ochil Hills of Perthshire, and established a family seat there. In 1446 they built the exquisite little TULLIBARDINE CHAPEL, which remains today as one of the medieval jewels of Scotland.

Andrew Murray, younger brother of the 9TH LAIRD OF TULLIBARDINE, was made LORD STORMONT, and from him came the MANSFIELD MURRAYS OF SCONE.

# Marquess of Atholl
## 1631–1703

In 1604 John Murray was made EARL OF TULLIBARDINE. His son married the heiress to the earldom of Atholl, once a Stewart plaything, making their son the FIRST MURRAY EARL OF ATHOLL in 1629. His son John was created 1ST MARQUESS OF ATHOLL in 1676 by Charles II, in recognition of his support for the Stuart cause against the invasion of Scotland by Oliver Cromwell's forces. He was THE FIRST CAPTAIN-GENERAL OF THE ROYAL COMPANY OF ARCHERS. In 1685, on behalf of James VII, he put down a rising in Scotland led by the Earl of Argyll in support of the Monmouth Rebellion, and he allowed his troops to fight for the Jacobites at the Battle of Killiecrankie.

## 1st Duke of Atholl
### 1660–1724

John Murray, the son of the Marquess, supported William of Orange during the Glorious Revolution in 1688 but, like his father, was powerless to stop most of the Clan Murray of which he was Chief joining Bonnie Dundee at Killiecrankie. In 1703, on the death of his father, he was made IST DUKE OF ATHOLL by Queen Anne.

The Duke's second son James Murray, who would become 2ND DUKE OF ATHOLL (1690–1764), stayed clear of the Jacobite uprisings, but three of James's brothers each commanded a regiment of Atholl men under the Earl of Mar during the 1715 rebellion. William Murray, Marquess of Tullibardine, the heir to the dukedom, was subsequently stripped of his titles and rights by the Hanoverians. Middle brother Lord Charles Murray was captured at the Battle of Preston, while the youngest, Lord George Murray, went on to be the Young Pretender's Lieutenant-General during the 1745 uprising.

When Bonnie Prince Charlie landed in Eriskay in the Outer Hebrides in 1745, William Murray was one of the Seven Men of Moidart who landed with him. After raising their standard at Glenfinnan they marched on the Murrays' own Blair Castle, which guarded the route from the Highlands, and Duke James was forced to flee, while William entertained the Prince at his ancestral home.

## Lord George Murray
### 1694–1760

William's younger brother George joined the rebels at Perth and became their key military strategist, executing a brilliant victory against the Hanoverians at the Battle of Prestonpans. He advised against Bonnie Prince Charlie's headlong invasion of England, finally persuading the other commanders to make the Prince turn back at Derby. Murray then managed to pull off the difficult retreat to Scotland and even secured another fine victory over the English at Falkirk.

On 15 March 1746, Lord George Murray laid siege to his own family's home, Blair Castle, which was garrisoned by government troops, but didn't have time to press home the attack before being called away to Culloden. This was THE LAST-EVER SIEGE OF A CASTLE IN BRITAIN.

Prince Charles once again ignored Murray's advice not to make a stand against the Duke of Cumberland or, if determined on it, to make a stand somewhere other than the moors at

Culloden. In the end Murray's men were the only group to escape the slaughter relatively unscathed. Lord George Murray retired to Holland, where he lived out his life in exile.

## 6th Duke of Atholl
### 1814–94

GEORGE MURRAY, 6TH DUKE OF ATHOLL, founded the ATHOLL HIGHLANDERS in 1839 to provide himself with a grand retinue and bodyguard with which to attend the Eglinton Tournament. When his wife had Queen Victoria to stay, Her Majesty was so delighted with the chivalrous treatment she received that she presented the Atholl Highlanders with their own colours and granted them the right to bear arms – today they remain Britain's only legitimate private army.

## 8th Duke of Atholl
### 1871–1942

JOHN STEWART-MURRAY, 8TH DUKE OF ATHOLL, fought at the Battle of Khartoum and raised the Scottish Horse regiment for the Boer War in 1900. His wife Kitty, who became known as the 'Red Duchess',

because of her support for Loyalist Spain and general opposition to Neville Chamberlain's Conservatives, was elected as MP for Kinross and West Perthshire in 1923, becoming THE FIRST SCOTTISH WOMAN MP, and in 1924 was appointed by Stanley Baldwin as Parliamentary Secretary to the Board of Education, THE FIRST-EVER FEMALE CONSERVATIVE MINISTER.

## Blair Castle

BLAIR CASTLE was actually begun by John Comyn, Lord of Badenoch. In 1296 he sneaked on to the lands of the Strathbogie Earl of Atholl, who was busying himself on crusade, and put up a small tower with immensely thick walls from which to go hunting and exercise power in the district. On his return the Earl complained to Alexander III and Comyn was forced to turn over the tower to Atholl, who realised at once what a splendid site this was on which to build a home. It has been the seat of the Atholls of all persuasion ever since, and the original tower, known as Cummings's tower, still stands at its heart. The castle was extended in the 15th and 16th centuries, garrisoned by both the Great Montrose and Bonnie Dundee (who is buried nearby), and rebuilt by the 2nd Duke of Atholl after his brother Lord George Murray had laid siege to it in 1745. In the 19th century Blair was made into a Scottish baronial edifice by DAVID BRYCE (1803–76), also known for Fettes College and Torosay Castle on Mull.

## Some Notable Murrays

WILLIAM MURRAY, 1ST EARL OF MANSFIELD (1705–93), judge and FIRST SCOT TO BECOME LORD CHANCELLOR OF GREAT BRITAIN. His affection and respect for his black adopted daughter Dido Elizabeth Belle, natural daughter of his nephew Sir John Lindsay and a black slave girl, no doubt influenced his courageous and momentous verdict in favour of the runaway slave James Somerset in 1772, which was THE FIRST IMPORTANT STEP TOWARDS THE ABOLITION OF SLAVERY.

GENERAL JAMES MURRAY (1721–94), British army officer who fought at the

*William Murray,*
*1st Earl of Mansfield*

Battle of Quebec in 1759. He was made military governor of Quebec and was later appointed as the FIRST GOVERNOR-GENERAL OF CANADA, during which time he was criticised for being too soft on the French.

THE REVD LORD GEORGE MURRAY (1761–1803), second son of the 3rd Duke of Atholl, and inventor of the SHUTTER TELEGRAPH. In 1796 Murray developed a system of pivoting shutters that could encode messages letter by letter and transmit them via a chain of relay stations positioned on high ground about 11 miles (18 km) apart. Using Murray's shutter telegraph, messages could be sent between the Admiralty in London and the navy ships in Portsmouth harbour in a matter of minutes. After the Napoleonic Wars this system was replaced by the French semaphore system invented in 1791 by Claude Chappe.

SIR JOHN MURRAY (1841–1914), oceanographer. After studying geology at Edinburgh University, Murray took part in the four-year Challenger Expedition to study the oceans. In 1883 he set up BRITAIN'S FIRST MARINE LABORATORY in Edinburgh and then moved it to Millport on Great Cumbrae as the Scottish Marine Station. He invented the term 'OCEANOGRAPHY', was the FIRST OCEANOGRAPHER and discovered THE MID-ATLANTIC RIDGE.

SIR DAVID MURRAY, chairman of Glasgow Rangers Football Club, was born in 1951. He made his fortune in the steel industry and despite losing both legs in a car crash in 1976 he has gone on to build up a huge business empire. In 1996 he established the Murray Foundation to help amputees.

ANDY MURRAY, tennis player, born in Dunblane in 1987. In 1996, while attending the Dunblane Primary School, he took refuge in the headmaster's study during the Dunblane massacre in which 16 children and a teacher were shot dead. Murray was THE FIRST SCOT EVER TO PLAY ON THE CENTRE COURT AT WIMBLEDON and has got further in the championship than any Scot before. In 2005 he became BRITAIN'S YOUNGEST-EVER DAVIS CUP PLAYER, competing in a doubles match against Israel.

# Gleneagles

❖

Gleneagles does not mean glen of eagles, but comes from the Gaelic 'eigeis', meaning a learned man, or possibly 'eaglais', a church, and so means either the 'glen in which a learned man lived' or the 'glen of the church'. The celebrated hotel and golf resort of Gleneagles is a Victorian construction that purloined the name from the genuine Gleneagles as described below.

# Haldanes

❖

Gleneagles has been the home of the HALDANES since the late 12th century when SIR ROGER DE HAUDEN is recorded as having a charter of lands in Perthshire. He was a descendant of the French knight SIR BERNARD DE HAUDEN who, in the mid 12th century, had obtained the lands of HAUDEN in the Borders. The name Haldane is derived from these lands.

GLENEAGLES CASTLE was begun in the 13th century, and in the next century Sir Bernard de Haldane (1340–1401) acquired more land at Gleneagles by exchanging some of his estate in Lanarkshire. By the start of the 15th century the head of the family felt proprietorial enough to call himself SIR JOHN HALDANE OF GLENEAGLES (1401–56).

A later Sir John Haldane of Gleneagles (1481–1513) was killed at Flodden, and another Sir John died fighting for the Covenanters at the Battle of Dunbar in 1650. The latter Sir John is believed to have begun the present GLENEAGLES HOUSE in 1624.

Parliament of Great Britain. He lost money in the disastrous Darien Scheme and fought at the Battle of Killiecrankie for the Hanoverians. He married MARY DRUMMOND, whose family opened SCOTLAND'S OLDEST FREE LENDING LIBRARY in INNERPEFFRAY in 1680. Amongst the library's treasures is the French pocket bible carried into battle by the great Marquess of Montrose, and which bears his signature.

In the mid 18th century, Union Jack's son Mungo extended Gleneagles House, adding two wings and leaving a space in the centre for the main house. This was never built, but the Gleneagles House of today, while less grand than intended, is an attractive example of rambling, unpretentious Scottish architecture.

## Union Jack

JOHN HALDANE OF GLENEAGLES (1660–1721), known as 'UNION JACK', was a staunch supporter of the Union in 1703, and was rewarded with a seat in the first

## Colours and Limes

In the late 18th century ADMIRAL ADAM DUNCAN, 1ST VISCOUNT CAMPERDOWN (1731–1804), victor of the Battle of Camperdown and a cousin of the 18th Laird, inherited Gleneagles through

an entail executed by Robert Haldane of Airthrey and Gleneagles in 1766. To commemorate Camperdown, an avenue of lime trees was planted, which still leads down to the house today.

The Battle of Camperdown, in 1797, was a British naval victory over a Dutch fleet attempting to break out of the ports of northern Holland to support a French invasion of Ireland. During the battle part of the mast on Admiral Duncan's flagship *Venerable* was shot away, along with the Admiral's flag. Lowering the flag was a sign of surrender, and so a quick-thinking sailor, Jack Crawford, climbed up what was left of the mast and nailed the flag back on to the top. From this action we get the expression 'to nail your colours to the mast'.

Admiral Duncan's example was an inspiration to Lord Nelson, who carried a miniature of Duncan in his cabin while at sea.

The Gleneagles estate under the entail reverted to a Haldane – JAMES BRODRICK CHINNERY-HALDANE – in 1918, when the 4th Earl of Camperdown renounced his rights.

# *Brodrick Chinnery-Haldane*

James's son BRODRICK became a society photographer, described by Cecil Beaton as the 'founder of modern society photography'. He was one of the few allowed to take photographs of the reclusive George Bernard Shaw, once showered the Aga Khan with exploding glass and was doused in champagne by the Duke of Westminster. Amongst those he photographed were Marlene Dietrich, Charlie Chaplin, Noël Coward and Vladimir Nabokov. He appeared in a number of films including *Murder at Monte Carlo*, with Errol Flynn, and *Get Your Man*, with Rex Harrison. He used to stand on his head for five minutes every morning to ensure his hair would keep growing.

The present Laird of Gleneagles is MARTIN HALDANE OF GLENEAGLES, who was born in 1941.

# Some Notable Haldanes

RICHARD HALDANE, 1ST VISCOUNT HALDANE (1856–1928), was co-founder of the London School of Economics (LSE), and in 1905 he was appointed Secretary for War in Sir Henry Campbell-Bannerman's government. Tasked with reorganising the military, he created the GENERAL STAFF, established the TERRITORIAL ARMY as a reserve unit and devised the idea of the EXPEDITIONARY FORCE. He twice served as Lord Chancellor, once for the Liberals and once for Labour, and for relaxation translated the work of the German philosopher Schopenhauer.

ELIZABETH HALDANE (1862–1937), sister of Viscount Haldane, was SCOTLAND'S FIRST FEMALE JUSTICE OF THE PEACE.

## *John Scott Haldane* 1860–1936

Showing similar courage to Sir Humphrey Davy, inventor of the safety lamp, John Scott Haldane experimented on himself to learn about the effect of gases on the human body, often locking himself into a sealed chamber and breathing in various cocktails so that he could record their effect on his mind and body. In the First World War he went to the Western Front to try to identify the newfangled poison gases being used by the Germans, and this led to his invention of the GAS MASK.

While doing his research into respiration as Professor of Medicine at Oxford University, Haldane devised a decompression procedure for deep-sea divers, which allowed them to return to the surface without getting the 'bends'. This technique was utilised in the recovery of a cargo of gold from the wreck of the *Lusitania* in 1920. In 1908 he published the FIRST SET OF DECOMPRESSON TABLES in his own magazine the *Journal of Hygiene.*

His son John Haldane was also a distinguished medical research scientist, and his daughter Naomi Mitchison a popular feminist writer who published over 70 books and lived to be 101.

*Well, I never knew this*
*about*
**PERTHSHIRE FOLK**

ADAM FERGUSON (1723–1816), 'THE FATHER OF MODERN SOCIOLOGY', born in Logierait. As Professor of Moral Philosophy at Edinburgh University, he introduced the study of human beings in groups, rather than as individuals, and developed the science we now call 'SOCIOLOGY'.

CAROLINA OLIPHANT, BARONESS NAIRNE (1766–1845), born in 'the auld hoose of Gask'. As the daughter of one of the most ardent Jacobite families, she was named Carolina in honour of Bonnie Prince Charlie. She grew into a remarkable beauty and was known as the 'Flower of Strathearn', or sometimes the 'White Rose of Gask'. Carolina expressed her love of the romance and dashing chivalry associated with the Jacobite memory by writing songs under the *nom de plume* Mrs Bogan of Bogan. Many became classics, such as 'Charlie is My Darling' and 'Will Ye No' Come Back Again?'

HELEN DUNCAN (1897–1956), medium, and THE LAST PERSON TO BE JAILED UNDER THE WITCHCRAFT ACT, born in Callander. She displayed the 'gift' of a medium as a child and from an early age travelled throughout Britain conducting seances. In 1941, while living in Portsmouth during the Second World War, she was purportedly 'visited' at one of her seances by the spirit of a sailor who announced that he had just gone down 'in the Barham'. HMS *Barham* was not reported lost until several weeks later, as the Admiralty had wanted to keep the sinking secret to protect morale and mislead the enemy. In 1944 Duncan was arrested at a seance and tried by a jury at the Old Bailey under the Witchcraft Act

of 1735. She was found guilty and sentenced to nine months in Holloway Prison.

COLONEL DAVID STIRLING (1915–90), founder of the SAS, born at Keir House, his family's ancestral home. Educated at Ampleforth and Cambridge, he was commissioned into the Scots Guards and was training on Mount Everest at the outbreak of the Second World War. He volunteered to join an experimental commando unit in 1940, and when it was disbanded he went to his superiors with the idea for a special operations unit of small groups that could be parachuted behind enemy lines. Stirling's new 'L Detachment, Special Air Service Brigade' (later just the SAS) operated throughout the North Africa campaign, causing immense damage to Rommel's fighting ability and contributing greatly to the first major British victory of the Second World War. Stirling himself was captured in 1943 and spent the rest of the war as a prisoner in Colditz. Stirling's cousin, SIMON FRASER, 15TH LORD LOVAT, was one of the first commandos (*see* Inverness-shire). Stirling's nephew, ARCHIE STIRLING (b.1941), a successful theatre producer, was married to the actress DIANA RIGG.

DENIS LAWSON, actor, born in Crieff in 1947. He portrayed pilot Wedge

Antilles in the original *Star Wars* film trilogy and played John Jarndyce in the BBC adaptation of Dickens's *Bleak House* (2005). He is uncle to Ewan McGregor.

EWAN McGREGOR, actor, born in Crieff in 1971. He played the lead role in *Trainspotting* (1996) and portrays the young Obi-Wan Kenobi in the *Star Wars* film series.

*Denis Lawson*

# Renfrewshire

---

ERSKINE ✦ EARL OF MAR ✦ SOME NOTABLE ERSKINES
✦ CLAN MONTGOMERY ✦ SOME NOTABLE MONTGOMERIES
✦ WALLACE ✦ SOME NOTABLE WALLACES

*Paisley Town Hall, completed in 1882,*
*when Paisley was the thread-making capital of the world.*

◄ RENFREWSHIRE FOLK ►

Robert Tannahill ✦ Peter Dodds McCormack ✦ George Reid
✦ Samuel Wilson ✦ James Goodfellow ✦ Gregor Fisher

# Erskine

◆◆◆◆

The name ERSKINE means 'green rising ground' and was used to describe an area on the south bank of the River Clyde west of Glasgow. The first person known to have adopted the name was HENRY DE ERSKINE, owner of the barony of Erskine in the time of Alexander II (1214–49).

The Erskines were staunch supporters of Robert the Bruce at Bannockburn, at which time Robert of Erskine was Chamberlain of Scotland, and Bruce's son David II made another Robert of Erskine Keeper of the Castle of Stirling, an office held by the Chief of the Erskines to this day.

The Erskines were descended from Robert the Bruce's brother Thomas, Earl of Mar, last of the Gaelic Earls or Mormaers of Mar, and when Alexander Stewart, the 1st Earl of Mar of the second creation, died in 1435 the Erskines tried to reclaim the title, but were denied it by the Stewarts. They were forced to settle for the title Lord Erskine instead.

The 4TH LORD ERSKINE was a friend to James IV and died with him at Flodden in 1513. His son was given custody of the infant James V, and a tradition of Erskine guardianship over the young monarchs was established. THE 5TH LORD ERSKINE accompanied Mary Queen of Scots to France when she was a baby and in gratitude she finally made his son, the 6TH Lord Erskine, THE 1ST EARL OF MAR OF THE SEVENTH CREATION and THE 17th EARL OF THE ORIGINAL CREATION. It was this Earl of Mar who built the magnificent MAR'S WARK beneath the castle walls in Stirling.

# Earl of Mar

◆◆◆◆

JOHN ERSKINE, 2ND AND 18th EARL OF MAR (1558–1634), was guardian to young James VI, but being only young himself was rather pushed aside by the regent, the Earl of Morton. Erskine felt that James was falling into the wrong hands and in 1582 became involved in the Raid of Ruthven, when James was kidnapped and held hostage in Huntingtower Castle for almost a year. For his part in this Erskine was exiled, but he was later restored to favour and in 1601 was entrusted with the task of reassuring Elizabeth I that James would make a good successor. In 1603 he accompanied James to London.

John Erskine, Earl of Mar was married to the daughter of the Earl of Buchan, and his younger son James became 7th Earl of Buchan. Both titles of Mar and Buchan remain with the Erskines today. In 1628 he built Braemar Castle in Aberdeenshire.

JOHN ERSKINE, 6TH AND 22ND EARL OF MAR, was forever changing sides and hence was known as 'Bobbing John'. He was Secretary of State for Scotland under Queen Anne and was one of the main architects of the 1707 Act of Union, along with the 'Union Duke' (of Queensberry).

After the Union he travelled to London in confident expectation of receiving a plum job in the Hanoverian government, but was rebuffed in firm Teutonic manner and took immediate umbrage. He returned to Scotland, recruited 10,000 men and in 1715 raised his standard at Braemar, in Aberdeenshire, declaring for James Stuart, the Old Pretender, and thus launching the 1715 Jacobite uprising. Alas, he was not a good general, rushed his fences and was fought to a standstill at the Battle of Sheriffmuir, despite having a larger army. By the time the Old Pretender had realised what was going on and hurried over from France to land at Peterhead and meet up with Mar, their cause was lost, and the two tramped back into exile in France. The earldom was lost too, and was not restored to the Erskines until 1824.

The present incumbent is JAMES ERSKINE, 14TH EARL OF MAR, who was born in 1949 and is CHIEF OF CLAN ERSKINE.

The original earldom of Mar was split from the newer creation in the 19th century and is today held by MARGARET ALISON, 30TH COUNTESS OF MAR of the first creation, who is CHIEF OF CLAN MAR.

## Some Notable Erskines

JAMES ERSKINE, LORD GRANGE (1679–1754), whose brother John, the 6th and 22nd Earl of Mar, raised the rebellion in 1715. James was terrified of being exposed as a Jacobite by his estranged wife, Rachel Chiesley, so one night in 1732 he smuggled her out of Edinburgh, sedated and hidden in a sedan chair, and transported her by diverse ways to the tiny and remote Monach Islands, west of North Uist and thence, just to make sure, to St Kilda, the most isolated spot in Britain. She was left there for seven years before finally being allowed to return to civilisation on Skye, where she died, completely mad, in 1745.

THOMAS ERSKINE, 6TH EARL OF KELLIE (1732–81), known as 'Fiddler Tam'. He studied music under the elder Johann Stamitz in Mannheim and became a virtuoso violinist and composer. He wrote at least a dozen symphonies, of which ten have recently come to light at Kilravock Castle in Nairnshire, and he is at last being recognised as one of the great composers of the 18th century. In 1774 he arranged and composed a suite of minuets for THE FIRST GARDEN PARTY EVER HELD IN BRITAIN, Lord Stanley's *fête champêtre* at the Oaks in Epsom. Like so many musicians, Erskine was partial to a tipple and he founded a drinking club in Edinburgh called the Capillaire Club. Here his nose became so red that one of his fellow members, the playwright Samuel Foote, suggested he should take it into the greenhouse to ripen the cucumbers.

## Colonel Robert Erskine
## 1735–80

COLONEL ROBERT ERSKINE was an engineer, an inventor and a map maker. After studying at Edinburgh University he became an engineer and developed a number of 'elevating pumps' such as a CONTINUAL STREAM PUMP and a CENTRIFUGAL HYDRAULIC ENGINE.

He thus invented HYDRAULICS, for which achievement he was elected a fellow of the Royal Society.

In 1771 he was asked to go to America to rescue a bankrupt ironworks in New Jersey and found himself caught up in the American Revolution. Sympathetic to the American cause, he formed his workers into a militia and asked what he could do.

His first contribution was to design a spiked marine barrier that could be thrown across the Hudson River to prevent British ships moving upriver to cut off New England from the rest of the colonies. The success of this project brought Erskine to the attention of George Washington, who appointed him as Geographer and Surveyor General of the Continental Army in 1777. In this capacity he drew over 275 detailed maps of the northern theatre of war, showing natural features as well as roads and buildings. These proved invaluable to Washington and are still historically valuable to geographers today. They can be seen in the Erskine Dewitt Map Collection at the New York Historical Society.

GENERAL SIR GEORGE 'BOBBIE' ERSKINE (1899–1965) commanded the 7th Armoured Division (the 'Desert Rats') in the Second World War, during the advance from Tripoli to Tunis in 1943 and throughout the short campaign in Italy in that same

year. He also led the division at the invasion of Normandy in 1944. Although renowned as a man of integrity and considerable courage, he was partially blamed (unfairly) for the setback at Villers-Bocage in June 1944, and was asked to fall on his sword by Montgomery, along with the corps commander, General Bucknall. He later served as Commander-in-Chief, East Africa, during the Mau Mau rebellion in Kenya, and as Governor of Jersey.

## Clan Montgomery

The MONTGOMERY name can be traced back to a 9th-century Viking called Gomeric, who sailed from Norway and settled in the Calvados region of Normandy. He fortified a hilltop as his home and this became known as 'Mont Gomeric'.

Fast forward to the 11th century, and ROGER DE MONTGOMERIE accompanied his relative William the

Conqueror to England, and was rewarded with great lands, including estates on the Welsh Marches which today make up Montgomeryshire.

The first record of a Montgomery in Scotland comes in 1165 with ROBERT MONTGOMERY (1103–78), grandson of the above Montgomerie, who was granted the lands of Egglisham (Eaglesham) by his father-in-law, Walter the Steward.

The French spelling of the name was gradually anglicised to Montgomery and the family name can now be spelt both ways. A number of branches of the Montgomeries availed themselves of the Ulster Plantations in the early 17th century and established a strong presence in Ireland, where they still hold lands today.

## Sir John Montgomery

In the late 14th century, SIR JOHN MONTGOMERY, 9TH OF EAGLE-SHAM, married Elizabeth, heiress to Sir Hugh de Eglinton, brother-in-law of Robert II, and obtained the vast baronies of Eglinton and Ardrossan.

In 1388 this same Sir John, with his own hands, captured Henry Percy (Hotspur) at the Battle of Otterburn, and with the ransom he received for Percy's release he built POLNOON CASTLE, at the top of the hill in Egglisham, now disappeared.

It was Sir John's grandson, ALEXANDER MONTGOMERIE (d.1470), who became 1ST LORD MONTGOMERIE, and Sir John's great-grandson HUGH, 2ND LORD MONTGOMERIE (1460–1545), who became 1ST EARL OF EGLINTON.

In 1769 ALEXANDER MONTGOMERIE, 10TH EARL OF EGLINTON (1723–69), decided to transform the scattered farms and houses around Polnoon Castle into a smart new village. He had recently been travelling on the Continent, where he had been impressed by a small town constructed in an 'A' shape. Egglisham now became Eaglesham, with two streets, Polnoon and Montgomery, climbing the steep hill to meet at the castle, with the 'A' being completed by a cross street called Mid Road.

In that same year Montgomerie was accidently shot dead when confronting a young poacher on his Ardrossan estate.

During the Second World War Eaglesham briefly found fame when Hitler's deputy Rudolf Hess parachuted into a field on the edge of the village, hoping to find the Duke of Hamilton, and was arrested by a local farmer.

In 1960 Eaglesham became SCOTLAND'S FIRST CONSERVATION VILLAGE.

# Some Notable Montgomeries

RICHARD MONTGOMERY (1736–75), America's first national hero. A brigadier general in the Continental Army during the invasion of Canada in 1775, Montgomery was struck down by musket fire while leading the assault on Quebec, THE FIRST AMERICAN GENERAL TO DIE IN THE AMERICAN REVOLUTION. The monument raised to him not long afterwards in New York City was THE FIRST AMERICAN WAR MEMORIAL, and THE FIRST SCULPTURE EVER COMMISSIONED BY THE US GOVERNMENT. It was commissioned by Benjamin Franklin while he was in France and now stands outside St Paul's Chapel across the road from the former site of the Twin Towers.

BERNARD MONTGOMERY, 1ST VISCOUNT MONTGOMERY OF ALAMEIN (1887–1976), Second World War field marshal known as 'Monty'. He commanded the 8th Army in

North Africa, achieving victory over Rommel at the Battle of El Alamein in 1942, of which Winston Churchill said, 'Now this is not the end. It is not even the beginning of the end. But it is, perhaps, the end of the beginning.' Montgomery went on to command the Allied ground forces during Operation Overlord, the invasion of Normandy in 1944. A spiky character, he was not always popular with his fellow generals, but was immensely popular with his troops.

Memorable Quote:
*'One of the great laws of war is Never Invade Russia.'*

COLIN MONTGOMERIE, professional golfer, born in 1963. Considered to be one of the best players never to win a major, he has come second five times, and in the 1990s he dominated the European Tour, finishing first in the Order of Merit every year from 1993 to 1999. He played for the European team in the Ryder Cup eight times and never lost a singles match. He was appointed as captain of the 2010 European Ryder Cup team.

## *Wallace*

WALLACE comes from the Old French word 'waleis', meaning Welshman, and it seems likely that the first Scottish Wallaces came north from Wales in the 10th or 11th century. The first name on record, RICHARD WALENSIS, can be found on a charter of 1160, and the parish of Riccarton appears to be named after him. Richard's grandson had two sons, the youngest of whom, Malcolm, was given the lands of Elderslie. Malcolm's son was the great Scottish patriot, William Wallace.

## Some Notable Wallaces

*This is the truth I tell you: of all things freedom's most fine.*
*Never submit to live, my son, in the bonds of slavery entwined.*
Proverb (said to have been told to William Wallace by his uncle)

SIR WILLIAM WALLACE (1274–1305), a young nobleman who used guerrilla tactics to clear southern Scotland of English rule after many Scottish nobles signed allegiance to Edward I in the Ragman Rolls of 1296. In September of that year he joined forces with Andrew Murray, whose men had risen in the north, and together they achieved a stunning victory over the English army at the Battle of Stirling Bridge. Murray was badly wounded and died not long afterwards, but Wallace became Guardian of Scotland, in the cause of John Balliol, until he was defeated by Edward I at the Battle of Falkirk the following year. Some years later, after being betrayed while in hiding, he was captured, taken to London and executed, his head placed on a spike above London Bridge.

WILLIAM WALLACE (1768–1843), bookbinder and mathematician, became Professor of Mathematics at Edinburgh University. He invented the PANTOGRAPH, a mechanical device used to copy a figure or plan on a different scale, and advised on the foundation of the Observatory on Carlton Hill in 1792.

ALFRED RUSSEL WALLACE (1823–1913), explorer and naturalist who, in the early 1850s, proposed his own theory of natural selection, prompting Charles Darwin to go public with his Theory of Evolution. A keen explorer, Wallace identified the Wallace Line in Malaysia, dividing Indonesia into two parts, one where the animals are related to those in Australia and one where they are of Asian origin. He was also THE FIRST 'ENVIRONMENTALIST' to show concern about how man's activity might be harming the planet.

*Well, I never knew this*
*about*
**RENFREWSHIRE FOLK**

## Australia Fair

ROBERT TANNAHILL (1774–1810), known as the 'weaver poet', born in Paisley. In 1805 he wrote a poem called 'Thou Bonnie Wood of Craigielea', which was put to music in 1818 by James Barr. In 1894, in Victoria, Australia, Christina Macpherson heard the tune played by the town band at the annual Warrnambool steeplechase. She later played what she could remember of the music to Andrew B. Banjo Paterson; he put some words to it, and so came into being Australia's national song, 'Waltzing Matilda'.

PETER DODDS McCORMACK (1834–1916), composer of the Australian national anthem, 'Advance Australia Fair', born in Port Glasgow, the son of a seaman.

GEORGE REID (1845–1918), Australia's fourth prime minister, born in Johnstone. He emigrated to Sydney with his family when he was 13.

*George Reid*

During the war of 1812, meat supplier SAMUEL WILSON, whose parents emigrated to New York from Greenock, would stamp the barrels of beef he was sending to the US Army with the letters US, for identification. When Wilson's delivery men handed over the barrels they would say 'Here's your meat from Uncle Sam [Wilson]'. The soldiers imagined the men were referring to the government, and that is how the phrase came to be used as slang for the US government.

JAMES GOODFELLOW, inventor, born in Paisley in 1937. He came up with the concept of an AUTOMATIC TELLER MACHINE (ATM) for use with an encrypted card and PIN (personal identification number) while working for Smiths Industries in Glasgow. There is much unresolved debate as to whether it was Goodfellow or John Shepherd-Barron (*see* Ross and Cromarty) who invented the cash machine and PIN number. Shepherd-Barron's was the first machine to be installed, by Barclays Bank in 1967, but Goodfellow's technology has proved to be more practical in the long run.

GREGOR FISHER, born in Glasgow in 1954 and brought up in Neilson. Best known for his character Rab C. Nesbitt, he is also fondly remembered for his portrayal of a bald man having his photo taken in the advertisement for Hamlet cigars.

# Ross and Cromarty

———✦✦◆✦✦———

ROSS ✦ EARLS OF ROSS ✦ ROSSES OF BALNAGOWAN
✦ BALNAGOWAN CASTLE ✦ SOME NOTABLE ROSSES
✦ CLAN MACKENZIE ✦ TWO EARLS ✦ EARL OF SEAFORTH
✦ BRAHAN SEER ✦ BRAHAN CASTLE
✦ SOME NOTABLE MACKENZIES ✦ CLAN MUNRO
✦ SOME NOTABLE MUNROS

*Foulis Castle, ancestral seat of the
Clan Munro for 800 years.*

◄ ROSS AND CROMARTY FOLK ►

David Urquhart ✦ Peter Fraser ✦ John Shepherd-Barron

# Ross

T he name Ross comes from the Gaelic word 'ros', meaning promontory, and defines the dominant physical feature of Easter Ross. The CLAN ROSS and the EARLS OF ROSS share a progenitor but became separated in 1372 when William, 5th Earl of Ross, died without a male heir.

# Earls of Ross

T he first recognised Mormaer or EARL OF ROSS, from 1225 to 1251, was Ferquhard mac an t-sagairt ('son of a priest'), who was from a family of lay abbots of Applecross. As a reward for helping Alexander II crush an uprising in Moray and Ross in 1215 he was created Earl of Ross around 1225.

His son William, 2nd Earl of Ross, did much to assist the capture of the Hebridean islands from the Norwegians, and under the Treaty of Perth in 1266 received the overlordship of Skye and Lewis. He married Jean Comyn, daughter of William Comyn, Earl of Buchan.

This line ended in 1372 when William, 5th Earl of Ross, died leaving no son; the title passed through his daughter Euphemia to Walter Leslie, and eventually both Donald, Lord of

the Isles, and the House of Stewart laid claim to it by marriage. The Battle of Harlaw Hill was fought between them in 1411 to decide the issue, and although it ended in a bloody draw, the earldom of Ross ended up with the Stewarts.

# Rosses of Balnagowan

T he 5th Earl of Ross's half-brother Hugh of Rarichies took over as Chief of Clan Ross when the Earl died in 1372, but by then, in the ancient Pictish fashion, the earldom of Ross had already gone elsewhere through the female line. So Hugh took on the name of his own lands and became HUGH ROSS OF BALNAGOWAN. This Hugh Ross built the core of the original fortified tower house of Balnagowan.

For the next 300 years the Rosses of Balnagowan remained Chiefs of the Clan until DAVID ROSS, 12TH OF BALNAGOWAN, died penniless and in debt in the Tower of London, after being captured fighting for Charles Stuart at the Battle of Worcester. His son David contributed to the debt by rebuilding the castle and adding a wing, and he then died in 1711 without children, leaving Balnagowan to go to Charles Ross of Hawkhead.

The chiefship then took a tortuous descent through a female line and various cousins until it ended up with Ross of Pitcalnie, a direct descendant of the David Ross of Balnagowan who had lost the castle in 1711.

Although the chiefship of Clan Ross is no longer in the hands of the Rosses of Balnagowan, BALNAGOWAN CASTLE is still regarded as the ancestral seat of Clan Ross.

# Balnagowan Castle

S IR CHARLES ROSS, 21ST LAIRD OF BALNAGOWAN (1872–1942), was a keen shot and designed high-velocity rifles, well regarded by sportsmen. In 1910 he produced the ROSS RIFLE, a military rifle for use by the Canadian army in the First World War, which turned out to be somewhat unreliable and actually more dangerous to the soldiers who were firing it than the enemy. Before

this had become apparent, however, Sir Charles made a lot of money out of the rifle, and when the Inland Revenue demanded a modicum of tax Sir Charles promptly declared the Balnagowan estate to be US territory and therefore beyond their reach. Although a noble attempt, it didn't work, and the resultant financial losses, allied to two expensive divorces, left Balnagowan in a parlous state.

When Sir Charles died in Florida in 1942, the castle and estate passed to his third wife, an American who, along with her second husband Francis de Moleyns, tried to run Balnagowan as a sporting venture. This was not a great success and by the time Francis died in 1964 Balnagowan was very run down.

In 1972 Harrods owner Mohammed Fayed bought the Balnagowan estate and he has renovated and refurbished the castle, returning it to its former splendour.

# Some Notable Rosses

BETSY ROSS (1752–1836), seamstress, who is alleged to have sewn THE FIRST 'STARS AND STRIPES' FLAG after a surprise visit from three members of the Continental Congress, George Washington, Robert Morris and her husband's uncle, George Ross. They arrived with a rough design, which she asked them to redraw in her back parlour using five-pointed stars instead of six-pointed ones, because five-pointed stars could be cut out in one snip of the scissors. Robert Morris and George Ross both signed the Declaration of Independence; George Washington did not, because in July 1776 he was otherwise engaged commanding the Continental Army in New York.

SIR RONALD ROSS (1857–1932) trained as a doctor at St Bartholomew's Hospital in London and in 1881 joined the Indian Medical Service, where he made a special study of malaria. In 1897 he made the breakthrough discovery that malaria is transmitted by mosquitoes. He returned to Britain in 1899 and became Professor of Tropical Medicine at Liverpool University. In 1902 he was THE FIRST BRITON EVER TO BE AWARDED A NOBEL PRIZE in any discipline, in his case for medicine. He is the grandfather of the present Chief of Clan Ross.

# Donald J. Ross
## 1872–1948

D ONALD ROSS, golf course designer, born in Dornoch. Apprenticed as a carpenter, he began by making clubs for the members of his local club at Dornoch, eventually becoming the club's professional and green-keeper. After studying with Old Tom Morris at St Andrews he emigrated to America in 1899 to take up a job at Oakley Country Club in Massachusetts. In 1900 he was appointed professional at the Pinehurst Resort and here began his career in course design.

He was one of the most prolific golf course architects of all time, designing more than 400 courses. His most celebrated course is the Pinehurst No. 2 course, which hosted the 1936 PGA Championship, two US Open Championships and a Ryder Cup. Others are Oakland Hills, Seminole and Oak Hill in New York.

He helped found, and served as FIRST PRESIDENT OF, THE AMER-ICAN SOCIETY OF GOLF COURSE ARCHITECTS, in 1946.

NELLIE TAYLOR ROSS (1876–1977), Governor of Wyoming, 1925–7, and THE FIRST WOMAN STATE GOVERNOR in US history.

ALEXANDER (ALEC) ROSS (1881–1952), golf professional, winner of the US Open championship in 1907, was born in Dornoch.

HAROLD ROSS (1892–1951), journalist and founder, in 1925, of one of America's most influential magazines, the *New Yorker*. Ross began the magazine with his wife, Jane Grant, in a house in Manhattan's 45th Street and remained its editor for 25 years until his death.

JERRY ROSS, astronaut, born in 1948, who shares the record number of Space Shuttle missions – seven – with Franklin Chang-Diaz, and also holds the record for the number of space walks, with nine.

# Clan Mackenzie

The Mackenzies are of Celtic stock and their name comes from the Gaelic MacCoinneach, meaning 'son of Kenneth' – Kenneth being an English translation of Coinneach, which means 'the fair one' – therefore 'son of the fair one'.

The first mac Coinneach was COINNEACH MACCOINNEACH or Kenneth, son of Kenneth, whose ancestors had come over from Ireland in 1261 and later been granted the barony of Kintail in Wester Ross, on the mainland across from Skye. This was in return for helping Alexander III against the Norwegian King Haakon.

Coinneach Mac Choinnich was the 3rd Baron Kintail, and his stronghold was the famous castle of EILEAN DONAN, sited on a small island in Loch Duich, which has become a picture-book icon of Scotland, although somewhat pretti-fied since the 12th century.

The Mackenzies rose steadily in power and influence until by the 14th century their lands spread right across Ross from east to west, and they moved their seat to Kinellan, near Strathpeffer, where they later built BRAHAN CASTLE.

The Mackenzies remained loyal to the Stewart monarchs. Iain Mackenzie, 9th Chief, fought at Flodden and Pinkie and somehow survived, and the Mackenzies also supported Mary Queen of Scots and James VI.

## Two Earls

The 12th Chief, KENNETH MACKENZIE (1569–1611), was made LORD MACKENZIE OF KINTAIL by James VI in 1609 and secured for himself and his heirs the whole island of Lewis. He married Ann Ross, daughter of George Ross of Balnagowan, and in 1623 their son Colin became EARL OF SEAFORTH. Their great-nephew George was made EARL OF CROMARTIE by Queen Anne in 1703.

## Earl of Seaforth

COLIN, 1ST EARL OF SEAFORTH (1596–1633), built Brahan Castle. His heir died young and the title went to Colin's brother George (d.1651).

## Brahan Seer

George's son KENNETH, 3RD EARL OF SEAFORTH (1635–78), employed Kevin Mackenzie from Lewis, the fabled BRAHAN SEER, as a labourer on the estate at Brahan Castle. The Brahan Seer was said to have predicted many things, such as the success of Strathpeffer as a spa – 'crowds of pleasure and health seekers shall be seen thronging its portals' – and North Sea oil – 'black rain that will bring riches to Aberdeen'. More pertinently, he predicted the extinction of the Seaforth line, when the last Seaforth would see all his sons die before him.

The Brahan Seer's foresight didn't do him much good. One of his prophesies upset the 3rd Earl's wife and she had him burned to death in a barrel of tar . . .

The Seaforth earldom was indeed lost soon afterwards when the 5th Earl of Seaforth was stripped of his title and estates after taking part in the 1715 Jacobite rebellion.

In 1797 FRANCIS MACKENZIE,

great-grandson of the 4th Earl, was made LORD SEAFORTH but, spookily, all of his four sons predeceased him and the title became extinct on his death in 1815.

The Brahan Seer's last prediction was that the Seaforth possessions would be 'inherited by a white-coiffed lassie from the east and she is to kill her sister'.

Lord Seaforth's eldest daughter, who inherited Brahan Castle, married Admiral Hood, and was stationed out in the East Indies with him. When he died in 1816, she returned to Brahan wearing, as was traditional, the Indian white coif of mourning. A few years later she was driving out in a pony carriage with her sister when the horses bolted and the carriage overturned. Lady Hood's sister was thrown out and died of her injuries. The Mackenzie Monument, 1 mile (1.6 km) west of Brahan House, marks the spot where this happened and the Brahan Seer's final prophesy came true.

was also at Brahan, in 1778, that Kenneth Mackenzie, grandson of the 5th and last Earl, raised a regiment of Highlanders that became the SEAFORTH HIGHLANDERS.

Brahan Castle was demolished in 1951, but the stables were transformed into Brahan House, where it is possible to stay. The grounds are open to the public.

## Some Notable Mackenzies

SIR ALEXANDER MACKENZIE (1764–1820), explorer, born in Stornoway, who emigrated to Canada and worked in the fur trade. He discovered the Mackenzie River in Canada's Northwest Territories in 1789.

OSGOOD MACKENZIE (1842–1922), garden architect, who created the Inverewe Gardens in Wester Ross in 1862, now run by the National Trust for Scotland.

## *Brahan Castle*

◆◆◆

BRAHAN CASTLE was the traditional home of the Seaforths, Chiefs of the Clan Mackenzie. It was at Brahan that the Jacobite Mackenzies swore allegiance to the English Crown, becoming THE FIRST OF THE DEFEATED CLANS TO DO SO, and it

SIR COMPTON MACKENZIE (1883–1972), author of the novel *Whisky Galore!* about the sinking of the SS *Politician*, which became a 1949 Ealing comedy film. Also the Highland novels such as *Monarch of the Glen*, which inspired the BBC television series starring actor Alastair Mackenzie, born in 1970, in the lead role of young laird Archie MacDonald.

KELVIN MACKENZIE, media executive, born 1946. During his editorship of the *Sun* from 1981 to 1994 the newspaper became Britain's best-selling tabloid.

# Clan Munro

The Munros came to Scotland from Ireland in the 11th century to fight for Malcolm II against the Norse. The name Munro comes from the Gaelic and would appear to mean 'man from Ro', Ro being the name of a river in Ireland. Their leader, and the first Chief of Clan Munro, was Donald, son of the O'Caan Ro's, and he was granted land in Easter Ross which he called Foules after Loch Feul in Ireland. He built himself a motte and bailey castle, the remains of which can still be seen in the grounds of the present-day Foulis Castle, itself built in the 18th century.

The Munros have now lived at FOULIS CASTLE for over 800 years and it remains the seat of CLAN MUNRO.

# Some Notable Munros

GENERAL SIR HECTOR MUNRO (1726–1805), Commander-in-Chief of India in 1864–5. On his return, as a means of providing employment, he built a monument on the summit of Fyrish Hill, near his Novar estate, representing the gates of Negapatnam, an Indian city that he had taken from the Dutch in 1781.

EBENEZER MUNRO (1752–1825), the Lexington Minuteman, who is thought to have fired 'the shot heard around the world', the first shot of the American War of Independence, at the Battle of Lexington in Massachusetts on 19 April 1775. Scot Robert Munroe was one of the seven minutemen who fell in the first return fire, ordered by Major John Pitcairn from Dysart in Fife.

> Minutemen were a type of advance guard, dedicated members of the militia who were expected to turn up at the scene of an emergency within minutes to take charge until the main body of the militia could arrive.

JAMES MONROE (1758–1831), 5th President of the United States and great-grandson of a Scottish Covenanter deported to the Americas in the 17th century during the religious persecutions under Charles II. He was the last president to have fought in the American War of Independence, hence his nickname of 'Last Cocked Hat'. He threw the Spanish out of Florida and drew up the Monroe Doctrine:

*The American Continents by the free and independent condition which they have assumed and maintain, are henceforth not to be considered as*

*subjects for future colonisation by any European Power.*

SIR HUGH MUNRO (1856–1919), mountaineer, who made a list of all the mountains in Scotland over the height of 3,000 ft (914 m). Such mountains are now known as Munros.

DONNIE MUNRO, rock musician, born 1953. He joined the folk-rock band Runrig as lead singer in 1974.

*Well, I never knew this*
*about*
## ROSS AND CROMARTY FOLK

DAVID URQUHART (1805–77), diplomat, born in Cromarty. In 1831 he was sent with the British legation to Turkey to help determine the border between Turkey and Greece. He became a great supporter of Turkey and spoke out against British involvement in the Crimean War

(1854–6), believing Turkey did not require help fighting the Russians. In his book *The Pillars of Hercules* (1850) he advocated the use of Turkish baths and went on to oversee the construction of BRITAIN'S FIRST TURKISH BATHS in London's Jermyn Street.

PETER FRASER (1884–1950), politician, born in Hill of Fearn, near Tain. He emigrated to New Zealand in 1910 and founded the New Zealand Labour Party in 1916, becoming prime minister in 1940. He was in office throughout the Second World War and until 1949, as NEW ZEALAND'S LONGEST-SERVING LABOUR PRIME

MINISTER. He was influential in the founding of the United Nations in 1945.

JOHN SHEPHERD-BARRON (1925–2010), inventor, was born in 1925 and lived near Tain. He began work with the banknote printing firm De La Rue in the early 1960s. Irritated by the fact that he couldn't get hold of any money at the weekend, he dreamed up the concept of a self-service machine, rather like a chocolate bar dispenser, that would instead dispense cash – the idea coming to him while he was lying in the bath. The FIRST AUTOMATED TELLER MACHINE (ATM), based on Shepherd-Barron's concept, was installed at a branch of Barclays Bank in Enfield in 1967, and the first customer was the actor Reg Varney from the TV series *On the Buses*. Shepherd-Barron apparently decided on using a four-figure PIN number after discussing the matter at the kitchen table with his wife, who told him that four figures was the longest string of numbers she could memorise.

The Paisley-born inventor James Goodfellow has also been credited as the inventor of the cash machine and PIN number (*see* Renfrewshire). The debate still rages.

# Roxburghshire

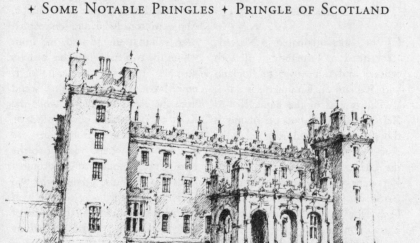

*Floors Castle, seat of the Dukes of Roxburghe and the largest inhabited castle in Scotland.*

## ◄ ROXBURGHSHIRE FOLK ►

# Duke of Roxburghe

The title DUKE OF ROXBURGHE is derived from the now decayed royal burgh of Roxburgh, and is held by the INNES-KER family.

# Clan Kerr

The KERS originated in Norway, settled in Normandy in the 10th century and came over to England with William the Conqueror in 1066.

The origins of the name Ker or Kerr are unclear, but the name is thought to be derived from either the Norse 'kjarr', meaning copse, or 'cearr', the Gaelic for left-handed. Since the Kers came originally from Norway, the Norse derivation would seem most likely. However, the Ker family do have a tradition of left-handedness. Sir Andrew Kerr, who led the Kerrs at the Battle of Flodden in 1513, was left-handed, and trained his men to fight left-handed as well, since it was a good way of confusing the enemy. Several of the Kerr family homes are built for left-handed use, particularly the 16th-century FERNIEHURST CASTLE, which has a famous 'Left-Handed Staircase' spiralling the wrong way.

The first Ker to appear in Scotland was JOHN KER, a hunter of Swynhope, whose two sons Ralph and John settled near Jedburgh around 1330, and from whom the two main branches of Kers descend. THE KERS OF FERNIEHURST, now MARQUESSES OF LOTHIAN, descend from the eldest son Ralph, while the KERS OF CESSFORD, now DUKES OF ROXBURGHE, descend from John.

Over the next 200 years or so the Kers gained in influence and acquired lands and honours, although the two sides of the family were constantly at war with each other. At the Battle of Langside in 1568 SIR THOMAS KER OF FERNIEHURST fought for Mary Queen of Scots while SIR WALTER KER OF CESSFORD lined up with the Earl of Moray, representing James VI. The feuding was finally resolved with the Union of Crowns in 1603 when Anne Kerr of Cessford married William Kerr of Ferniehurst. From Anne and William descended the Earls of Lothian, while Sir Walter Cessford's son Robert became Earl of Roxburghe.

*Ferniehurst Castle*

# Earl of Roxburghe

ROBERT KER had long been a staunch ally of James VI and accompanied the King to London for the Union of Crowns in 1603. In recognition of his loyalty James made Robert EARL OF ROXBURGHE in 1616, and the Earl continued to support the Stuarts when Charles I inherited his father's throne, being appointed Keeper of the Privy Seal of Scotland in 1637. In 1642, when Charles attempted to arrest five members of the House of Commons at Westminster, it was the Earl of Roxburghe who held open the door of the chamber for the King.

Stripped of his position as Keeper of the Privy Seal after Charles's execution in 1649, the Earl returned to FLOORS, his new estate at Kelso, where he died the following year. Floors, which until the Reformation of 1560 had belonged to the monks of Kelso Abbey, was given to him by James VI.

# Dukes of Roxburghe

WILLIAM Drummond, the 1st Earl's grandson by his daughter Jean, became 2ND EARL OF ROXBURGHE, and changed his surname to Ker. William's grandson

John became the 5TH EARL OF ROXBURGHE (1680-1741) on the death of his older brother Robert in 1696. John became Secretary of State for Scotland in 1704 and was influential in bringing to fruition the Union with England for which he was rewarded by being made DUKE OF ROXBURGHE, THE LAST-EVER CREATION OF THE SCOTTISH PEERAGE.

He is said to have remarked that his greatest honour in life was to be one of the six pall-bearers at Sir Isaac Newton's funeral in Westminster Abbey in 1727.

The 3rd Duke died without an heir, and after a bit of a spat the title worked its way down to SIR JAMES INNES OF THAT ILK, descended from the 1st Earl via his mother. On becoming 5TH DUKE OF ROXBURGHE Sir James changed his surname to INNES-KER – which meant that he ceased to be Chief of Clan Innes since he now had a double-barrelled name. (To be chief you are required to bear simply the name of the clan, i.e. Innes.)

The present holder is GUY INNES-KER, 10TH DUKE OF ROXBURGHE, who was born in 1954 and lives at Floors Castle, by Kelso in Roxburghshire.

# Some Notable Kerrs

ROSE KERR (1882–1944), pioneer of the Girl Guide movement in Britain

## Roxburghe Club

JOHN, 3RD DUKE OF ROXBURGHE, was rebuffed in marriage by Christina Sophia Albertina, oldest daughter of the Duke of Mecklenburg-Strelitz whose younger sister Charlotte was engaged to marry King George III. Apparently, for an older sister to marry someone of lower rank than a younger sister is not considered done. Instead, the Duke devoted his life to collecting books, and after his death in 1806 his library, the finest private library in existence at the time, formed the basis of THE WORLD'S FIRST BOOK CLUB, the exclusive ROXBURGHE CLUB, founded in 1812. Its membership, which is restricted to 40, has included Sir Walter Scott, Arthur Balfour, J.P. Morgan and Sir Paul Getty.

and co-founder of the World Association of Girl Guides and Girl Scouts (WAGGGS). She rebuffed a proposal of marriage from the founder of the Boy Scouts, Robert Baden-Powell, in 1905, instead marrying REAR ADMIRAL MARK KERR, commander of the Greek navy at the start of the First World War. As THE FIRST BRITISH FLAG OFFICER TO BECOME A PILOT, in 1914, he was instrumental in the development of the Air Ministry and the Royal Air Force.

CAPTAIN RALPH KERR (1891–1941), captain of the Royal Navy's largest battleship HMS *Hood* when she was sunk by the *Bismarck* on 24 May 1941.

DEBORAH KERR, CBE (1921–2007), actress and star of one of the most

mention of a person of that name in the 12th century, during the reign of Alexander III, when ROBERT DE HOPPRYNGIL witnessed a charter to the hospital of Soutra.

## Smailholm Tower

iconic moments in film, in which she and Burt Lancaster roll about in the breaking waves on a beach in Hawaii, in *From Here to Eternity* in 1953.

Memorable Quotes:
*'Personally, I think if a woman hasn't met the right man by the time she's 24, she may be lucky.'*

*'Years from now, when you talk about this, and you will, be kind.'*

JIM KERR, born 1959, lead singer with the band Simple Minds, who have achieved five No. 1 albums in the UK and one No. 1 single, 'Belfast Child'.

## Pringles

The name PRINGLE comes from the lands of Hoppringhill which lie some 10 miles (16 km) north of Melrose. Hopringhill is an old Norse word meaning 'enclosed valley of the round hill', and we first come across

By the end of the 14th century the Pringles, who were followers of the Earls of Douglas, had settled mainly around SMAILHOLM, 4 miles (6.5 km) north-west of Kelso. There they built themselves a magnificent peel tower in a remote and dramatic setting atop a rocky crag called Lady Hill, with wide views over the surrounding countryside.

SMAILHOLM TOWER passed to the Scott family in 1645 and they built a small house in the courtyard, where they lived for about 50 years before moving to a more comfortable house they put up nearby at Sandyknowe.

The author Sir Walter Scott spent a lot of time at Sandyknowe as a boy, staying with his grandfather in the shadow of Smailholm Tower, and it was here that he fell under the spell of ballads from the Scottish Borders. In his later years Scott brought the artist John Turner here to make a sketch of the tower for his *Poetical Works*. Smailholm also appears in Scott's epic poem *Marmion*, and this inspired the photography pioneer

William Fox Talbot to follow in Scott's and Turner's footsteps and produce THE FIRST-EVER COFFEE-TABLE PHOTOGRAPHIC TRAVELOGUE BOOK, *Sun Pictures in Scotland*, in 1845.

## Some Notable Pringles

SIR JOHN PRINGLE (1707–82), physician. As physician to the Earl of Stair, British field marshal at the time of the Battle of Dettingen in Bavaria in June 1743, Pringle negotiated an agreement with the French commander, the Duc de Noailles, that military hospitals on both sides should be considered as neutral territory and sanctuaries for the sick and wounded, and should be protected as such by both sides. This concept formed the

---

### Pringle of Scotland

The Scottish Borders are known as the birthplace of the British knitwear industry, and Pringle is one of the oldest and most recognisable names in knitwear across the world. In fact, the very name 'knitwear' was invented by Pringles in 1905, to describe knitted garments worn as outerwear.

The association of Pringles with the woollen industry goes back to 1540 when a Pringle was responsible for overseeing the shearing, storage and transportation of the wool from the King's sheep.

PRINGLE OF SCOTLAND was established in Hawick in 1815 by Robert Pringle to manufacture knitted hosiery. In 1870 Pringle began producing the cashmere (from fine Kashmir goats' wool) for which it has become renowned, and in the 1930s a new two-piece cardigan was designed which was teamed up with a single string of pearls to create the classic British look, 'TWINSET AND PEARLS'.

---

basis for the constitution of the modern INTERNATIONAL RED CROSS. In 1752 Pringle married the daughter of Dr William Oliver, inventor of the Bath Oliver biscuit.

THOMAS PRINGLE (1789–1834), abolitionist and poet known as 'the FATHER OF SOUTH AFRICAN POETRY'. Born near Kelso, he emigrated to South Africa, where he wrote THE FIRST ENGLISH-LANGUAGE POETRY DESCRIBING SOUTH AFRICA'S SCENERY AND PEOPLES and edited two newspapers critical of the colonial government. An anti-slavery article he wrote for one of the newspapers came to the attention of the abolitionist Zachary Macaulay, and when Pringle returned to England he was appointed secretary of the Anti-Slavery Society, being instrumental in its successful campaign to abolish slavery throughout the British Empire.

JAMES HOGARTH PRINGLE (1863–1941), surgeon and inventor of the 'PRINGLE MANOEUVRE' used in abdominal operations.

PRINGLES, popular potato snack born in Ohio in 1968. In common with many other Border families a number of Pringles emigrated to North America, sometimes via Ireland, and settled in the United States. One such family ended up in Cincinnatti, Ohio, and gave their name to a suburban street, PRINGLE DRIVE. When Procter and Gamble were looking for something to call their new potato snack, they scoured the Cincinnatti phone book for a good name and landed on Pringle Drive – it sounded snappy and had the added advantage of incorporating the first two letters of Procter and the last two letters of Gamble. Little did Robert de Hoppryngil know what he was starting all those years ago in the Scottish Borders.

Memorable Quote:
*'Once you pop, you can't stop.'*

*Well, I never knew this*
*about*
# ROXBURGHSHIRE FOLK

*Success to Mr J. Graham Henderson,*
*  who is a good man,*
*And to gainsay it there's few people can,*
*I say so from my own experience,*
*And experience is a great defence.*

*He is a good man, I venture to say,*
*Which I declare to the world without*
*  dismay,*
*Because he's given me a suit of Tweeds,*
*  magnificent to see,*
*So good that it cannot be surpassed in*
*  Dundee.*

*The suit is the best of Tweed cloth in*
*  every way,*
*And will last me for many a long day;*
*It's really good, and in no way bad,*
*And will help to make my heart feel*
*  glad.*

Lines in Praise of Mr J. Graham
Henderson of Hawick in the
county of Roxburghshire' by William
McGonagall (the world's worst poet)

SAMUEL RUTHERFORD (1600–61),
Presbyterian theologian and author,
born in Nisbet. In 1627 he became
minister of Anworth in Kirkcudbrightshire, where he is commemorated
with Rutherford's Monument, a granite
obelisk on a hill overlooking the town.
Although condemned for it at the time,
he is now celebrated for his political
tome *Lex Rex*, which argued for the
concept of the rule of law rather than
the divine right of kings. *Lex Rex*
inspired later political thinkers such as
Thomas Hobbes, John Locke and
Rousseau, and laid the foundations for
the Constitution of the United States
of America. In 1982 constitutional
attorney John W. Whitehead started a
new civil liberties organisation inspired
by *Lex Rex*, which he called the
RUTHERFORD INSTITUTE. This achieved
national prominence in 1997 by helping
the Arkansas state employee Paula Jones
to sue President Clinton for sexual
harassment and winning her an out-
of-court settlement.

JAMES BROWN (1709–88), traveller
and linguist who wrote a dictionary
of Persian grammar, born in Kelso.

JAMES BALLANTYNE (1772–1833) and
John Ballantyne (1774–1821), printers
of the works of Sir Walter Scott, both
born in Kelso.

MARY SOMERVILLE, née Fairfax (1780–1872), scientist, born in the manse at Jedburgh. She found fame by translating scientific works into language that ordinary people could understand, and published a number of books herself on the science of mathematics and astronomy. Mary Somerville and Caroline Herschel, sister of Sir William Herschel, the astronomer who discovered Uranus, were the FIRST WOMEN TO BE ADMITTED TO THE ROYAL ASTRONOMICAL SOCIETY, in 1835. Indirectly Somerville became the FIRST 'SCIENTIST', when William Whewell invented the term in a review of her 1834 tract 'On the Connexion of the Sciences'. Oxford University's SOMERVILLE COLLEGE is named after her.

SIR WILLIAM FAIRBAIRN (1789-1874), engineer, born in Kelso, helped to build the Kelso Bridge. His speciality was the experimental study of the strengths of metals, and he conceived the idea for Robert Stephenson's iron tubular Britannia Bridge across the Menai Straits and the Conwy railway bridge in Wales. He went on to become a builder of iron boats including the *Lord Dundas*, the first steamboat on the Forth and Clyde Canal and prototype for the world's first practical steamboat, the *Charlotte Dundas*.

DAME ISOBEL BAILLIE (1895–1983), soprano, born in Hawick. Her signature work was Handel's *Messiah*, which she performed over 1,000 times. She was THE FIRST BRITISH PERFORMER TO SING IN THE HOLLYWOOD BOWL, in 1933.

Memorable Quote:
*'Never sing louder than lovely.'*

BILL McLAREN, rugby commentator known as the 'voice of rugby', born in Hawick in 1923. A talented player himself, he was on the verge of being called up to play for Scotland when he was struck down and nearly killed by tuberculosis. After two years in a sanitorium he was saved by an experimental drug, Streptomycin.

# Selkirkshire

---

BUCCLEUCH ✦ SCOTT ✦ LORD OF BUCCLEUCH
✦ DUKES OF BUCCLEUCH ✦ STOLEN MADONNA
✦ GREAT SCOTTS ✦ AMERICAN SCOTTS

*Bowhill, christened 'Sweet Bowhill' by*
*Sir Walter Scott, is the oldest ancestral home*
*of the Scott family, now Dukes of Buccleuch.*

◄ SELKIRKSHIRE FOLK ►

James Hogg ✦ Mungo Park ✦ Isabella Shiels ✦ Tom Scott
✦ Murray of Fala Hill

## Buccleuch

Buccleuch lies on the Rankle Burn, a tributary of the Tweed, some 10 miles (16 km) west of Hawick, and gives its name to the dukedom belonging to the Scott family, owners of the lands since the 12th century.

There is a romantic story about how Buccleuch came by its name, which tells of two brothers from Galloway who came to Rankleburn, in the royal forest of Ettrick, and were given employment by the keeper. When the King of Scotland Kenneth MacAlpin came to hunt in the forest, he became separated from his attendants and was thrown from his horse when it slipped on the muddy ground. MacAlpin found himself in great peril, face to face with the stag at bay, when John, one of the Galloway brothers who had been following the chase on foot, sprang to the rescue, seizing the buck by its antlers and throwing it across his back, before laying it at the feet of the King. From that time the place has been known as the Buck's cleuch, or Buck's glen, and John the Scot was granted the land in perpetuity.

## Scott

The family name of the DUKES OF BUCCLEUCH is SCOTT.

Previously the Romans had given the name Scotii to Gaelic raiders from Ireland.

The first true record of the name Scott is found on the foundation charter of Selkirk of 1120, which is witnessed by one Uchtred 'filius Scot', that is Uchtred, 'the son of a Scot'. He was described in that way to distinguish him from others with the same Christian name, who were probably Saxons or Normans.

RICHARD LE SCOTT signed the Ragman Rolls of 1296, swearing fealty to Edward I, and was confirmed to his lands of Rankleburn and Buccleuch in Selkirk. His son Michael was knighted by David II and it is from Michael's eldest son Robert that the Buccleuch line of Scotts descends.

## Lord of Buccleuch

WALTER SCOTT, 1ST LORD SCOTT OF BUCCLEUCH (1565–1611), was knighted by James VI in 1590 and appointed Keeper of Liddesdale and Warden of the West Marches.

In 1596, in his capacity as Keeper, Buccleuch rode to the rescue of KINMONT WILLIE ARMSTRONG, a border reiver who had been captured in Liddesdale by the English warden Sir Thomas Scrope and imprisoned in Carlisle Castle. This was in violation of an agreed truce, so Buccleuch gathered together a small raiding party of Scotts and Armstrongs, and one April night during a violent storm, they crossed into England over the swollen River Eden and broke into the supposedly invincible castle by undermining part of the wall near the postern gate. After overpowering the surprised sentries, and while Buccleuch stood guard, his men hurried along to Armstrong's cell, smashed down the door and released the prisoner. They all then fled, shouting and roaring to make the guards think they were a much larger force, swam back across the river and made for the border.

Armstrong remained free for the rest of his life, but the incident almost caused war between Scotland and England. Buccleuch surrendered himself to the authorities and was taken to London, where he came up before Elizabeth I. When the Queen demanded to know how he dared to be so presumptuous, Buccleuch replied, 'What is it that a man dare not do?' Elizabeth was impressed. 'With ten thousand such men,' she said, 'our brother in Scotland might shake the firmest throne in Europe!'

The story of the raid is recorded in a well-known ballad called 'Kinmont Willy', which appears in Sir Walter Scott's *Minstrelsy of the Scottish Border*.

# Dukes of Buccleuch

Buccleuch's son Walter was created 1ST EARL OF BUCCLEUCH in 1619. His granddaughter Anne, who became the 4th Countess of Buccleuch after her older sister Mary died at the age of 13, married Charles II's illegitimate son the Duke of Monmouth, and on their wedding day they were made DUKE AND DUCHESS OF BUCCLEUCH.

Monmouth was executed after his attempt to gain the throne from his uncle James II ended in defeat at the Battle of Sedgemoor in 1685, and when Anne died in 1732 her titles passed on to her grandson Francis Scott, who became 2nd Duke of Buccleuch.

HENRY SCOTT, 3RD DUKE OF BUCCLEUCH, was tutor to Adam Smith, author of the economist's bible *The Wealth of Nations*, and was FIRST PRESIDENT OF THE ROYAL SOCIETY

OF EDINBURGH. In 1767 he married Lady Elizabeth Montagu, daughter of the Duke of Montagu, and changed the family name to MONTAGU-SCOTT. He also eventually became the 5th Duke of Queensberry, inheriting the title from his cousin the 4th Duke, or 'Old Q', and so added Douglas as well, becoming MONTAGU-DOUGLAS-SCOTT.

The 9th Duke dropped the surname Montagu-Douglas-Scott for himself and his eldest son in 1974 because, as Chief of Clan Scott, he preferred to be just Scott. The Clan Scott seat is Branxholm Castle, near Hawick in Roxburghshire.

was stolen from his Dumfriesshire home, Drumlanrig Castle, by thieves posing as tourists. The picture was painted around 1510 for Floriamand Robertet, Secretary of State to Louis XII of France, and had been in the Buccleuch family for more than 250 years. The Duke loved it so much that he would put it in the boot of his car and take it with him as he moved between his various homes. The loss broke his heart and sparked a worldwide search, with the painting being placed on the FBI's list of ten most wanted stolen artworks. It was finally recovered in 2007, from a solicitor's office in Glasgow, one month after the 9th Duke had died.

## Stolen Madonna

In 2003 the 9th Duke was robbed of his most treasured possession, a painting by Leonardo da Vinci called *Madonna of the Yarnwinder*, which

## 10th Duke

The current Duke of Buccleuch is RICHARD SCOTT, 10TH DUKE OF BUCCLEUCH AND 12TH DUKE OF QUEENSBERRY. He is the largest private landowner in Britain, owning BOWHILL HOUSE in Selkirkshire (for the Scott line), DRUMLANRIG CASTLE in Dumfriesshire (for the Douglas line), and BOUGHTON HOUSE in Northamptonshire (for the Montagu line). A former seat, Dalkeith Palace in Midlothian, which was bought by the 2nd Earl of Buccleuch in 1642, is currently leased out to the University of Wisconsin.

# Great Scotts

SIR WALTER SCOTT (1771–1832), poet, author and creator of the modern Scottish image.

THE REVD THOMAS SCOTT (1747–1821), one of the founders of the CHURCH MISSIONARY SOCIETY and patriarch of the great architectural Scotts. . .

Grandson GEORGE GILBERT SCOTT (1811–78), architect of St Pancras Station and the Albert Memorial. Great-grandson GEORGE GILBERT

SCOTT JUN. (1839–87), architect of Dulwich College, Christ's College and Peterhouse, Cambridge. He suffered from mental health problems and alcoholism, and died of cirrhosis of the liver in a bedroom of his father's masterpiece, the Midland Grand Hotel at St Pancras Station.

Great-grandson JOHN OLDRID SCOTT (1841–1913), architect for the restorations of Hereford Cathedral and St Albans Cathedral.

Great-great-grandson GILES GILBERT SCOTT (1880–1960), architect of Liverpool Cathedral, Battersea and Bankside power stations (the latter now Tate Modern), and designer of the iconic red telephone kiosk.

Great-great-grandson ADRIAN GILBERT SCOTT (1882–1963), architect for the restoration of Mount Edgcumbe House, Cornwall, and St James's Anglican Church, Vancouver.

Great-great-great-niece ELISABETH SCOTT (1898–1972), designer of the Shakespeare Memorial Theatre at Stratford, THE FIRST IMPORTANT PUBLIC BUILDING IN BRITAIN TO BE DESIGNED BY A FEMALE ARCHITECT.

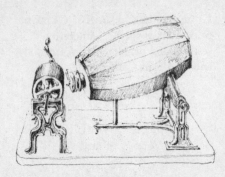

EDOUARD-LÉON SCOTT (1817–79), inventor of the earliest-known sound recording device, the PHONAUTOGRAPH, patented in 1857. In 2008 a recording of the French folk song 'Au Clair de la Lune', sung by Scott's daughter and recorded on a phonautograph in 1860, was discovered in Paris. It is THE OLDEST-KNOWN RECORDING OF BOTH MUSIC AND A HUMAN VOICE. There is a persistent story, never proved but nonetheless mouth-watering, that Scott visited the White House at the start of the American Civil War and made a recording of Abraham Lincoln – which may have later been destroyed by Thomas Edison as he was trying to play it back. Or maybe not. The search for this, the 'holy grail' of the recording world, continues.

ROBERT FALCON SCOTT, 'Scott of the Antarctic' (1868–1912), polar explorer.

ALFRED ANGAS SCOTT (1874–1923), founder of the SCOTT MOTORCYCLE COMPANY. Born in Bradford, England, but brought up and educated in Melrose, Scott designed, built and produced his first motorcycle in 1908, a very advanced model that incorporated water cooling, telescopic forks and a low-slung, lightweight duplex frame. In 1910 a Scott was the first two-stroke motorcycle ever to complete a full Isle of Man TT course under race conditions, and in 1911 another Scott, ridden by Frank Phillip, achieved the TT lap record with an average speed of 50.11 mph (80.63 kph). Scott motorcycles were the fastest machines in 1912, 1913 and 1914, winning the event in 1912 and 1913. Scott died from pneumonia contracted after riding home from a potholing expedition in wet clothes on one of his motorcycles. Scott motorcycles ceased production in 1978, and vintage models are highly sought after.

SIR RIDLEY SCOTT, film director, born 1937. His work includes the famous Hovis advert (1973), *Alien*

(1979), *Blade Runner* (1982), *Thelma and Louise* (1991), *Gladiator* (2000) and *American Gangster* (2007).

DOUG SCOTT, CBE, mountaineer, born 1941. He was THE FIRST BRITON TO CLIMB MOUNT EVEREST and made the FIRST-EVER ASCENT OF THE SOUTH-WEST FACE OF EVEREST, in 1975.

TONY SCOTT, film director, brother of Ridley Scott, born 1944. His films include *Top Gun* (1986), *Days of Thunder* (1990), *Crimson Tide* (1995) and *Spy Game* (2001).

BON SCOTT (1946–80), lead singer of Australian rock band AC/DC, born in Kirriemuir.

SELINA SCOTT, newsreader and TV presenter, born 1951.

## American Scotts

WINFIELD SCOTT (1786–1866), US Army general. Known as the 'Grand Old Man of the Army', he was the LONGEST-SERVING ACTIVE GENERAL IN AMERICAN HISTORY.

RANDOLPH SCOTT (1898–1987), film actor and leading man who starred in *Last of the Mohicans* (1936), *High, Wide and Handsome* (1937), *The Desperadoes* (1943) and *Ride the High Country* (1962).

GEORGE C. SCOTT (1927–99), film actor and director, who won an Oscar for Best Actor in 1970 for his portrayal of General Patton in the film *Patton – Lust for Glory*.

DAVID RANDOLPH SCOTT, commander of the 1971 Apollo 15 mission, born in Texas in 1932. During the mission he became the seventh person to walk on the Moon, and THE FIRST PERSON TO *DRIVE* ON THE MOON.

WILLARD HERMAN SCOTT JNR., weatherman on NBC's *The Today Show*, born 1934. He was the creator of Ronald McDonald, and the first person to play him on screen.

*Well, I never knew this*
*about*
## SELKIRKSHIRE FOLK

JAMES HOGG (1770–1835), poet known as the 'Ettrick shepherd', born at Ettrick Hall in the Yarrow valley. He, Sir Walter Scott and William Wordsworth, all guests of Tibbie Shiels (*see* below), the formidable hostess of St Mary's Cottage, overlooking St Mary's Loch, are thought to have gone together to visit the ruins of Tushielaw up the Yarrow valley, the home of Scott's kinsman, freebooter Adam Scott, known as 'King of the Border' or 'King of Thieves'. Local tradition says Adam was hanged by James V from the branch of an ash tree that grew within the walls of Tushielaw, the same ash tree from which Adam himself had hanged so many poor wretches in his time. The tree has perished, but an entry in *Chambers' Gazetteer* of 1832 states: 'It is curious to observe that along its principal branches there are yet visible a number of nicks, or hollows, over which the ropes had been drawn wherewith he performed his numerous executions.'

MUNGO PARK (1771–1806), African explorer and FIRST EUROPEAN TO SEE THE RIVER NIGER, born at Foulshiels, son of one of the Duke of Buccleuch's tenant farmers.

TIBBIE, OR ISABELLA, SHIELS (1783–1878), who is buried in the churchyard in Ettrick, moved to St Mary's Cottage in 1823, with her husband, a mole catcher. He died the following year and for the next 50 years Tibbie supported herself (and, initially, her six children) by taking in lodgers. Even though she only had beds for 13 people, she would take in anything up to 35 guests at a time. St Mary's Cottage, now much extended, still takes in travellers today, and is known as TIBBIE SHIELS' INN.

TOM SCOTT (1854–1927), historical artist known as 'the Borders painter'.

He was born in Selkirk in a house where the Selkirk Institute now stands. His romantic style was drawn from the Arts and Crafts movement, and his subjects are mainly depictions of Border landscapes and legends.

MURRAY OF FALA HILL (1940–52), Scottish terrier, owned by US President Franklin D. Roosevelt and named after Roosevelt's Scottish ancestor John Murray of Fala Hill. Fala was present at FDR's famous fireside chats and at the President's meeting with Winston Churchill and Soviet Ambassador Litvinov in Washington in 1941. In September 1944 Roosevelt gave a speech to the teamsters union which became known as the 'Fala' speech, in which FDR protested at outrageous rumours being circulated about him by stating that Fala was deeply hurt by the attacks. A statue of Fala is incorporated into the Franklin D. Roosevelt Memorial in Washington, DC, and Fala is the only presidential pet to receive such an honour.

# Stirlingshire

✦◆✦◆✦

Stirling Castle ✦ Stirling Stewarts ✦ Stewarts
✦ Bute ✦ Stewart Titles ✦ Royal Stewarts
✦ House of Stewart ✦ Dukes of Albany ✦ James
✦ Earl of Moray ✦ Mary Queen of Scots
✦ Union of Crowns ✦ Pretenders ✦ Stuart Queens
✦ Some Notable Stewarts ✦ Acting Stewarts

*Stirling Castle, gateway to the Highlands*
*and principal centre of the Royal Stewarts.*

◄ Stirlingshire Folk ►

Alexander 'Greek' Thompson ✦ Andrew Greig Barr ✦ John Grierson
✦ John Damian de Falcuis ✦ Willie Carson

# Stirling Castle

The Stirling Castle we see today is very much a Stewart creation, begun by the first Stewart kings, Robert II and Robert III, and expanded into a grand Renaissance palace, particularly by James IV. It has played an important role in the history of the Royal House of Stewart.

# Stirling Stewarts

In 1437, after JAMES I was murdered at Perth, Queen Joan brought the six-year-old JAMES II to Stirling for safety. In 1452 James slew the Earl of Douglas at Stirling and threw his body out of the window.

JAMES III was probably born at Stirling in 1451 (some historians think he may have been born at St Andrews in 1452), and during his reign undertook extensive rebuilding of the castle.

In 1488 he was killed by persons unknown after the Battle of Sauchieburn, which was fought out less than 2 miles (3 km) away over the same ground as the Battle of Bannockburn. His opponent that day was his own son, the 14-year-old JAMES IV.

JAMES IV built the Chapel Royal and the GREAT HALL at Stirling, THE GRANDEST MEDIEVAL HALL IN SCOTLAND.

JAMES V was born at Stirling and, no doubt goaded by his French wife Mary of Guise, transformed the castle into a splendid palace to rival those in France.

James's daughter, the infant MARY Queen of Scots, was crowned in the Chapel Royal at Stirling and in 1561 celebrated mass there, to the extreme agitation of many Protestants, notably John Knox.

In 1566 Mary's son, the future JAMES VI, was christened in the Chapel Royal at Stirling, to the accompaniment of the FIRST RECORDED PUBLIC FIREWORKS DISPLAY IN BRITAIN. The following year, after Mary's abdication, he was crowned in the Church of the Holy Rood close to the castle.

In 1594 James VI rebuilt the Chapel Royal, and his son PRINCE HENRY was christened in the new building.

# Stewarts

The Stewarts descend from WALTER FITZALAN, grandson of Flaad Fitzalan, seneschal or steward to the Count of Dol in Brittany, who came over to England with William the Conqueror. Walter Fitzalan accompanied David I to Scotland, where the King gave him lands in Renfrewshire and appointed him as 1st Hereditary High Steward of Scotland.

Walter's grandson, another Walter, adopted the surname Stewart, from his hereditary position as Steward.

# Bute

Walter Stewart had three great-grandsons, of whom one became the Earl of Menteith while the eldest, Alexander, married the heiress to the Lord of Bute.

Alexander's eldest son James became Lord of Bute.

# Stewart Titles

Alexander's youngest son, JOHN OF BONKILL, was killed at the Battle of Falkirk in 1298, supporting William Wallace. John had four sons.

Through the three younger sons the Stewarts picked up the Earldoms of Angus, Lennox and Galloway.

# Royal Stewarts

John of Bonkill's eldest son, ALEXANDER STEWART, became 5th High Steward. His son Walter, the 6th Steward, commanded the left wing of the Scottish forces at the Battle of Bannockburn and later married Marjorie, the daughter of Robert the Bruce. Their son Robert became the first of the long line of Stewart monarchs, Robert II, in 1371.

# House of Stewart

The Stewarts ruled in Scotland, and later in England, for almost 350 years until the death of Queen Anne in 1714. They provided 11 kings and three queens, beginning with Robert II (1371–90), son of Walter Stewart, 6th High Steward, and Princess Marjorie, daughter of Robert the Bruce (Robert I). Robert II's fourth son was the notorious 'Wolf of Badenoch'. Next came his son Robert III (1390–1406), who created his brother Robert the 1st Duke of Albany.

# Dukes of Albany

# James Stewarts

Albany is a territorial term referring to that part of Scotland north of the River Forth that formed the kingdom of the Picts. The title DUKE OF ALBANY, first conferred in 1398, is SCOTLAND'S OLDEST DUKEDOM and has been used intermittently for younger sons of the Scottish, and later British, royal family. James VII, before he became king, was the Duke of York and Albany, and in that guise gave his name to Albany, the state capital of New York.

ROBERT STEWART, 1ST DUKE OF ALBANY (1340–1420), had to act as regent for his father Robert II, who was old and infirm, and for his brother Robert III, who was incapacitated after an accident and apparently died of grief after the capture of his young son James I by the English. In fact Albany, who wanted the throne for his own son, had organised the kidnap himself.

His son was MURDOCH STEWART, 2ND DUKE OF ALBANY (1362–1425). He was executed on Heading Hill next to Stirling Castle in 1425, along with his own sons Walter and Alexander, by James I, in revenge for the 1st Duke's machinations.

JAMES I (1404–37) spent 18 years in captivity in England, during which he wrote one of the early great works of Scottish literature, *The Kingis Quiar*, a semi-autobiographical poem about his imprisonment inspired by his love for Joan Beaufort, cousin of Henry VII. In 1424 Joan became his Queen. James was murdered in Perth at the behest of his uncle, Walter Stewart, Earl of Atholl.

JAMES II (1437–60) was just a teenager when William, 6th Earl of Douglas, and his brother were beheaded in front of him at the 'Black Dinner' in Edinburgh Castle, so that their great-uncle the Earl of Avondale, one of James's guardians, could inherit the Douglas title. James later spent much of his reign trying to rid himself of the Douglases, and in 1452 he did just that, inviting the 8th Earl of Douglas to his own 'black dinner' at Stirling Castle and running him through with his dagger. James tried in vain to ban golf, in 1457, and was killed while besieging Roxburgh Castle when one of his beloved cannons exploded.

JAMES III (1460–88) married Margaret of Denmark and received Orkney and Shetland as surety for a dowry. Thus Scotland reached its greatest territorial extent during his reign. He was defeated by his own son James at the Battle of Sauchieburn and murdered shortly afterwards, while in hiding, probably by one of his son's nobles. He is buried at Cambuskenneth Abbey, just east of Stirling.

JAMES IV (1488–1513) is regarded as the most successful of the Stewart monarchs. A cultured man, he was also the last monarch to speak fluent Gaelic. He married Margaret Tudor, daughter of Henry VII, and it was this marriage that led ultimately to the Union of the Crowns in 1603. James was killed along with nine earls, 14 lords, many Highland chiefs and one-third of the Scottish army at the Battle of Flodden in 1513, THE LAST BRITISH MONARCH TO BE KILLED IN BATTLE.

JAMES V (1513–42) fathered three illegitimate sons before he was 20 and sired at least 7 illegitimate children by different mothers. He liked to wander around Scotland in disguise as 'Gudeman of Ballenguich' (meaning farmer of a place in Stirling), but was usually recognised because of his bright red hair (*see* Fife). He resurrected the Auld Alliance with France, married the French Mary of Guise and encouraged the persecution of Protestants, including the first Protestant martyr Patrick Hamilton. After his defeat by Henry VIII at Solway Moss he retired to Falkland Palace a broken man, distressed at having no male heir, and lamenting the fate of the House of Stewart: 'It came wi' a lass, it'll gang wi' a lass.' He was almost right,

*Cambuskenneth Abbey*

but a bit previous. The Stewarts began with Marjorie, daughter of Robert the Bruce, and ended with a woman too – not his own daughter Mary, but Anne, over a century later.

*Falkland Palace*

## Earl of Moray

J ames V's illegitimate son the EARL OF MORAY was a Protestant convert who was opposed to his sister Mary's marriage to Lord Darnley, and was part of the plot to murder her secretary Rizzio. Two years after defeating Mary at the Battle of Langside in 1568, he became THE FIRST RECORDED VICTIM IN BRITAIN OF AN ASSASSINATION BY FIREARM,

when he was shot by a supporter of Mary, James Hamilton, in Linlithgow.

## Mary Queen of Scots
### *1542–87*

M ary was also Queen of the French for two years while married to the Dauphin. At that time she changed the spelling of her name to Stuart since 'w' is not used in French.

Her second husband, HENRY STUART, LORD DARNLEY (1545–67), was her first cousin and they shared a grandmother, Margaret Tudor, sister of Henry VIII. It was this line of descent that made their son James VI a legitimate heir to the English throne.

Handsome but vain, Lord Darnley, son of Matthew Stuart, Earl of Lennox, instigated the murder of Mary's favourite David Rizzio in 1566, and the next year was himself found strangled in the garden of the Kirk o'

Fields in Edinburgh, after the house was blown up. The prime suspect was Mary's third husband, the EARL OF BOTHWELL (1536–78).

## Stuart Monarchs after the Union of Crowns, 1603

JAMES VI OF SCOTLAND (reigned 1567–1625) and I OF ENGLAND (1603–1625). He acceded to the English throne on the death of Elizabeth I. Known as the 'wisest fool in Christendom', he was the target, in 1605, of Guy Fawkes's Gunpowder Plot.

CHARLES I (reigned 1625–49). The LAST KING TO BE BORN IN SCOTLAND and THE LAST BRITISH MONARCH TO BE BEHEADED.

CHARLES II (reigned 1649–85). THE LAST KING TO BE CROWNED IN SCOTLAND, at Scone in 1651. Although exiled from England between 1651 and 1660 and deposed in England, he remained King of Scotland all that time. After the Restoration in England he was known as 'the Merrie Monarch'.

JAMES VII AND II (reigned 1685–89). THE LAST STUART KING until over-

thrown by the Glorious Revolution, which placed William and Mary on the throne. His final attempt to retake the throne ended in defeat at the Battle of the Boyne in Ireland in 1690, an event that has moulded Irish politics to this day.

## Pretenders

JAMES FRANCIS EDWARD STUART (1688–1766). The Old Pretender, son of James VII. After the failure of the 1715 uprising he lived the rest of his life in Rome.

CHARLES EDWARD STUART (1720–88). Bonnie Prince Charlie, the Young Pretender, son of the Old Pretender. After defeat at Culloden in 1745, he fled to France with the aid of Flora MacDonald and spent the rest of his life in France and Italy. He is buried in St Peter's Basilica in the Vatican.

## Stuart Queens

MARY II (reigned 1689–94). Daughter of James VII, she reigned with her husband and cousin William of Orange, AS THE ONLY JOINT BRITISH MONARCHS in history. William reigned as sole monarch for eight years after Mary's death.

ANNE (reigned 1702–14). Sister of Mary II and the FIRST SOVEREIGN

OF THE UNITED KINGDOM OF GREAT BRITAIN. Because she died without an heir she was THE LAST OF THE STUART MONARCHS. The crown went to her second cousin, George I, of the House of Hanover, who was a descendant of the Stuarts through his maternal grandmother, Elizabeth, daughter of James VI.

## Some Notable Stewarts

FRANCES STUART, 'LA BELLE STUART' (1647–1702), Duchess of Richmond and Lennox. Mistress of Charles II, she was described by Samuel Pepys as 'the greatest beauty I ever saw' and was the model for BRITANNIA on the coinage and statues.

DUGALD STEWART (1753–1828), philosopher and exponent of 'common sense'. Dugald was the first to describe Edinburgh as 'the Athens of the North'.

JOHN McDOUALL STUART (1815–66), Australian explorer, born in Dysart. Trained as a civil engineer, he emigrated to Australia when he was 23 and found work as a surveyor. He completed a number of expeditions into the interior of Australia, but his greatest achievement came in 1861–2 when he became THE FIRST MAN TO CROSS AUSTRALIA FROM SOUTH TO NORTH, from Adelaide to the Indian Ocean at Chambers Bay, to the east of what is now Darwin. His journey opened up the Northern Territory and determined a route for the overland telegraph line, which in 1872 connected Australia to the rest of the world for the first time. Stuart's name is commemorated by Mount Stuart, which was thought at one time to mark the centre of Australia, Stuart's Creek and the Stuart Highway, which runs from Adelaide to Darwin through Alice Springs, more or less following the route Stuart took in 1861.

Memorable Quote:
*'Today I find, from my observations of the sun, that I am now camped in the centre of Australia.'*

ANDY STEWART (1933–94), comedian and singer, known for his television show *The White Heather Club* and warmly remembered for the hit song 'Donald Where's Your Troosers'.

SIR JACKIE STEWART, racing car driver known as the 'Flying Scot', born in 1939. He is THE ONLY BRITON TO WIN THREE FORMULA ONE WORLD CHAMPIONSHIPS, in 1969, 1971 and 1973. In 1997 he launched the Stewart Grand Prix Formula One team, which achieved one pole position, at the French Grand Prix in 1999, and one win, when Johnny Herbert drove to victory in the European Grand Prix at the Nurburgring, also in 1999. The team was sold to Jaguar for the following season and is now Red Bull.

ROD STEWART, rock singer renowned for his husky voice, born 1945. An apprentice footballer with Brentford, he soon turned to music and came to prominence first as lead singer of the Jeff Beck Group and then of the Faces. He has had six No. 1 hits and 24 top ten singles including 'Maggie May' (1971), 'Sailing' (1975) and 'Do Ya Think I'm Sexy?' (1978). He is renowned for his relationships with statuesque blondes: actress Britt Ekland, first wife Alana Hamilton, model Kelly Emberg, second wife Rachel Hunter and third wife Penny Lancaster.

HAMISH STUART, singer and guitarist in rhythm and blues group the Average White Band, born 1949.

DAVE STEWART, musician, best known for founding the Eurythmics with Annie Lennox, born 1952.

## Acting Stewarts

JAMES 'JIMMY' STEWART (1908–97). Remembered for classic films such as *Mr Smith Goes to Washington* (1939), *Harvey* (1950), *Rear Window* (1954), *The Spirit of St Louis* (1957), *Vertigo* (1958) and *Shenandoah* (1965). He won an Oscar in 1941 for Best Actor in *The Philadelphia Story* and a Lifetime Achievement Award in 1985. He also had a distinguished war record. While flying B-24 Liberators out of England he earned the Distinguished Flying Cross with two Oak Leaf Clusters, the Air Medal with three Oak Leaf Clusters, and the French Croix de Guerre with Palm.

Memorable Quotes:
*'If I had my career over again? Maybe I'd say to myself, speed it up a little.'*

*'It's well done if you can do a part and not have the acting show.'*

*'When it came to kissing, Harlow was the best.'*

STEWART GRANGER (1913–93). Born James Stewart, he had to change his name so as not to be confused with the American film actor of that name (*see* above). Best remembered for *King Solomon's Mines* (1950), *The Prisoner of Zenda* (1952) and *North to Alaska* (1960).

PATRICK STEWART, born in 1940. A distinguished Shakespearian actor, he is most widely known for his role as Captain Jean-Luc Picard of the starship *Enterprise* in *Star Trek: The Next Generation*, from 1987 to 1994.

Memorable Quote:
*'Make it so.'*

*Well, I never knew this*
*about*
## STIRLINGSHIRE FOLK

ALEXANDER 'GREEK' THOMPSON (1817–75), architect, born in Balfron. Regarded by many as the best of Victorian Glasgow's architects, Thompson drew inspiration from classical Greek architecture, hence the nickname 'Greek'. His three churches in Glasgow, Caledonia Road (now a shell), St Vincent Street and Queens Park, are all landmarks, while Holmwood House in Cathcart is owned by the National Trust for Scotland.

## Andrew Greig Barr
◄── 1872–1903 ──►

ANDREW GREIG BARR, inventor of 'Scotland's other national drink', Irn Bru, 'made in Scotland from girders', was born in Falkirk. Andrew's father

Robert was a cork cutter in Falkirk, supplying the town's bottling trade, who moved into producing fizzy water and lemonade when the cork trade declined. In 1887 Robert's eldest son, also Robert, set up a branch of the fizzy drinks business in Glasgow, and such was its success that Robert Junior persuaded his brother Andrew to leave his bank job and come and help run the company. In 1901 Andrew introduced his legendary Iron Brew, made from his own secret recipe, and A.G. Barr and Co. Ltd took off.

Andrew did not live to see his company grow into BRITAIN'S BIGGEST MANUFACTURER OF SOFT DRINKS. He died of pneumonia in 1903 aged just 31.

In the 1930s, Irn Bru as it became known (they were forced to change

the name since it was not actually 'brewed'), was transported around the streets of Falkirk by a magnificent Clydesdale horse called CARNERA, reputed to be THE BIGGEST HORSE IN THE WORLD.

JOHN GRIERSON (1898–1972), 'Father of the Documentary', was born at Deanston near Doune. A graduate of Glasgow University, Grierson was fascinated by the psychology of propaganda, and in

### First Flight

In 1507, in the days of James IV, JOHN DAMIAN DE FALCUIS, the Abbot of Tongland, flung himself from the walls of Stirling Castle, intending to fly to France with the help of a pair of wings made from chicken feathers. This attempt at Scotland's first flight ended in a dunghill because, as the Abbot explained as they carried him back up the hill to set his broken leg, the chicken feathers were attracted to the dung.

Almost exactly 400 years later, not far away in a field at Causeway-head, two brothers actually did achieve SCOTLAND'S FIRST FLIGHT. In 1909 HAROLD BARNWELL soared for nearly 260 ft (80 m) above a field beneath the towering Wallace Monument, in a proto-type aeroplane designed by his brother FRANK BARNWELL. Their feat is commemorated today by a silver granite sculpture set on top of a cairn that was unveiled on the site in 2005.

Harold became chief test pilot for Vickers but was killed during the First World War in 1917. Frank went on to become chief designer for the Bristol Aeroplane Company, where he was responsible for the BRISTOL FIGHTER and the BRISTOL BLENHEIM bomber.

1926, in an article for the *New York Sun* about Robert Flaherty's film *Moana*, he introduced the term 'documentary', which he later defined as the 'creative treatment of actuality'. He went on to make a number of films about ordinary British life, the first of them, *Drifters* (1929), about the herring fishermen of the North Sea. He ended his career as Head of Film for UNESCO.

WILLIE CARSON, jockey, born in Stirling in 1942. He was champion jockey five times, won 17 classics and rode 100 winners in a season 23 times.

# Sutherland

---◆◆◆◆---

CLAN SUTHERLAND ✦ EARLS OF SUTHERLAND
✦ DUKES OF SUTHERLAND
✦ SOME NOTABLE SUTHERLANDS
✦ CLAN MACKAY ✦ PIPER MACKAY

*Dunrobin Castle, seat of the Clan Sutherland and the
largest house in the north of Scotland.*

◄ SUTHERLAND FOLK ►

Lieutenant-General Hugh Mackay of Scourie ✦ Alistair Forbes-Mackay
✦ Fulton Mackay ✦ James Mackay

# Clan Sutherland

The name Sutherland comes from the Norse Sudrland, meaning either the land to the south of, or the southern lands of, the Norse earldom of Orkney and Caithness. Up until the late 11th century this territory was populated, if at all, by a combination of hardy Norsemen and intrepid, Gaelic-speaking Celts.

At the start of the 12th century, the Celtic Scots began to be driven north by the Norman Scots accompanying King David I on his return from exile, and many of them ended up in Sutherland. In 1150 David came north himself to put down the pesky Norse and gave out large tranches of land to those who helped him do so.

One of these was a Flemish mercenary nobleman by the name of FRESKIN DE MORAVIA – Moravia being Moray, where his father Olec had been given land at Duffus.

Freskin's job was to clear the Norse out of Sutherland, and this he did. Indeed, he is credited with killing THE LAST NORSEMAN by hurling a horseshoe at him during a final battle near Dornoch in 1150.

Freskin's son WILLIAM DE MORAVIA continued the good work on behalf of William the Lion, as did his descendants, and eventually the family were granted large swathes of Sutherland from which they took their family name.

The Chief of Clan Sutherland is, to this day, whoever holds the title of Earl (or Countess) of Sutherland, regardless of the family name, and the Clan seat is DUNROBIN CASTLE, near Golspie, which sits on the site of the castle constructed by the 1st Earl.

# Earls of Sutherland

The 1ST EARL OF SUTHERLAND was WILLIAM DE MORAVIA (d.1248), who was elevated to the title by Alexander II in 1228. This makes Sutherland THE OLDEST SURVIVING BRITISH EARLDOM. William's son WILLIAM, 2ND EARL OF SUTHERLAND (c.1247–1325), fought on the side of Robert the Bruce at the Battle of Bannockburn in 1314 and signed the Declaration of Arbroath in 1320.

*Dornoch Castle*

WILLIAM, 4TH EARL OF SUTHER-
LAND, married Princess Margaret,
eldest daughter of Robert the Bruce,
by his second wife, Elizabeth de
Burgo. Margaret was full sister to King
David II, and David chose her son
John, his nephew, to succeed him to
the Scottish throne, in preference to
Walter Stewart, husband of the Bruce's
daughter by his first marriage, Princess
Marjorie. John died in 1361, however,
ten years before King David, and so
Walter and Marjorie's son Robert
came to the throne as Robert II and
founded the Royal House of Stewart.
Had John Sutherland lived, Scottish
history would have taken a very
different course.

JOHN, 9TH EARL OF SUTHER-
LAND, died childless in 1514 and the
title devolved upon his sister Elizabeth, who married Adam Gordon,
second son of the Earl of Huntly, and
so the family name of the Earls of
Sutherland became Gordon.

JOHN GORDON, 16TH EARL OF
SUTHERLAND (1661–1733), changed
the family name back to Sutherland,
and so it remained until William
Sutherland, 18th Earl (1735–66), died
without sons. After a famous struggle
('the Sutherland peerage case'), which
established the validity of the earldom
to pass through the female line, the
title settled on his one-year-old
daughter Elizabeth, 19th Countess of
Sutherland (1765–1839).

# Duke and Duchess of Sutherland

In 1785 Elizabeth married the
fabulously wealthy George Leveson-
Gower, heir to the Marquess of
Stafford. He was British ambassador
to France during the French Revolution, and he and his wife were arrested
and held for a while for trying to help
Marie Antoinette and her son escape.

In Scotland they are remembered,
without much affection, for presiding
over the 'Sutherland' Clearances of
the early 18th century, when the
Countess and her factor Patrick Sellar
were alleged to have behaved with
high-handed ruthlessness in moving
crofters off the land they had worked
for generations, to make way for
sheep-farming.

Elizabeth had kept the earldom of
Sutherland and in 1833, six months
before he died, her husband was
created 1ST DUKE OF SUTHERLAND.
He is controversially commemorated

by a huge statue on Beinn a'Bhragaidh overlooking Golspie.

Their son George, 20th Earl and 2nd Duke of Sutherland, took the family name of Sutherland-Leveson-Gower.

GEORGE SUTHERLAND-LEVESON-GOWER, 5TH DUKE OF SUTHERLAND (1888–1963), was life patron and first chairman of the British Film Institute from 1933 to 1936. In 1958 the BFI created the Sutherland Trophy in his honour, which is today awarded annually to the maker of the most original and imaginative first film shown at the London Film Festival.

When the 5th Duke died, the earldom, along with the Sutherland estates and Dunrobin Castle, passed to his niece Elizabeth, 24th and current Countess of Sutherland, while the dukedom went to a distant cousin, John Egerton.

# Some Notable Sutherlands

## *Thomas Sutherland 1834–1922*

THOMAS SUTHERLAND, shipping magnate and banker, was born in Aberdeen, the son of an unsuccessful businessman. Watching the marine activity in Aberdeen harbour

gave him an enthusiasm for ships, and he found a job as a clerk in the London office of P&O. After swiftly proving his abilities Sutherland was sent to Hong Kong and ended up managing P&O's Asian operation. He began regular steam services to Nagasaki and Yokohama in Japan, the only Japanese cities open to the British at the time, and in 1863 opened THE LARGEST DOCKYARD IN ASIA, the Hong Kong and Whampoa Dock Company.

In the aftermath of the Second Opium War (1856–60) Sutherland saw the need for a bank to finance the burgeoning trade between China and Europe, and in 1865 he founded the HONGKONG AND SHANGHAI BANKING CORPORATION, to be run on 'sound Scottish banking principles'.

In 1881 Sutherland became chairman of P&O, a position he held for 30 years until his death.

HSBC, as it is now called, has since grown into one of the world's biggest banks and financial institutions.

GRAHAM SUTHERLAND (1903–80), artist. His most talked-about work was his portrait of Winston Churchill, painted in 1954 to be given to the great man as an 80th birthday present from both Houses of Parliament. When Churchill unveiled the picture, which he disliked, he remarked, 'The portrait is a remarkable example of modern art. It certainly combines force and candour . . .' It was destroyed on the orders of Lady Churchill the following year. Sutherland's most celebrated work, completed in 1962, is BRITAIN'S LARGEST TAPESTRY, *Christ in Glory*, which hangs behind the altar in Coventry Cathedral.

DAME JOAN SUTHERLAND, CBE, opera singer known as 'La Stupenda', born in 1926.

RANALD SUTHERLAND, Lord Sutherland, born in 1932, graduated from Edinburgh University and was called to the Bar in 1956. He has been a judge since 1985 and was the presiding judge in the trial of the man accused of blowing up Pan AM Flight 102 over Lockerbie in 1988.

DONALD SUTHERLAND, Canadian film actor, born 1935. He has starred in over 100 major films, such as *M*A*S*H* (1970), *Klute* (1971), *Don't Look Now* (1973), *The Eagle Has Landed* (1976), *Eye of the Needle* (1981), *Disclosure* (1994) and *The Italian Job* (2003).

KIEFER SUTHERLAND, actor and son of Donald, born in 1966. His maternal grandfather, Tommy Douglas, who led North America's first socialist government and introduced universal public healthcare to Canada, was born in Camelon, near Falkirk. Sutherland is widely known for playing the lead role in the ground-breaking television series *24*, in which he plays government agent Jack Bauer.

# Clan Mackay

CLAN MACKAY is one of the oldest of the Gaelic Scots clans and can claim descent for the Irish King Niall. The name Mackay means 'of Aedh' or 'son of Aedh', Aedh being a grandson of King Niall.

In the early 8th century the Mac Aedh left the kingdom of Dalraida in Ireland with other tribes and settled in what is now Argyllshire. Over the centuries many of them moved up through the Great Glen and settled in the kingdom of Moray, some attaining the position of Mormaer, until their power was broken by David I, and they were banished across the mountains to Strathnaver, an area that stretched along the north coast from Caithness in the east to Cape Wrath in the west. Strathnaver now forms the northern portion of Sutherland.

The Mackays, as they became, ruled their lands from VARRICH CASTLE, under the mountainous presence of Ben Hope and Ben Loyal. Although it is now a ruin, Varrich, the oldest stone building in the north of Scotland, remains the spiritual home of the Clan.

The Mackays suffered greatly in the 'Sutherland' Clearances of the early 19th century. The 90-year-old Margaret Mackay was almost burned alive when her croft was set alight by the minions of Patrick Sellar, factor to the Countess of Sutherland. She was rescued but died five days later. Sellar was put on trial in Inverness, accused of arson and culpable homicide, but was acquitted.

Although their presence in Strathnaver is a fraction of what it was, north-west Sutherland is still known as Mackay country. There is a Clan Mackay Museum in Bettyhill – a village named, ironically, after the Countess of Sutherland, who built it to house the Mackays cleared off their crofting lands.

The present Clan Chief is HUGH WILLIAM MACKAY, 14TH LORD REAY, Baron Mackay, born in 1937, who lives in the *House of Tongue*.

# Piper Mackay

The Clan tune is 'Mackay's March', although there are several tunes associated with the Clan, including 'The White Banner of Mackay'.

The FIRST PIPER KNOWN OF IN A BRITISH ARMY UNIT was a Piper Mackay, recorded as being transferred from the Scots Brigade on the Continent to the Royal Scots when they were founded in 1633. (The Royal

Scots is THE OLDEST REGIMENT IN THE BRITISH ARMY.)

In 1758, during the French and Indian Wars, as a member of the 'Black Watch', Piper William Mackay led the ill-fated charge on the French Fort Ticonderoga, in what is now upper New York State.

In 1815, at the Battle of Waterloo, Piper Kenneth Mackay of the Cameron Highlanders won renown by marching out in front of the square during a cavalry charge and playing 'War or Peace'. He was personally presented with a set of silver pipes by the King, in recognition of his exceptional act of bravery.

PIPER ANGUS MACKAY (1813–59) was piper to Queen Victoria.

*Well, I never knew this*
*about*
**SUTHERLAND FOLK**

## Lieutenant-General Hugh Mackay of Scourie
### ◄ 1640–92 ►

As commander of the Scots brigade in Holland, Mackay returned to England to help James VII (James II of England) suppress the Monmouth Rebellion, but then refused to support the King against William of Orange, instead leading William's forces during the Glorious Revolution in 1688.

He was then sent to subdue the Jacobites as William's commander-in-chief in Scotland, and although he suffered a bad defeat at the Battle of Killiecrankie, the Jacobite leader Viscount Dundee was killed and Mackay was able to carry on and secure the Highlands, founding Fort

William, which he named after William of Orange, as a base from which to control the area.

Following his experience at Killiecrankie, where his men were overwhelmed by the charging Highlanders because they could not attach their bayonets quickly enough, Mackay invented the RING BAYONET, which allowed the rifle to be fired with the bayonet in place.

ALISTAIR FORBES-MACKAY (1878–1914), naval surgeon and Antarctic explorer. While a member of one of Ernest Shackleton's expeditions to the Antarctic in 1909, Mackay became one of the first three men to reach the south magnetic pole. He was ship's doctor on the tragic *Karluk* expedition to the Arctic, which began in 1913. The *Karluk* was crushed by the ice and all but one of the crew perished.

*Fulton Mackay*

FULTON MACKAY (1922–87), actor fondly remembered for his role as the deeply suspicious and authoritarian prison warder 'Mr Mackay' in the BBC television comedy series *Porridge*, starring Ronnie Barker, which ran from 1974 until 1977.

JAMES MACKAY, LORD MACKAY OF CLASHFERN, was born in 1927, the son of a railway signalman. He served as Margaret Thatcher's Lord Chancellor from 1987 and stayed in the role until 1997. Clashfern was his father's birthplace in Sutherland.

# West Lothian

DALMENY + PRIMROSE + EARLS OF ROSEBERY + HOPE
+ HOPETOUN + EARLS OF HOPETOUN
+ MARQUESSES OF LINLITHGOW + SOME HIGH HOPES

*Dalmeny House, home of the Earl of Roseberry,*
*birthplace of the Edinburgh Festival and the*
*first Tudor revival house in Scotland.*

◄ WEST LOTHIAN FOLK ►

James Douglas + John Cain + Lawrence Ennis + Dougal Haston
+ Bernard Gallacher + Michael Caton-Jones + Dario Franchitti

# Dalmeny

The village of DALMENY sits at the south end of the Forth Road Bridge and boasts THE FINEST ROMANESQUE CHURCH IN SCOTLAND as well as Scotland's FIRST GOTHIC REVIVAL DWELLING, DALMENY HOUSE, seat of the EARL OF ROSEBERY.

The Dalmeny Estate was acquired in 1662 by SIR ARCHIBALD PRIMROSE, clerk of the Privy Council, who bought what was then the barony of Barnbougle from the Earl of Haddington.

# Primrose

The word 'primrose' comes from the Old British 'pren ros', meaning 'tree of the moor'. The name Primrose derives from the lands of Primrose near Dunfermline, in Fife, where the first de Primrose, HENRY DE PRIMROSE, was recorded in 1490.

His grandson James was clerk of the Privy Council of Scotland, and his son SIR ARCHIBALD PRIMROSE (1616–79), lauded by Charles I for his 'fidelity, judgement and discretion', fought for the King in the Civil War, lost his estates to Cromwell, then had them restored at the Restoration and was knighted.

# Earls of Rosebery

When Sir Archibald bought Dalmeny in 1662, the property he moved into was a crumbling 13th-century tower house, BARNBOUGLE CASTLE, which sat right beside the Forth River and was forever flooding, but it would be many years before the Primroses were in a position to build themselves somewhere more suitable.

Sir Archibald's fourth son, also Archibald, supported William of Orange and was created 1ST EARL OF ROSEBERY (1664–1723) by Queen Anne in 1703, a title he took from Rosebery Topping, a hill on his wife's estate in Yorkshire.

His son, the 2ND EARL OF ROSEBERY (1691–1765), was something of a 'black sheep' who ran through the family money, was imprisoned for debt and riotous behaviour, and deserted his wife for a laundry-maid.

# 3rd Earl of Rosebery

His son, the 3RD EARL OF ROSEBERY (1729–1814), married a Norfolk heiress who helped to pay off his father's debts. Sadly, she died in 1771, and the Earl was never able to fulfil his dream of rebuilding Barnbougle into a spectacular triangular castle and harbour, as designed by his friend Robert Adam, which would have 'conjured up an image of the imperial palace at Spalato'.

The 3rd Earl was a proud man who liked to disguise his insipient baldness with a nest of wigs of varying lengths, and one can only imagine his agony at the dinner table when his children demanded to know why they couldn't have a grand house like their neighbour, the Earl of Hopetoun. 'What was good enough for my grandfather should be good enough for my grandchildren,' he would tell them while wringing out his wig after another wave had crashed in through the dining-room window and drenched him.

*Barnbougle Castle*

## 4th Earl of Rosebery

His son, the 4TH EARL OF ROSE-BERY (1783–1868), somehow managed to find the money to replace

Barnbougle Castle with a completely new Tudor Gothic house built nearby, to a design by William Wilkin, architect of the National Gallery in London. Rosebery's costs were somewhat defrayed by mulcting his brother-in-law Sir Henry Mildmay for substantial damages in compensation for 'alienating my wife's affections'. Mildmay had disguised himself as a fisherman, approached Barnbougle in a rowing boat at dusk and managed to slip into the castle apparently undetected. It was Mildmay's misfortune, however, that the Earl's younger brother, Frank Primrose, happened to be visiting. Alerted by the strong smell of fish, Frank spied muddy boot marks on the carpet and followed the trail all the way to Lady Rosebery's boudoir. Mildmay had to jump for his life out of the window, and next day Lady Rosebery was sent packing too.

The 4th Earl's heir, LORD DALMENY, FIRST LORD OF THE ADMIRALTY, anticipated the nanny state by telling the middle classes that they should get out and walk more for the sake of their health. Unfortunately he died of pleurisy as a result of walking back to Dalmeny from Edinburgh in the middle of winter, after a Turkish bath and pre-deceased his father.

# 5th Earl of Rosebery
## 1847–1929

Lord Dalmeny's son and heir Archibald Primrose chose to reveal his life's ambitions while still a boy at Eton. They were modest: to become Prime Minister, to win the Derby and to marry a Rothschild.

In 1878, by now 5TH EARL OF ROSEBERY, he married the richest woman in the world, Hannah, only child of Baron Meyer de Rothschild and beneficiary of his spectacular will, which included Mentmore Towers in Buckinghamshire. One ambition met.

In March 1894 he became Prime Minister, succeeding William Gladstone. Two ambitions met.

In June that same year he achieved the first of three Derby wins, with a horse called Ladas II. Game, set and match.

Ladas II was named in honour of his first racehorse, Ladas, which he had bought in 1869 while still at Oxford. Since it was against the rules for an Oxford undergraduate to own a horse, Rosebery was given the choice – the horse or your degree. He chose the horse.

Lord Rosebery's term as Prime Minister was brief, lasting only 15 months, during which time he opposed Irish Home Rule and created the Scottish Office. A serious insomniac, he took to riding round London in the middle of the night in a primrose-coloured carriage, and refurbished Barnbougle Castle as a retreat and a home for his huge library. He was THE RICHEST BRITISH PRIME MINISTER IN HISTORY.

Rosebery was distraught when his wife Hannah, by whom he had four children, died in 1890, and was saddened further when the Marquess of Queensberry cast aspersions on Rosebery's relationship with the Marquess's son Lord Alfred Douglas, Oscar Wilde's friend 'Bosie'.

Rosebery's youngest son, CAPTAIN NEIL PRIMROSE, who was born at Dalmeny, died in Palestine in the First World War at the third Battle of Gaza, leading one of the last British cavalry charges.

The 5th Earl of Rosebery died in 1929 to the strains of the 'Eton Boating Song' and is buried in the lovely old church at Dalmeny.

Dalmeny House remains the seat

of the Primrose Clan and home to the Clan Chief, presently the 7th Earl of Rosebery. It contains one of the most extensive art and furniture collections in the world, bolstered by many items from the Rothschild collection retained from the forced sale of Mentmore Towers in 1977 to meet death duties.

Memorable Quotes:
*'The British Empire is a common-wealth of nations.'* (From a speech in Adelaide, Australia, in 1884)

*'A gentleman will blithely do in poli-tics what he would kick a man downstairs for doing in ordinary life.'*

*'It is beginning to be hinted that we are a nation of amateurs.'* (Address at Glasgow University in 1900)

## Hope

Hope is a Scottish name that comes from the Old English word 'hop', meaning 'small valley', and the Hopes originate from JOHN DE HOP of Peeblesshire, whose name is found on the Ragman Rolls of 1296.

The next Hope to have made a mark is another John de Hope, who escorted James V's first wife Magdalene to Scotland from France in 1537 and then settled in Edinburgh, where

his descendants became respectable lawyers and businessmen.

His grandson, SIR THOMAS HOPE OF CRAIGHALL (1573–1646), was appointed Lord Advocate by Charles I in 1626 and contributed much to Scottish law with his *Minor Practicks*, published in 1726 and still referred to today. He is particularly remembered for drafting the National Covenant. His younger brother Henry went into banking and was ancestor of the line that founded Hope & Co. Bank in Amsterdam.

## Hopetoun

Sir Thomas's younger son SIR JAMES HOPE (1614–61) made a fortune out of the lead mines his wife Anne Foulis inherited, at Leadhills in Lanarkshire, and was the first to style himself 'of Hopetoun', which was the old name for Leadhills.

Their son JOHN HOPE was thus enabled to buy a large portion of the Abercorn estate from the Setons in 1678, where he planned to build a fine home for his family.

Before he got the chance, four years later in 1682, John was lost at sea when the frigate *Gloucester*, which was bringing the Duke of York (later James VII) to Scotland, was shipwrecked off the Norfolk coast. John gave up his seat in the lifeboat to the Duke (and, it is said, to the Duke's dogs) and perished.

## *Earls of Hopetoun*

J ohn's widow Lady Margaret Hamilton went ahead and commissioned Sir William Bruce to design a comfortable house in the classical style for her son Charles (1681–1742). In 1703 he was created IST EARL OF HOPETOUN by Queen Anne, who was no doubt grateful for the sacrifice Charles's father had made for her own. Charles married the sister of the Marquess of Annandale, who bequeathed his renowned art collection to Hopetoun, and in 1721 the Earl asked William Adam to enlarge the house, which he did by adding the magnificent façade and sweeping colonnades, while Robert and John Adam completed the interior. By the time it was finished, Hopetoun was THE LARGEST COUNTRY HOUSE IN SCOTLAND.

It was from this 'Scottish Versailles' that future Earls of Hopetoun and later Marquesses of Linlithgow went out and played their part on the world stage.

The 4th Earl of Hopetoun, GENERAL SIR JOHN HOPE (1764–1823), distinguished himself in the Peninsular War, completing the successful evacuation of British troops from Corunna after the death of Sir John Moore in 1808. He was also a governor of the Royal Bank of Scotland, and his statue stands outside Dundas House in St Andrew Square in Edinburgh.

During the 4th Earl's time, in 1822, Hopetoun House was the setting for the first visit of a reigning British monarch to Scotland for 170 years when George IV came to stay. The King's tour was stage-managed by Sir Walter Scott to promote the new Romantic image of Scotland, and

throughout the trip George wore Highland dress, which had been banned from 1745 until 1782 after the Jacobite rebellions. While he was at Hopetoun, the King knighted the artist Henry Raeburn in the State Drawing Room.

## Marquesses of Linlithgow

The 7TH EARL OF HOPETOUN, JOHN HOPE (1860–1908), served as THE FIRST GOVERNOR-GENERAL OF AUSTRALIA, from 1901 to 1902. He was created 1ST MARQUESS OF LINLITHGOW in 1902.

His son VICTOR HOPE, THE 2ND MARQUESS OF LINLITHGOW (1887–1952), was THE LONGEST-SERVING VICEROY OF INDIA, from 1936 to 1943. His second son, John Hope, married the daughter of novelist Somerset Maugham, while his

youngest daughter Doreen was mother to horse-riding champion Lucinda Green (b.1953), who won the Badminton Horse Trials a record six times on six different horses.

His son, CHARLES HOPE, 3RD MARQUESS OF LINLITHGOW (1912–87), served with the 51st Highland Division during the Second World War, was captured at Dunkirk in 1940 and held prisoner at Colditz.

## Some High Hopes

PROFESSOR JOHN HOPE (1725–86), botanist, was appointed to the Regius Chair of Botany at the University of Edinburgh and served as King's Botanist. He was the first botanist in Britain to apply Carl Linnaeus's system of plant classification and is credited with introducing RHUBARB to Britain.

PROFESSOR THOMAS HOPE (1766–1844), chemist and son of Professor John Hope (*see* above), was appointed to the Chair of Chemistry at the University of Edinburgh. In 1793 he examined some samples of a new substance uncovered by French prisoners working in the lead mines on the Ardnamurchan Peninsula in Argyllshire and realised it was a completely new element. He called it STRONTIUM, after the village of Stronian where it was discovered. He was also the FIRST CHEMIST TO

DEMONSTRATE THAT WATER EXPANDS WHEN FROZEN.

ADMIRAL SIR GEORGE JOHNSTONE HOPE (1767–1818), grandson of the 1st Earl of Hopetoun, commanded HMS *Defence* at the Battle of Trafalgar in 1805.

ADMIRAL SIR JAMES HOPE (1808–81), son of Admiral Sir George Johnstone Hope (*see* above), commanded the Royal Navy fleet in China during the Second Opium War from 1856 to 1860, and rose to be admiral of the fleet. Not long before his death he married Elizabeth Cotton as his second wife. Lady Hope was an evangelist who later claimed that she had visited the naturalist Charles Darwin on his deathbed in 1882 and heard him recant his Theory of Evolution and accept Jesus Christ as his Saviour. This became a huge story, particularly in America, but was refuted by Darwin's children.

LESLIE TOWNES HOPE (1903–2003), better known as Bob Hope, comedian and actor who starred in *The Cat and the Canary* (1939), *My Favourite Blonde* (1942) and *The Paleface* (1948). He is best remembered for sparring with Bing Crosby in *The Road to Singapore* (1940) and its six sequels.

Memorable Quotes:
*'You know you are getting old when the candles cost more than the cake.'*

*'I do benefits for all religions – I'd hate to blow the hereafter on a technicality.'*

*Well, I never knew this*
*about*
## WEST LOTHIAN FOLK

JAMES DOUGLAS (1675–1742), anatomist and physician to George II's consort Queen Caroline, was born in West Calder. As a result of his groundbreaking anatomical investigations there are several anatomical terms that bear his name, including the Douglas pouch, Douglasitis, Douglas abscess, Douglasfold, Douglas line and Douglas septum.

JOHN CAIN, OR KANE (1860–1934), first self-taught artist to be exhibited in a museum. Born in West Calder, he emigrated to Pittsburgh, Pennsylvania, in 1879 and supported himself with a variety of jobs while he learned to sketch the local scenery. After losing a leg in a railway accident he began painting railway carriages, but left his family when his baby son died in 1904. For the rest of his life he wandered around Pittsburgh painting the urban landscape and his memories of his Scottish boyhood. His bold, original, primitive style was at first dismissed as childish, but he slowly built up a popular following and was finally accepted for exhibition at the Carnegie Museum of Art in 1927, when he was 67. He had a one-man show in New York in 1931, and he and the wife he had abandoned were reconciled for his final years. Today his works are almost priceless.

LAWRENCE ENNIS (1870–1938), chief engineer who oversaw construction of the world's widest long-span and tallest steel arch bridge, the Sydney Harbour Bridge, which opened in 1932. He was born in West Calder.

Memorable Quote:
*'Working on a bridge invigorates the poorest intelligence and captivates the imagination of everyone concerned.'*

DOUGAL HASTON (1940–77), mountaineer, born in Currie. Haston was THE FIRST MAN TO CLIMB THE NORTH FACE OF THE EIGER BY THE MOST DIRECT ROUTE, or *direttissima* (1966), the FIRST TO CLIMB THE SOUTH FACE OF ANNAPURNA (1970), and the FIRST TO CLIMB EVEREST BY THE SOUTH-WEST FACE (1975). He died in an avalanche while skiing alone in Switzerland, garrotted by his own scarf.

BERNARD GALLACHER, golfer, born in Bathgate in 1949. In 1969, aged 20, he became the youngest player up to that time to represent Great Britain in the Ryder Cup. He was non-playing captain of the European Ryder Cup team three times, in 1991, 1993 and 1995, when he finally led them to victory. Gallacher was the second Ryder Cup captain to be born in Bathgate after ERIC BROWN (1925–86), who captained the British team in 1969 and 1971.

MICHAEL CATON-JONES, film director, born in Broxburn in 1957. His films include *Scandal* (1989), *Memphis Belle* (1990), *Doc Hollywood*

(1991), *Rob Roy* (1995), *The Jackal* (1997) and *Basic Instinct 2* (2006).

DARIO FRANCHITTI, racing driver, born in Livingston in 1973. Winner of the Indianapolis 500 in 2007, he married American actress Ashley Judd at Skibo Castle, in Sutherland, in 2001.

# Wigtownshire

THE SHIRE ✦ EARLS OF WIGTOWN
✦ SOME NOTABLE FLEMINGS

*Old Place of Mochrum, two typical Scottish tower houses dating from the 15th century, joined to create a classic Scottish home.*

◄ WIGTOWNSHIRE FOLK ►

Sir John Ross ✦ John Ramsay McCulloch

# The Shire

Wigtownshire forms the western part of the old kingdom of Galloway, and is known locally as the Shire, to distinguish it from the 'Stewartry' of neighbouring Kirkcudbrightshire which, in turn, loosely makes up the eastern portion of Galloway.

## Earls of Wigtown

The 1st Earl of Wigtown was MALCOLM FLEMING, guardian of Robert the Bruce's son, the boy King David II. When David returned from exile in France in 1341, he gave Malcolm lands in Wigtownshire and created him EARL OF WIGTOWN, as a means of establishing the power of the Bruce family in the territory of their main rivals the Balliols.

When Malcolm died in 1363 the title passed to his grandson Thomas, who had been made a hostage of Edward III, King of England, during the struggle for Scottish independence, and was almost bankrupted by having to pay his own ransom. He sold his earldom to Archibald 'the Grim' Douglas, which not only raised some money for Fleming, but conveniently solved the problem of jurisdiction that had been caused by

Archibald's elevation to the resurrected lordship of Galloway, which contained Wigtown within its boundaries.

The earldom remained with the Douglas family until 1455, when the 9th Earl of Douglas was accused of plotting against James II and stripped of his title and lands.

In 1606 the title was resurrected for JOHN FLEMING, a member of the family who originally held it, and survived until the death of the 7th Earl in 1747 when it became extinct.

Flemings are descendants of the Fleming merchants who came from Flanders and settled throughout Britain from the 11th century.

## Some Notable Flemings

JOHN FLEMING (1785–1857), Britain's first zoologist. In 1822 he published *The Philosophy of Zoology* and in 1828 *British Animals*, in which he argues that climate change drastically affects the evolution of plant and animal life in a particular region.

SIR SANDFORD FLEMING (1827–1915), 'the Father of Standard Time', was born in Kirkcaldy. He emigrated to Canada with his brother at the age of 18 and became a surveyor. An early achievement, in 1851, was designing CANADA'S FIRST STAMP, the Threepenny Beaver, and ten years later he began surveying the route of the

Canadian Pacific Railway and was present when the 'last spike' was driven in at Craigellechie in 1885. Now that people were able to travel vast distances at high speed, the problem of time became a factor if people were to know when the train was going to arrive or leave. Up until then, noon was when the sun stood right overhead wherever you happened to be, which was earlier in the east and later in the west. Fleming proposed a universal system of time, based on a world map divided into 24 zones; within each zone the time would be the same, and there would be a one-hour difference between zones, with Greenwich as the prime meridian. With some modifications Sandford Fleming's STANDARD TIME came into effect on 1 January 1885.

ROBERT FLEMING (1845–1933), banker, born in Dundee. After working for a while as a clerk in Dundee, Fleming spotted that America, which was rebuilding after the American Civil war and expanding rapidly westwards, could provide excellent investment opportunities for the vast amounts of money being made from Dundee's flourishing jute industry. In 1873 he set up the Scottish American Investment Trust, which proved highly successful, particularly in the high returns it made from the American railway companies. He moved to London and opened a merchant bank, Robert Fleming & Company, which by the time of his death had become the largest investment trust company in the City of London.

SIR ALEXANDER FLEMING (1881–1955), pharmacologist celebrated for the discovery of penicillin in 1928. After returning to his research laboratory in St Mary's Hospital, in Paddington, after a long holiday, he noticed a mould on an unwashed culture dish that appeared to have killed off the bacteria. He managed to isolate the active substance produced by the mould, and having identified it as being from the genus Penicillum he christened it penicillin. He was awarded the Nobel Prize for Medicine for his discovery in 1945.

Memorable Quote:
*'When I woke up just after dawn on September 28, 1928, I certainly didn't plan to revolutionise all medicine by discovering the world's first antibiotic, or bacteria killer.'*

PETER FLEMING (1907–71), soldier, travel writer and grandson of banker Robert Fleming. He served in the Grenadier Guards at the start of the Second World War and was asked to help set up the Auxiliary Units, a secret army of civilian volunteers who would form Britain's resistance in the event of invasion. He was also head of 'D' Division, responsible for covert operations in South-East Asia. After the war he travelled widely in South America and Asia, and wrote numerous bestselling travel books. He was married to actress Celia Johnson, star of *Brief Encounter*, and they had three children, including actress Lucy Fleming. He used to love walking on Rannoch Moor, in Argyll, where there is now a memorial cairn set up in his memory.

IAN FLEMING (1908–64), creator of James Bond, younger brother of Peter and grandson of banker Robert Fleming. He picked up the ideas for many of his plots while serving as a naval intelligence officer during the Second World War, although Bond himself is based more on his brother Peter than himself. Ernst Stavro Blofeld is said to be based on Ernst Blofeld, father of author John Blofeld, an acquaintance of Fleming's at his London club Boodles. The name James Bond was taken from the American ornithologist of the same name whose book was lying around Fleming's home in Jamaica. Sales of the James Bond books took off when President Kennedy included *From Russia with Love* on his list of favourite books. Fleming also wrote the children's story *Chitty Chitty Bang Bang* for his only son Caspar, who died of a drugs overdose in 1975.

AMARYLLIS FLEMING (1925–99), renowned cellist and teacher. She was the daughter of artist Augustus John by his mistress Eve Fleming, the mother of James Bond author Ian Fleming.

TOM FLEMING (b.1927), actor, theatre director and television commentator, most familiar for his commentary for the BBC on state occasions such as royal weddings, the Queen's silver jubilee, and the Remembrance Day service from the Cenotaph. He also began commentating for the Edinburgh Review in 1966.

*Well, I never knew this*
*about*
WIGTOWNSHIRE FOLK

# Sir John Ross
────◄ 1777–1856 ►────

JOHN ROSS was born in Kirkholm on the North Rhins, near Stranraer, the son of a Protestant minister, and joined the navy at the age of nine as a volunteer. After spending some time with the merchant marine and the East India Company, he rejoined the Royal Navy in 1799 and fought through the Napoleonic Wars, rising by 1812 to the rank of captain.

In 1818 Ross was asked by the Admiralty to lead one of the first expeditions to search for the fabled Northwest Passage around the top of Canada, and investigate the findings of an early 17th-century English explorer William Baffin, after whom Canada's largest island (and the fifth largest in the world) is named.

Ross reached Baffin Bay and then faced a choice of three exits to the west, eventually deciding to try the southernmost, Lancaster Sound. This would later be proved the correct route, but Ross, like others before him, suffered from seeing mirages of distant mountains, which led him to think he was sailing into a bay, and against the wishes of his officers, who included Sir Edward Parry, he turned back. His reputation as an Arctic explorer was damaged by the episode and he had to seek out a private sponsor for his next expedition. After some years he eventually persuaded Sir Felix Booth, the distiller of Booth's gin, to back an expedition, and in 1829 Ross set sail for the Arctic in a paddle steamer called *Victory*. It was the first time steam power had been employed in polar exploration.

This time Ross, accompanied by his nephew, James Clerk Ross (1800–62), who would later go on to become a celebrated Antarctic explorer, sailed

250 miles (400 km) further north than anyone before and discovered the northernmost point of mainland America, naming it Boothia Peninsula in honour of his sponsor. The expedition became caught in the ice off the peninsula and had to spend three winters at a place they called Port Felix, passing the time by mapping as much of the terrain as they could. They were aided by the local Inuits, who taught them how to make sledges which they then used to explore further. It was on one of these sledging explorations, in the winter of 1830–31, that James Clerk Ross discovered the north magnetic pole.

In May 1832 they decided to leave the *Victory* behind and take one of the ship's boats back to where Edward Parry had abandoned his ship the *Fury* on a previous expedition. They were able to survive a fourth winter by making a shelter from the remains of the *Fury* and living off the ship's supplies, and then in August 1833 they were rescued by a whaler in Lancaster Sound – amazingly, it was the *Isabella*, the ship that Ross had commanded on his first expedition in 1818.

His reputation restored by the discovery of the magnetic pole and by surviving for a record four and a half years in the Frozen North, Ross eventually retired to his boat-shaped home in Stranraer, the North West Castle.

There he stayed until 1850 when, at the age of 72, he led one of the fruitless expeditions to discover the fate of Sir John Franklin.

*Stranraer*

JOHN RAMSAY McCULLOCH (1789–1864) was born in Whithorn on his father's estate. In 1817 he helped to found the *Scotsman* newspaper and became its first editor. He later joined the *Edinburgh Review* as economics editor and through his column expounded his belief in the classical Ricardian school of economics – a free trade economic theory created by David Ricardo that built upon the theories laid out in Adam Smith's *The Wealth of Nations*. McCulloch's major work, *Principles*, published in 1825, is considered the first comprehensive textbook of economics, and he also compiled some of the earliest accounts of the history of economic thought.

# Index of People

# Index of Places

# ACKNOWLEDGEMENTS

My thanks to the team at Ebury, Carey Smith, Vicky Orchard, Caroline Craig and editor Steve Dobell. Special thanks to Robert and Margaret Bolam for the use of their beautiful house and hospitality.